DARKNESS
BRAVO

A SOLDIER REMEMBERS

1966–1967
1968–1969

Edward R. Fedrick

ISBN 978-1-63630-470-0 (Paperback)
ISBN 978-1-63630-471-7 (Digital)

Covenant Books, Inc.
11661 Hwy 707
Murrells Inlet, SC 29576
www.covenantbooks.com

This book is dedicated to my wonderful wife, Louise, without whose assistance and encouragement, this book would not have been possible.

I also dedicate this book to the fine young men of Bravo Company and the entire Darkness Battalion. They answered their country's call and performed their duty.

GLOSSARY

AK-47—A fully automatic 7.62x39 Russian-made assault rifle with thirty-round magazines.

APC—An armored troop carrier with tracks and a .50-caliber machine gun.

ARVN—The South Vietnamese Army or a soldier in that army.

BAR—An automatic .30-06 rifle used by the USA in WWII and the Korean War.

battalion (B)—A unit that contains three or four rifle companies and Headquarters Company.

Brigade—A unit that contains three battalions.

caliber—Size of a bullet fired by a weapon, such as a 7.62 mm is a .308 caliber.

Cavalry—A cavalry unit with tanks and armored personnel carriers.

CIB—Combat Infantry Badge. Awarded to an infantry soldier that has been in combat.

I Corps—The northern quarter of South Vietnam. US Marines fought here.

II Corps—An area that included the Central Highlands of Vietnam. The Fourth Division, 173rd Airborne Brigade and 101st Airborne Division were here.

III Corps—An area that included Saigon and northwest to the Cambodian border. The First Infantry Division and the Twenty-Fifth Infantry Division were here.

IV Corps—An area known as the Mekong Delta. The US Ninth Division was stationed there.

Chinook helicopter—A huge helicopter capable of carrying a platoon of troops.

Cloverleaf—A two-man patrol that moves a short distance from the main body.

Cobra helicopter—A high-tech gunship.

COL—A Colonel O-6 who commands a brigade of three thousand to four thousand soldiers.

combat patch—The patch of the unit a soldier served with in combat worn on right shoulder.

Company—An infantry company should have about 180 men, usually had about 120.

Corporal—An E-4 like a specialist 4 except a corporal is an NCO and has command authority. During the Vietnam War, infantry soldiers were not promoted to this rank. There were two corporals in Bravo Company when I arrived in 1966, but they were demoted sergeants.

C rations—Meals in cans that the soldiers carried with them in the field.

DI—Drill Instructor who trains new troops.

dusted off—When a wounded soldier is taken out of the combat area by helicopter for medical attention.

green tracers—Enemy bullets with green paint on the tips.

Gooks—North Vietnamese Army soldier or Viet Cong soldiers.

105 howitzer—A large American artillery cannon with a barrel diameter of more than four inches.

155 howitzer—A very large American artillery cannon, self-propelled or towed by truck. Has a barrel diameter of more than six inches.

75 mm howitzer—An artillery cannon used by NVA and VC forces, usually on wheels—with a barrel diameter of three inches.

Huey helicopter—Troop carrying helicopter that was introduced in the early 1960s.

Infantry—Ground troops.

infantry regiment—Old unit description used in the '40s and '50s which includes around two thousand men.

LT (a first or second lieutenant)—A platoon leader or Company Executive Officer.

LTC—A Lieutenant Colonel. The Commanding Officer of a battalion of five hundred to seven hundred men.

LZ—Landing zone, an opening in the jungle where we land helicopters.

hot LZ—Area where troops on helicopters are brought in with the enemy shooting at them in a barrage of gunfire.

M-1—An eight-shot semiautomatic .30.06 rifle used by USA in WWII and Korean War.

M-14—Fully automatic, twenty-shot, 7.62 rifle used by the USA early in Vietnam.

M-16—Fully automatic, twenty-shot, 5.56 rifle used by USA, prone to jamming early in the war.

M-60—A belt-fed 7.62 machine gun, weighs twenty-three pounds when empty.

M-72—A short light rocket launcher that is thrown away after firing.

M-79—A single-shot, break-down grenade launcher.

M-1 carbine—A small light caliber US rifle used in WWII and Korea, used by the Viet Cong early in the Vietnam War.

60 mm mortar—A small weapon that can be carried.

82 mm mortar—An enemy medium-sized mortar.

81 mm mortar—A US medium-sized mortar.

4.2 mortar—A very large US mortar.

NCO—A noncommissioned officer or different levels of sergeant.

NVA—North Vietnamese Army.

place guard—A unit that guards a perimeter while other units are on patrol.

Platoon—An infantry unit that should be forty-three men but was seldom over thirty.

Pathfinders—A special unit that sends two-man patrols deep in enemy areas.

PX—Post Exchange.

Quarter Cavalry—The First Squadron of the Fourth Cavalry Regiment in the First Division.

Regiment—A unit containing three battalions, could be over two thousand men.

red tracers—USA bullets with red paint on the tips.

RPD-56—An enemy machine gun that fires same round as the AK-47.

RPG-7—An enemy shoulder-fired rocket launcher.

saddle up—Infantry troops putting on web gear getting ready to move out.

SFC-E7—Sergeant First Class E-7 who is usually a platoon sergeant.

SGT—A sergeant E-5, supposed to be in charge of a five-man team but usually leads a squad.

SKS—A Russian-made light ten-shot semiautomatic rifle, fires same round as an AK-47.

SPC4—Rank between private first class and sergeant.

SPC5—Same pay grade as a sergeant E-5 but is not an NCO.

SSG—Staff Sergeant E-6, should be a squad leader.

Stevedores—Soldiers who unload ships.

sticks of men—Number of soldiers set to ride on a helicopter.

sticks of helicopters—Number of helicopters set to land at the same time.

Squad—An infantry rifle squad is supposed to be ten men, but it seldom is.

Tanks—USA used M-48 tanks in Vietnam, armed with a cannon and two machine guns.

VC—Viet Cong (Vietnamese Communist).

white mice—Army of the Republic of Vietnam Military Police. They wear white caps.

CHAPTER 1

In the Army Now

Christmas 1965 and New Year's Day 1966 are over in Memphis, Tennessee. I'm six months out of high school and eighteen years old. My high school buddy, Dave Wing, and I have joined the Army. I had gone to college for one semester and worked from 6:00 p.m. until 2:00 a.m., each night loading trucks at the Sears warehouse on Broad Street. Needless to say, I have performed poorly in school. Dave has just been working and is drafted, so we go down and join the Army together on the "buddy system."

We are due to catch the train at Memphis for Fort Benning, Georgia, for basic training. My mother, stepfather, and one of my stepbrothers drive me down to the train station. Dave's mother, father, and brother drive him down. Dave's brother and my step-brother have both served a hitch in the army. They were both stationed in Germany—his brother in the military police and my step-brother in a transportation unit.

We arrive at the train station and meet the other guys heading to the army. There are thirty-six of us in all. Six of us enlisted, and the other thirty were drafted. A big older red-haired recruit is placed in charge of us all. He was married but with no children, so he was drafted. Instead of proceeding with the draft, he chose to enlist in hopes of avoiding being assigned to the Infantry. He has all of our paperwork. There is a tall lanky guy with black hair from Dyersburg, Tennessee, named Travis Nunnery who seems like a nice guy. He's also married, and his wife will soon be pregnant. He's been drafted but has no intention of giving the army more than two years. He and I would be in the same squad in Vietnam.

Our train arrives, and we board after saying goodbye to our families. Each two men have their cabin with two bunks inside. It's tight in the little cabin, and Dave is bigger than I. It is late as the train departs, so we hit the rack. I go right to sleep and awake later in the night as we go around a bend, and I am pressed against the wall. I roll over and go right back to sleep.

The morning comes; and we arrive in Birmingham, Alabama, and change trains. We travel the rest of the way sitting in seats in coach. We even get to go to the dining car for a meal. So far this isn't bad.

We arrive at Columbus, Georgia, and there is a bus waiting on us to take us out to Fort Benning. We arrive, and there is a large sergeant E-5 waiting on us. He assigns us to a WWII-type older barracks. We each grab a bunk, and then they feed us at the mess hall.

The next morning, we begin processing. We get all our hair cut off. We are issued uniforms and boots. We then take three days of written tests to see which job we would be best suited. I was a little concerned when the test showed that of the more than a hundred jobs in the army, I would be best suited for the infantry. I did get a high GT (general test) score. I hope it will balance out my infantry score.

We pack our civilian clothing and ship them home. They did not want us to have any civilian clothing. This made it harder for any of us to go AWOL. The sergeant who is herding us around keeps telling us that when we got to Harmony Church for basic training, the drill instructors would not be nice to us. We didn't believe him. After all, he is an Army Sergeant, and he has been firm but decent to us.

The fifth day, we load on buses with our duffle bags and drive to Harmony Church. It's cold and spitting a little snow. As we approach the parking lot, we see them, about ten soldiers in overcoats and wearing Smoky Bear hats. They were walking back and forth and appear high-strung. I got a very bad feeling. The buses stop and two or three of the DIs enter each bus. They are all screaming and cursing us. Some of the words I had never heard, and I thought I was a *tough* streetwise guy.

The DIs shove and kick us off the buses and form us up in a formation. They never stop screaming and cursing. They call us some names I've never heard. They get in our faces screaming and spewing spit. I realize that I've made a major mistake, but it's too late now.

They assign us barracks and bunks and never stop screaming. I find that Dave and I are in the same company but different barracks. It seems that every few seconds, they tell us to drop for push-ups as a punishment for some violation. We are all in shock. They run us around the company area and keep screaming. They feed us, giving us about four minutes to eat.

They put us to bed, and it seems that I've just gone to sleep when they wake us beating on garbage can lids. They have us out, and we have the "daily dozen." It's a series of very hard calisthenics. They scream at us and belittle us. Some of the guys who have never played sports are having a very hard time. The DIs then form us up, and we run for two miles. Some of the guys fall out, but the DIs are on their case screaming and kicking them in the butt. This is a nightmare. I did not know that people could be this bad to other people.

My new army boots rub a hole in the back of my left ankle. I go on sick call, and they bandage my ankle and put me on "profile." I will have to wear low-quarter shoes the rest of basic training and wear a bandage on my ankle until I am out of basic training. This doesn't keep me from running two miles in formation each morning in low-quarter dress shoes.

One of our DIs is an old leathery staff sergeant E-6 from Senatobia, Mississippi, named SSG Loyce Graham. He had entered the army in 1946 after WWII. He had fought in the Korean War and had been awarded the Silver Star, a very high award for an enlisted man to receive. He also has the Combat Infantry Badge.

This shows that he has fought in ground combat as an infantryman. If a soldier has fought in two wars, he is given a star on top of his CIB.

Staff Sergeant Graham lets us know that he will train one more cycle of troops after us and then retire. I tell him if he reenlists and goes to Vietnam, he will most likely make sergeant first class E-7 and receive a star on his CIB. He smiles a frosty smile at me and says, "Young soldier, I would rather be a retired E-6 with a 'plain' CIB than a dead E-7 with a star on my CIB." I understand what he is saying and just nod.

Toward the end of our training, we have the obstacle course. It's crawling under barbed wire with live machine gun fire passing six feet over our heads. It's raining heavily that day, and the DIs tell us that we will have to leave one man in each barracks as a barracks guard while the rest of the company does the course, rain, mud and all. The DIs tell me that due to the open wound on my ankle that I will be barracks guard for my barracks. I'm relieved. I did not want to get muddy.

I remain in the barracks sitting where I can see both doors as the rain falls even harder outside. Then I hear the trucks pulling up outside. Then the guys started coming in the barracks. They are covered in mud, even their rifles. They all go into the showers, rifles and all, and wash the mud off. They then clean and oil their rifles and clean up their mess. I'm glad I didn't have to go.

A few days before graduation, we get our orders. Dave Wing will go to Military Police School at Fort Stewart, Georgia. I will go to infantry school at Fort Polk, Louisiana. Well, I've done it now. I'm going to be a foot soldier, and there is a major ground war going on.

We graduate from basic training and head home for a few days. Dave and I ride a Greyhound bus back to Memphis and spend a few days with our families.

I check into how to get to Fort Polk, Louisiana. I find that Trans Texas Airways has a flight that goes from Memphis to Leesville, Louisiana. That's the little town near Fort Polk. I've never flown, so this would be my first, and I would get there much quicker than on a bus. I make reservations, and on the day, I go to the airport and board the plane. It's a DC3 prop job. There are only eighteen passenger seats, and some of the others are soldiers like me. The plane lands five times before we get to Leesville. I become air sick and throw up the entire flight.

We land at Leesville and I deplane. I see more than five hundred soldiers, all in their khaki uniforms, sitting on their duffle bags and waiting on transportation out to Fort Polk. That's when it hits me. All these guys are going to infantry school. This ground war thing is getting very real.

We arrive at our new company headquarters and find that we will be housed in WWII barracks. The catch is that no one has lived in these barracks since WWII, a total of twenty-one years. The first week we will live in the barracks while we refurbished and paint them. This week they consider a zero week and does not count on our nine weeks of infantry training. We have been pumping each other up, telling each other that we know that most of us will go to Vietnam but some troops will have to go to Germany or Korea. The first day of training, we are all sitting in bleachers when an old sour-looking Sergeant First Class E-7 steps up to the podium and looks us over. In a loud voice, he says, "I want you people to listen to me and remember what I say. None of you men is going to Germany. None of you men is going to Korea. Every damn one of you are going to Vietnam and to an infantry unit." I look around at my fellow soldiers and see that some of them are quietly crying. Well, at least now we know for sure. I have noticed that one of the guys in the company is Jim Swick. He was in my company for basic training but in a different platoon. In this infantry training company, he is also in a different platoon. I will find later that he is in my company in Vietnam but in a different platoon. He's an average-sized guy with black hair from West Virginia. He's always seemed like a really nice guy, and I've considered him a "distant friend."

One of our trainers is a very old staff sergeant, in his midforties. He is short and a little stocky with a star on his CIB. We learn that he has fought in WWII and the Korean War. He runs the two miles with us every morning, and I wonder how he can do it. I'm running in my boots now, and I'm glad that I don't stand out in a crowd. One day, the old SSG tells us that he's had orders for Vietnam come down so he has just returned from main post where he has put in his papers for retirement. I say, "But, Sergeant, if you went to Vietnam, you would get a second star on his Combat Infantry Badge and probably be promoted to Sergeant First Class E-7." He gives me a sideways look and says, "Troop, I know that you are not as dumb as you sound." He leaves the next day for retirement.

We get a new trainer. He is a young Specialist 4 just back from a tour in Vietnam with the 173 Airborne Brigade. They cut orders at company changing him from a Specialist 4 to a Corporal E-4. This makes him an NCO and gives him much more power. He's very approachable, however. He's in our age group and has been in the army less than two years. He's got his CIB on his shirt and the 173rd Combat Patch on his right shoulder. After we get to know him, a half dozen of us are talking with him at a firing range. I work up the courage and ask him what combat is like. He tells us that he's not been in combat. I'm shocked. He has just spent a year in Vietnam in an elite unit and has the Combat Infantry Badge. I ask him how he got the CIB if he had never been in combat. He says that they went on patrols every day or night and quite often they got shot at and they had shot back but he had not been in combat. I say, "Pardon me, Corporal, but if you got shot at a lot and you shot back, isn't that combat?" He seems stunned and says, "I never saw it that way. I guess I have been in combat."

Toward the end of our training, we spend a week on Peason Ridge. It will later be called Tiger Land. This is a solid week of sleeping on the ground and running around the woods in the day time and at night playing war games. Toward the end of the week, I realize that I'm coming down with poison ivy. I'm very allergic to this plant. When we get back to the barracks, I find that the rash is over my entire body, even between my toes and on my eyelids. I cannot sleep. I go to the hospital, and they admit me and start an IV. They cover me with hot, wet towels. I'm able to sleep for the first time in days. They keep me in the hospital for nearly a week until the rash resolves.

I return to the company hoping that I do not get recycled because I've missed nearly a week of training. I ask the company first sergeant, and he says that I have qualified with all weapons so I will graduate with the other guys. I'm relieved.

Graduation day comes, and we all have orders for Vietnam. We are all in our khaki uniforms, and our duffle bags are packed. We are in formation outside our barracks. They will truck us down to main post for a parade and graduation ceremony. We will leave our duffle bags where they are until after the ceremony. It's early June and very hot. I'm not looking forward to marching in the sun and standing in the sun while some General makes a long-winded speech. One of our trainers says that he needs a duffle bag guard. I shout that I will do it. He tells me to fall out and let nothing happen to all those bags. The company loads up on trucks and departs. There's a small shade tree beside the bags. I carry my bag over and place it against the tree. I sit on the bag, place my back against the tree, and go to sleep in the shade.

In a couple of hours, the company returns. They are sweat soaked and tired. I'm cool and have had a nap. We form up in formation, and the company commander says a few words. We then load on trucks, and they take us to Leesville to the bus station and airport. I arrive back in Memphis and spend a few days with my family. I drive down to central Mississippi and see more of my relatives. I'm so afraid that I'm saying goodbye to all of them forever.

The day comes for me to leave for Vietnam. My mother, grandmother, and stepfather take me to the airport. We wait at the gate until it's time for me to walk to the plane. I hug all of them, turn, and walk to the plane. I don't look back. I don't want them to see that I'm crying. After all, I've turned nineteen by now.

I get on the plane heading for Newark, New Jersey and Fort Dix. I run into a soldier on the plane in the same uniform as me but without the blue infantry rope on his right shoulder. He seems very happy. I find out that he is on his way home. The army has put him out for being unable to adjust to military life. I quit talking to him. I've nothing to say to a quitter like him.

I find myself sitting beside a gray-haired woman in her sixties. She is very talkative and is drinking mixed drinks. She finds out that I'm on my way to Vietnam and says that her husband and her brothers were in WWII. She gets a little teary-eyed and says she sure hates to see young men go off to war. She then tells me that she is sorry for being so emotional that she is just like my mother. I don't tell her that my mother is thirty-eight years old and both my grandmothers are younger than her.

We land at Newark, New Jersey and there is an Army sergeant and a driver collecting soldiers going to Vietnam. They bus us out to Fort Dix and assign us bunks in an old barracks. We have formation three times a day as names are called out for seats on planes heading "over there."

The second day, my name is called. I get my duffle bag and board the bus that takes us to the plane. We board the plane and find that it is a 707. Also, it has a half-dozen beautiful flight attendants who will make the trip with us. They will be feeding us and getting us cokes. Of course they are much older than we are. Some of them may even be twenty-five years old.

There are 160 slick-sleeved privates on the plane. About half of them I went through infantry training with at Fort Polk. It is good to know a lot of the guys, but none of us are happy campers. You could cut the fear with a knife!

We fly over the Canadian Rockies. They are beautiful from the air, but I would not want to fight in all those rocks and that snow. We land in Anchorage, Alaska, to gas the plane. We all get to deplane and go into the terminal. They have a stuffed polar bear standing there. He looks ten feet tall. I buy three postcards and send them to my mother and two grandmothers.

We board the plane and start flying over the Pacific Ocean in the dark. Most of us start sleeping in our seats. Much later, our plane lands in Japan to gas. Most of the guys don't wake up. I look out the window and watch the Japanese ground crew gassing the plane. I think that only twenty-one years ago, we were at war with these people.

We fly on in the dark, and after more hours, we land at the airport near Saigon. We deplane and smell Vietnam for the first time. It smells like rotten cantaloupes. They put us on buses to take us to Camp Alpha to process us "in country." We notice that the bus windows have a heavy wire mesh over them. One of the guys ask why that mesh is over the windows. The bus driver tells him it's to keep the gooks from throwing hand grenades into the bus. This is getting more real by the minute.

We arrive at Camp Alpha, and they assign us bunks in large tents and feed us at the tent mess hall. We then process, and I get orders to the First Infantry Division. They issue M-14 rifles and three loaded magazines to each of us. We then board trucks and head up the highway toward First Division Headquarters. There is a sergeant E-5 and a spec5 in the truck I'm on. They are griping because there is no machine gun on the truck. They check and find that all our M-14s are semiautomatic only.

They gripe that if we are ambushed on the road, we have no fully automatic weapons to break the ambush. I am really scared now.

We arrive at First Division Headquarters and are assigned to different battalions. About fifty of us are assigned to Second Battalion Eighteenth Infantry Regiment. We then truck to Base Camp Bearcat to the battalion headquarters. About thirty of the guys go to Charlie Company. About fifteen go to Alpha Company. Jim Swick, four others, and I go to Bravo Company. Maybe I've lucked out. We are replacements for openings in the companies made by either guys rotating home or guys getting killed. This makes me think that Bravo Company takes fewer causalities than the other two companies. I sure hope I'm right.

I have been hearing some of the other guys griping about "why are we here?" I have even been hearing some of the NCOs asking the same question. Apparently, they do not read. I have studied SEATO while in high school. That stands for Southeast Asia Treaty Organization. It's where a number of countries in East Asia and the USA have formed a treaty, whereas if any of the member countries are invaded by another power, then all the members will assist that country.

The North Vietnamese Army has invaded South Vietnam with hundreds of thousands of soldiers, and all the member nations have sent troops to assist the South Vietnamese. Australia, New Zealand, South Korea, Thailand and the Philippines have troops fighting in South Vietnam. The USA has the largest number of troops "in country," but then we are the much larger country.

Some have called this a civil war. It is not. When Vietnam split into two countries in 1954, more than eight hundred thousand people living in what had become North Vietnam fled to South Vietnam. Most of them were Catholics fleeing Communist dictatorship. In the South, less than one hundred thousand people fled North. Most of them were hard-core Communists. The North Vietnam Army trained these people, and in 1959, the North started infiltrating these people back into the South to their home villages. Their mission was to start the Viet Cong movement. Then in 1962, North Vietnam started sending regular North Vietnamese Army units down the Ho Chi Minh Trail through Laos and Cambodia to reinforce these insurgents. By 1965, this invasion of NVA Units had become a flood. The South Vietnamese then needed help from their allies to save their country from the invaders.

SEATO is to Asia what NATO is to Europe. NATO stands for the North Atlantic Treaty Organization, and all the countries of Western Europe and the USA belong. This keeps the Communists out of Western Europe just like SEATO is attempting to keep the Communists from taking over Southeast Asia.

I have always been amused by most people thinking that if you were assigned to a combat zone, then you must have seen combat and went "hand to hand" with the enemy. In Vietnam, this is certainly not correct. In Vietnam, it takes ten soldiers in support roles in order to field one soldier or marine out in the "bush" actively looking for enemy soldiers.

I have a friend from high school who is a clerk typist in Vietnam. He is stationed at the huge support base at Long Binh. He works in an air-conditioned office, typing. He has one day a week off. He lives in a barracks with hot showers and flush toilets. He has to pull "bunker guard" about once every two weeks and has to be issued a weapon for this detail. There is something like a quarter of a mile of barbed wire between the bunker line at Long Binh and the jungle. Long Binh does have rocket attacks on occasion, but it's not every day or even every week.

There are other clerks who work in an infantry unit, but they are back at base camp living in a large tent with no air-conditioning, flush toilets, or running water. The showers are cold and outdoors. These clerks tend to get more rocket and mortar fire in than the ones at Long Binh, but they are still not in the field sleeping on the ground for weeks or even months at a time activity searching each day for enemy troops.

Truck drivers may get a little sniper fire on the highways and on rare occasions are ambushed. But the truck drivers are usually able to return to a secure base camp each night with a cot and big tent.

Cooks are in the rear cooking and are subjected to the occasional rocket attack. Sometimes, a cook may take the large cans of hot chow to the field on a helicopter to the troops. The cook then returns to a secure area with the empty food containers on a helicopter. Stevedores unload the big cargo ships at Saigon or Cameron Bay. They work hard but have good living conditions.

The military police escort convoys on the highways and take sniper fire and are subjected to the occasional ambushes. They also drive their gun jeeps to assist other units in contact on the highways. They also police American soldiers in the big cities, which can be a tough job. But their living conditions are much better than that of the infantry.

The medics are a mixed bag. Some spend six months in the field with an infantry unit being subjected to the same dangers and poor living conditions as the grunts. Usually, these field medics are then assigned to a large hospital in the rear with great living conditions for the second six months of their tour. Some medics are lucky enough to spend their entire year in Vietnam in one of the large rear hospitals, where the grunt spends his entire year in the field living in a foxhole and subjected to the weather and the terrible fear of very close ground combat.

The artillery are usually located in a perimeter in the field with an infantry unit dug in around them, providing security. They get a lot of mortar and rocket fire incoming on their positions, as well as some small-arms fire. They are also subjected to a ground attack on rare occasions. They usually sleep on the ground in bunkers but are not out in the brush looking for the enemy.

The helicopter crews might be shot at more than the grunts. They may do more shooting than the grunts, but each day they return to base camp. There they have access to cold beer, hot chow, cold showers, and a bunk in a large tent.

The bottom line is the grunts could not do their jobs if it were not for all the support personnel in the rear supporting us and keeping us supplied. It is a team effort, but it's the grunt soldier or marine who is "the tip of the spear." Seventy-five percent of the causalities in Vietnam were from army or marine infantry units, which only made up nine percent of the troops in Vietnam. The grunts are out every day and night searching for enemy units. They are attempting to locate the enemy so they can engage and destroy them.

CHAPTER 2

First Squad Overrun

It is summer 1966. Bravo Company is "dug in" in the perimeter at Quan Loi Rubber Plantation up near the Cambodian border. Second Platoon is led by LT Robert Leary, and the platoon sergeant is John Hall. The Division has been in Vietnam for a year now, and most of the guys are seasoned veterans except new replacements coming in. A large number of the seasoned veterans are about to rotate back to the states.

The rubber trees are more than a foot thick, and the rows go on for miles. The French owners live in a big house inside the perimeter. The hundreds of rubber workers live in the close by village. There are a number of large enemy units that also work this area. Their sanctuaries in Cambodia are only a few miles away.

It is First Squad's night for ambush duty out in the rubber trees. As it gets on toward dusk, First Squad line up to move out. Sergeant Johnson is the squad leader, Frostbach will run point, and Mulchaney carries the radio. The machine gun crew is Kirkland as gunner, Charlie P. Livingston as assistant gunner, and Alston as ammo bearer. All three of the gun crew are black, so they call themselves "the soul gun." Grimsley is one of the riflemen, a tall white soldier with brown hair. My buddy Doug McVey will be going out. He is a tall sandy-haired soldier from Booneville, Mississippi, by way of Joiner, Arkansas. It will be his first night on ambush.

They move out into the growing darkness and move in and out among the rubber trees. They will be ambushing a dirt road that runs through the rows of trees. They will only be about three klicks (two miles) from the perimeter. In the dark, that is a very long way.

As they slowly move along in the dark, Frostbach thinks he sees two figures out in the darkness shadowing First Squad. He stops the patrol and informs the patrol leader what he thinks he has seen. The squad holds in place a while, looking and listening. They hear or see nothing. After a while, they move on toward their ambush site.

They reach their location and set up in four positions—three along the road and one watching to the rear. They are monitoring the road for enemy traffic. The guard watches are set up, and some men are on watch while others have gone to sleep.

Then it happens! A large enemy unit walks in on them from the rear and opens fire from very close range. The squad immediately takes causalities but strongly fights back. McVey is awakened by an enemy soldier standing over him firing down at him with an automatic weapon. McVey rolls away, and the enemy fire stitches the poncho he was lying on. The enemy is between First Squad's positions.

In the machine gun position, Kirkland is badly wounded by half a dozen rounds through his torso. He is completed neutralized and can only lay there and curse the enemy. Alston is mortally wounded and unconscious. Livingston takes over the machine and begins running belts of ammo through the gun. Mulchaney, on the radio, is badly wounded but is calling for help on the radio and attempting to fire his rifle with one hand. McVey has a claymore bag filled with a dozen or more hand grenades. He is throwing grenades and firing his rifle as fast as he can.

Back at the perimeter, Lieutenant Leary has the rest of the platoon lined up on the road, ready to respond to First Squad's call for help. The firing in the distance is unbelievably heavy. Everyone can hear the steady beat of that M-60 machine gun along with the enemy fire and our own rifles.

Lieutenant Leary advises on the radio that Second Platoon is ready to go, but the platoon is down to two squads and one machine gun. The other rifle squad and the other machine gun are the ones out there being overrun. The powers-to-be advise Lieutenant Leary to secure the perimeter that they are sending Third Platoon, which is at full strength. Reluctantly, Second Platoon takes back their positions on the perimeter.

Third Platoon line up and move out with Richardson running point. They move toward the sound of the guns while attempting to be as careful as possible. They do not want to get ambushed while going out to help First Squad.

Third Platoon reaches the scene and attacks into the rear of the enemy unit that is attacking First Squad. It is vicious, close work with the combatants within feet of each other. Richardson is firing and advancing like a whirlwind and is then hit by return enemy fire and falls dead on the battlefield.

Third Platoon's attack has disrupted the enemy unit, and they begin pulling out. Daylight breaks soon, and the results of the night's fight is plain to see. Sergeant Johnson, Frostbach, and Alston are dead. All the other members of First Squad are badly wounded except McVey, Livingston, and Grimsley. McVey is out of grenades and has his last magazine seated in his rifle. Livingston has only a very short belt of ammo left for the machine gun.

Third Platoon gathers up all the wounded and get them dusted off by helicopter to an army hospital along with the four dead Americans. The enemy unit has left five of their soldiers dead on the field. This indicates, along with blood trails and drag marks, that the enemy took many more dead and wounded than these five bodies that have been left behind. They bring a truck out from the perimeter to load the enemy bodies. They then take the enemy bodies and bury them. I would have left them lying among the rubber trees.

We have had three good men killed, and Third Platoon has lost one. We have a number of soldiers badly wounded, and the only wounded man who will ever come back to us is Mulchaney. The others' wounds are so severe that they will be shipped to an army hospital in Japan and from there to an army hospital in the States.

The Brass theorizes that at least a reinforced enemy platoon was involved in the action and possibly a full company. First Squad has made a good fight of it. Third Platoon also did an excellent job of reinforcing First Squad in the dark and putting the enemy unit to flight.

CHAPTER 3

July 1966

June 30, 1966

The First Squadron of the Fourth Cavalry of the First Infantry Division was ambushed off Highway 13 near the Cambodian border by the entire 271st Regiment from the Ninth Viet Cong Division. The Ninth Viet Cong Division was the premier enemy unit in III Corps in 1966. It was a full-time, well-trained unit with NVA advisers from the 101st NVA Regiment.

This was early in the war, and some of the enemy troops were armed with AK-47 assault rifles and SKS carbines, but the majority of the troops in this unit in the summer of 1966 were armed with M-1 carbines, M-1 rifles, and BAR automatic rifles. The enemy unit was also armed with 60 mm and 82 mm mortars. The enemy unit also had numerous B-40 shoulder-fired rockets that we later called RPGs. They were also well supplied with heavy 7.92 x .54 machine guns mounted on wheels. Bravo Company captured three of these heavy machine guns during this battle, and one of them was on display in front of Bravo Company's orderly room at Di An until the unit redeployed to Fort Riley in 1970.

The enemy soldiers in this unit at this time mostly wore what we called black pajamas with "bush hats" or no head covering at all. Most of the enemy troops wore Ho Chi Minh sandals made from tires or shower shoes and were supplied with web gear and packs with a mixture of American and NVA origins.

The first unit to reach the First of the Fourth Cavalry on June 30, 1966, was Bravo Company, Second, Eighteenth, followed closely by Alpha Company, Second, Eighteenth. SFC Bill D. Perry was the platoon sergeant for Bravo's Mortar Platoon.

LTC Herbert McChrystal was the battalion commander of the Second-Eighteenth and arrived on the battlefield with Alpha Company. Lieutenant Colonel McChrystal immediately relieved the company commander and first sergeant of Bravo Company because he did not believe they were performing correctly. Lieutenant Colonel McChrystal took personal command of Bravo Company and made SFC Bill D. Perry the acting First Sergeant of Bravo Company on the spot. Sergeant Perry remained in this position until he was promoted to First Sergeant E-8 in November 1966. "Top" Perry was then Bravo Company's permanent First Sergeant until he rotated home in April 1967.

"Top" Perry then took primary charge of Bravo Company's fight. He limped badly early in the fight, and the troops did not know if he was wounded or had a badly sprained ankle. We later learned he had been wounded early in the fight on June 30, 1966, but refused to be evacuated and fought for the next three days.

Bravo Company was moving to reinforce the Quarter Cavalry when our air assets observed an entire battalion of enemy troops in the brush and elephant grass setting up an ambush for the company. Bravo Company changed direction, and as the enemy attempted to move their ambush, they were hit with huge amounts of artillery fire and air strikes. This caused severe casualties in the enemy ranks. Bravo Company then attacked into the flank of the enemy battalion. Many enemy troops were wounded but still fighting. The company pushed into the enemy until a heavy enemy machine gun stopped Bravo Company's advance. The company was pinned down and completely stopped by this machine gun. SGT Ben Garza, Corporal George Arnold, and Specialist 4 Nix then flanked the enemy machine gun and overran it, killing the three-man gun crew. Bravo Company was then able to continue their advance.

"Top" Perry resupplied Second Platoon numerous times with ammo and water while under heavy fire. He was doing the same for the other platoons. If the company had not had this ammo and water, it would not have survived as a unit. "Top" Perry placed squads and platoons into defensive positions on numerous occasions and led squads and platoons on assaults all while under heavy enemy fire. He also, on at least two occasions, took out enemy strong points by over-running the enemy positions alone and shooting the heavily armed enemy soldiers face-to-face at point-blank range. "Top" Perry seemed to be running Bravo Company's fight from June 30 until July 2. Top Perry seemed to be giving all the orders and making all the decisions, and they all seemed to be correct. He seemed to completely ignore all enemy fire and was standing up giving orders each time he was observed.

After two days of the battle the 271st Regiment, Ninth VC Division was completely decimated, and then our battalion was attacked by a battalion from the 273rd Regiment, Ninth VC Division. This battalion was attempting to overrun Alpha and Charlie Companies of the Second, Eighteenth. Bravo Company then attacked into the flank of the enemy unit. The Second, Eighteenth had soundly defeated this unit by midmorning of July 2, 1966. By noon on July 2, 1966, army engineers had arrived on the scene and began digging huge trenches with bulldozers. Second-Eighteenth then carried the dead enemy soldiers to these trenches by hand and threw them in. The bulldozers then covered the bodies with dirt. Our unit was told at that time that there were over six hundred enemy dead on this battlefield. I have since read that the number of enemy dead was four hundred plus. I do not know which is correct, but I do know that the enemy dead was well into the hundreds.

The Second, Eighteenth also recovered hundreds of enemy weapons. The word around Bravo Company after the fight was that Top Perry had personally shot and killed seventeen enemy soldiers during the battle. I do not know if this is correct, but Top Perry was seen to shoot and kill several heavily armed enemy soldiers face-to-face at close range. It has always been felt that had it not been for Top Perry many more of Bravo Company soldiers would have been killed and wounded. We were also told at the time that a total of thirty-six American soldiers from our battalion and the Quarter Cav. were killed in the three-day fight. All the officers in our Charlie Company were either killed or wounded. Fortunately, our side had air superiority. The helicopter gunships and jet fighters aircraft really rained fire down on the enemy troops.

CHAPTER 4

The Firefight

Late July 1966

I'm a nineteen-year-old private more than a month in Vietnam. I've got seven months in the army and have been out of high school for thirteen months. I'm assigned to Second Squad, Second Platoon, Bravo Company, Second BN, Eighteenth Infantry Regiment, First Infantry Division. My team leader is SPC4 Dimas Ramirez. My squad leader is SGT Ben Garza. My platoon leader is 1LT Robert Leary, and the platoon sergeant is SFC John Hall.

We are working an area that has elephant grass and bushes. We've made no "contact" with the enemy in the last few days. We are hoping that it stays that way.

We have relieved another company in the perimeter that we are working from. It is one of the few times that I have seen barbed wire around a company perimeter out in the boonies.

It's our squad's night to pull an all-night ambush. I do not know about the other guys, but I'm afraid. There are nine of us in Second Squad. Garza is the squad leader. CPL George Arnold is the A-team leader and assistant squad leader. Travis Nunnery, Louis Sanders, and Liberato Gonzales make up Arnold's team. SPC4 Dimas Ramirez is the B-team leader. His team is made up of Charles Bicket, Scott, and me. We'll have De Jesus's machine gun crew out with us. De Jesus is the gunner, Bossier is the assistant gunner, and Jim Norberg is the ammo bearer.

Gonzales and Bicket are armed with M-79s. It's a short, fat-barreled weapon that fires a single explosive round that is half as powerful as an American hand grenade. It then breaks down like a single-barrel shotgun for reloading. Each shell for the M-79 weighs a half pound. An M-79 man usually carries at least forty rounds. De Jesus is carrying the M-60 machine gun. It's a 7.62 mm weapon that is belt fed. We usually carry at least nine hundred rounds for the machine gun. Each hundred-round belt weighs six pounds. The machine gun weighs twenty-three pounds empty.

The remaining nine of us are armed with 5.56 mm M-16 rifles. Only recently has the unit been given the M-16s and had their 7.62 M-14s taken away. No cleaning kits or cleaning rods came with the little rifles. The M-16 is prone to jamming. If it jams with a round in the chamber, the only way to un-jam it is with a cleaning rod down the muzzle. When I arrived in the squad, I noticed that Louis Sanders and Dimas Ramirez had each obtained a single section of a thin metal rod. They carry it along the left side of their rifles. There are two sections of baling wire around their rifles; one is just in front of the carrying handle, and the other is just behind the front sight. The metal rod is threaded through these two wires and rides very well on the left side of the rifle. Thus, when their rifles jam, which they will do, they can quickly clear the jam. They can also pass the jamming rods to other members of the squad. When I saw this, I wrote to my mother and asked her to send me a .22-caliber cleaning rod. I've just received it. It's not in one piece but in sections that are screwed together. I carry it in its plastic kit in one of the cargo pockets of my pants.

The battalion SOP (standard operational procedure) for the M-16 included that we are not to fire our rifles on automatic. If we do, they will jam in the first magazine; and if we fire on semiautomatic, they do not jam until the second or third magazine most of the time. I cannot believe that we have been armed with such undependable weapons.

Most of the men carry two ammo pouches on the front of their web belt. Each pouch carries four M-16 magazines with twenty rounds each. Three are side by side, and the fourth lies horizontal under the flap of the pouch. Most of the men have a thin green cloth bandolier that comes with seven twenty-round boxes of ammo for the M-16. Seven metal M-16 magazines fit perfectly into this bandolier. All this and one magazine in the rifle gives each man 16 magazines or 320 rounds. I am bigger than most men, and my waist is much thicker. I carry four ammo pouches on the front of my web belt along with the seven magazines in the bandolier and one in the rifle. This gives me 24 magazines or 480 rounds. We all carry four hand grenades.

Sergeant Garza briefs us before we leave the perimeter. We will ambush a trail about five hundred meters from the perimeter. De Jesus and his gun crew will be positioned facing the trail. Corporal Arnold, along with Nunnery and Scott, will set up about fifteen meters to the right of the machine gun. SGT Ben Garza, along with Gonzales and Sanders with the radio, will be about fifteen meters to the left of the machine gun. Ramirez, Bicket, and I will be about twenty meters behind the machine gun pulling rear security for the squad. Each position will put out a claymore antipersonnel mine. These mines are about nine inches long and five inches wide. Each one has two small bipod legs that can be pressed into the dirt. The mine is covered in green plastic. There are 720 steel ball bearings in the front of the mine and C-4 explosive in the back. An explosive cap is screwed into an opening on top of the mine. A hundred foot of wire covered with rubber goes back from the "cap" to the handheld detonator that we carry. The other end of the wire is then screwed into the detonator that is squeezed by hand. This sends the 720 steel balls out in a fan-shaped area to its front.

We move through the break in the wire of the perimeter just after dark and head out to our left. Our ambush position is to the right. We are hoping that if the "gooks" are watching that this will throw them off as to where we are heading. We head into the brush in column or two six-man files. The left file is made up of Sergeant Garza on point with Sanders behind him with the radio. Then it's

Ramirez, Bicket, me then Scott. The right file is Corporal Arnold on point with Nunnery next and then Gonzales. The machine gun crew follows Gonzales, De Jesus, Bossier, and Norberg.

The monsoon is overdue, and there's thunder and lightning in the distance. There is a feeling of rain in the air. We stop our forward progress every forty or fifty meters, and everyone faces out except Scott and Norberg in the back. They turn and watch our back trail. Garza and Arnold then confer about our direction of travel.

We change direction a number of times, again to confuse any enemy troops that may be watching us. It's not that hot this evening, but I'm soaked with sweat, and my mouth is dry. I'm trying hard to do the right thing and not screw up. I've only been here a month, so I'm pretty new at this; but then so are Bicket, Scott, Norberg, and Nunnery. The other seven guys are seasoned combat troops with months of experience.

After nearly an hour, we reach our destination. Sergeant Garza and Corporal Arnold quickly put everyone into their positions. Ramirez, Bicket, and I find ourselves in four-foot elephant grass looking out into a field of grass and a few bushes back toward our perimeter. Ramirez tells me to go with him to put out our claymore mine. We crouch as we move forward, trying to keep our helmets below the top of the grass. We move out about sixty feet; and Ramirez then takes the little mine from its cloth carrier, pops open the two little sets of bipods, and pushes them into the ground. He screws in the explosive cap, and then we head back to Bicket. Ramirez is laying out the wire from the claymore as we move back.

We get back to our position, and Ramirez screws the claymore wire into the detonator. The back blast from the little mine can also be deadly if you are only twenty or thirty feet behind the mine, but we are about sixty feet back in heavy grass, so we will be all right from the back blast.

Ramirez then sets up the guard shifts. He tells me that I have last watch. We have one wristwatch to pass around as we stand watch. I'm beat. I've filled sandbags all day. I don't say a word. I just take off my web gear and helmet and lie down in the grass with my head on my web gear and my rifle across my body. I hope it doesn't rain. I don't want to get wet. I'm instantly asleep.

A big storm must be coming in. A heavy volume of thunder and lightning has moved in on us and awakens me. I feel Bicket snatch my rifle from my hands, and as I sit up, I see Ramirez duck out into the elephant grass. I then realize what's happening. The three positions on the trail are in a heavy firefight. I grab Bicket's M-79, check it to be sure it's loaded, and close the breach. I crawl over to Bicket and ask him where Ramirez went. Bicket tells me that he went after the claymore mine.

After a few seconds, Ramirez ducks back into our position and puts the claymore back into its carrier. Just then Sergeant Garza fast crawls into our position. He grabs Ramirez and is about to tell him something when Ramirez growls at me to watch out and not look at him and Garza. I turn around, embarrassed, and watch out into the grass. I then tell Bicket to give me my rifle, and I give him his M-79.

I hear Garza tell Ramirez to take Bicket and me and move to a big tree with some bushes around its base about one hundred meters behind us. Garza says we are to set up a base of fire to cover the squad's rear. He also says if the gooks get between us and the perimeter, we are in trouble.

Ramirez tells me to move toward that tree with Bicket and he will cover our backs. I've put on my web gear and helmet, so I just stand up in a crouch and run toward that tree as hard as I can run. I expect bullets to hit me in the back at any second. I hear Bicket and Ramirez running behind me.

We reach the tree, and I turn around with the others. I'm on the left with Ramirez on the right and Bicket between us. We are all three-breathing hard through our mouths as we watch the muzzle flashes in the distance. The firing is very heavy. I can hear De Jesus's machine gun, Gonzales's M-79, and the other guys' M-16s. I also hear a lot of enemy carbines popping.

Then we see shapes running toward us. We ready our weapons in case it's an enemy squad attempting to cut us off from the perimeter. As they get closer, we can see, even in the dark, that it's Arnold, Nunnery, Scott, and the machine gun crew.

They are about to pass us when Ramirez shouts, "Arnold." They see us then and run over to our location. Arnold gasps that Garza is holding the enemy off. Just then we see three men running toward us through the grass. It's Garza, Sanders, and Gonzales. I can see Sanders's and Gonzales's faces in the moonlight. They are straining with every fiber in their bodies to run faster. Garza is running backward behind them, firing back at the enemy. Arnold shouts, "Open fire." We all open fire, half of us firing on each side of our running men.

I see carbine muzzle flashes near a couple of small bushes to my left behind Garza's men. I fire as fast as I can pull the trigger toward these muzzle flashes. I empty my magazine and drop it out of my rifle. I shove another magazine in and open fire again as fast as I can. Halfway through my second magazine, my rifle jams. I curse and grab my cleaning rod from my cargo pocket and begin to screw it together. I un-jam my rifle and finish my second magazine and a third one as well. I see a lot of enemy muzzle flashes now in the grass and bushes to our front.

Garza shouts to Arnold to take Nunnery, Gonzales, and the gun crew and pull back about seventy-five meters, and the rest of us will cover them. The six of them leave on the run with the other six of us firing away. My M-16 jams again in my fifth magazine, and I quickly clear the jam. Scott shouts to me that he needs a jam rod, and I pass him mine. He un-jams his rifle and passes my rod back to me. I see Sanders clearing a jam in his rifle with his jam rod. Bicket is steadily pulling out little shells from his single-shot M-79. The other five of us are firing as fast as we can in between jams.

Garza then shouts that he has mortar fire coming in from our perimeter. He tells Ramirez to take Bicket and Scott and pull back to Arnold's position. That leaves Garza, Sanders with the radio, and me. Damn, I'm scared! We are all three firing away, and my rifle jams for the third time. I curse and quickly clear the jam with my rod. We are still facing a lot of muzzle flashes from carbines. Garza shouts for us to get out of here. He doesn't have to tell me twice. I turn and run in the direction the other members of the squad have run. Sanders is running beside me. He's as tall as I am and a hundred pounds lighter, but he cannot pass me. I'm putting my whole self into my run. I glance back one time and see Garza running backward behind us firing back at the enemy.

Suddenly, a line of muzzle flashes goes off in our faces. I wet my pants and almost fall to the ground. I then realize that it's the rest of the squad on line giving us cover fire. Sanders, Garza, and I run in among them and turn and add our fire to theirs.

Our 81 mm mortars are now being fired from inside our perimeter. The rounds are impacting in the area of our ambush location. Garza shouts into the radio to drop the mortar fire another one hundred meters closer to us and to tell the guys on the perimeter not to shoot us when we get close. He then tells Arnold to take his half of the squad and move back to cover the rest of us. I'm firing as fast as I can pull the trigger, sometimes shooting at muzzle flashes and sometimes just spraying the elephant grass. It seems that the enemy will follow us all the way back to our perimeter.

The mortar rounds land closer to us, and the explosions rattle my teeth. Garza then shouts for all six of us to fall back to Arnold's position. We turn and run, and this time I'm ready when Arnold and the others open fire to cover us. We set up with all twelve of us on line and firing. Garza calls for the mortars to drop another one hundred meters and tells Arnold to pull back again. I'm firing as fast as I can and dropping my empty magazines into my cargo pockets. Damn! My rifle has jammed again. I clear it and keep firing. Garza then tells all of us to run as the mortar rounds fall very close to us.

We reach Arnold's position where De Jesus with the machine gun and Gonzales with his M-79 are putting out a blistering fire. I think I can see the perimeter in the distance. We are all firing when Garza shouts for Ramirez, Bicket, and Scott to run for the break in the wire. They leave at a dead run with the other nine of us firing cover. I empty a magazine and slam in another, and Garza is shouting on the radio to drop the mortars another one hundred meters. He then shouts for Arnold to take Gonzales and Nunnery and run for the break in the wire. They leave without a word. The other six of us are still firing when the mortars drop in close and rattle my teeth again. Garza shouts for De Jesus to take his gun crew and head for the wire. They leave with Garza, Sanders, and I still firing.

Garza then shouts for Sanders and me to run for the wire. He doesn't have to tell me again. I turn and run for the wire, and this time, Sanders passes me with his long legs really reaching out. As I get close to the break in the wire, I see PSG John Hall kneeling at the break in the wire waiting for us. Sanders runs through the break in the wire, and Sergeant Hall says something to him, and he answers. Then I am at the break in the wire. Sergeant Hall says, "Fedrick, are you okay?" I tell him I am and drop on one knee beside him. Then here comes Garza still running backward, covering us. As he gets to Sergeant Hall, he also drops down on one knee and has a coughing fit. Sergeant Hall grabs his arm and says, "Damn, Garza, boy, are you hit?" My heart stops. Garza can't be hit! How would we survive without him? Garza says, "No, Sergeant, I'm okay just out of breath." Relief floods over me—Garza is okay.

Garza and I then head to our foxholes, and Garza starts going from hole to hole, making sure that everyone is okay and getting an ammo count so we can get an ammo resupply. I quickly count my magazines and find that I have got only, ten loaded magazines left and fourteen empty ones. I've fired 280 rounds in that short fight.

Garza gets to me and asks if I'm okay and how much ammo I need. I tell him I'm fine and I need 280 rounds to fill my magazines. He asks, "You fired up fourteen magazines?" I tell him I did. He then asks me how many loaded magazines I have left. I tell him ten. He then leaves to give the ammo count to the platoon sergeant.

I hear Corporal Arnold talking. He's saying that there had to be a platoon of the enemy. He says if there was only a squad, they would have exchanged fire with us for a minute or two and then pulled out, but these people had tried to cut us off from the perimeter and pushed us hard. I'm amazed that none of us were hit with all the fire we took. I also wonder if we hit any of them. I also find out what started the fight. Arnold and Scott were sleeping in their position, and Nunnery was on watch when he heard people crawling in on him. He opened fire and was quickly joined by Arnold and Scott. Arnold tells Nunnery that in the future if he has time to wake the other guys in his position up first before he opens fire, then they can all throw grenades and then open fire. Learning this infantry combat is a step-by-step learning process.

Everything has gotten quiet now, and there's no firing. The mortar tubes have also quit putting out rounds. It seems that it is over for tonight. Ramirez and Bicket are in the foxhole with me, and we set up the guard shifts. I roll over and cover myself with my poncho just as the rain starts. I instantly go to sleep.

Daylight comes, and I reload all my magazines with fresh ammo. We all clean our weapons as best as we can using torn M-14 cleaning patches and the few rods we have. We try to clean the rifle chambers as best as we can, but they are recessed, and we have no bore brushes. We use oil and rags and toothbrushes but make a poor job of it.

We get finished with our weapons, and the word comes to saddle up. The entire Second Platoon will head out and check the area of our firefight. Lieutenant Leary heads out with First and Second Squads up front and Third Squad in the back with Platoon Sergeant Hall. We check the entire area and find no sign of the enemy or any sign that they took casualties, but the rain may have washed away the signs. We then move to our ambush location. All we find there are our expended shell casings and Nunnery's poncho liner with a number of bullet holes in it. Scott looks for his watch and cannot find it. The gooks must have picked it up. Scott starts griping about Nunnery losing his watch when Arnold tells Scott that Nunnery may have saved his life and to quit griping. Scott thinks a minute and then tells Nunnery that he is sorry and to not worry about the watch.

We patrol the area the rest of the day but find no sign of the enemy. I guess they don't want to tie into a full platoon of Americans. We pull back to the perimeter late in the day and set in. Third Squad has ambush tonight, so we are holding down the perimeter with just two men per foxhole. I find that I share a foxhole with SGT Ben Garza. We talk a little as darkness approaches. He tells me that I am lucky to be in this platoon, and I agree with him. He asks me how many "natural-born combat infantrymen" I think are in Second Platoon. I have no idea and have never heard the term before but guess that it must be about ten. Garza laughs and tells me no. He says there are nearly forty men in the platoon and a dozen or more of them are great soldiers and he would go anywhere with them but there are only three "natural-born combat infantry soldiers" in the platoon. I am shocked and ask him why so few. He tells me that is a lot. Most platoons only have one, and once in a blue moon, a platoon might have two. He says that a platoon having three is unheard of. That is why this platoon is so good in combat.

I have got to ask him who the three are. He tells me one is Specialist 4 Nix, a tiny, blond soldier in First Squad with four years in the army. The Second is CPL George Arnold in our squad; he's got nine years of service. The Third is Garza himself with four years of army time. He says this with no bragging, and after watching him work for the last month, I believe him. So we've got three, and two are in this squad. We also have a dozen others that are "great soldiers" in the platoon. I feel better about my chances of surviving.

CHAPTER 5

The Booby Trap

August 1966

I'm a nineteen-year-old private and have been with Second Platoon, Bravo, Second, Eighteenth for two months. I think I'm just starting to get my feet on the ground. We have a brand-new platoon leader, 2LT Charles Fletcher, and I think that he will work out well. My squad leader is SGT Ben Garza, by far the best squad leader that I have known before or since.

The platoon is on a daytime sweep outside Base Camp Bearcat. It's hot and muggy, and it rains often here in the monsoon season. The area we are patrolling is not jungle. It's a bushy area with occasional open areas.

It's the middle of the day, and word is passed down the files to take a break for noon chow. Each of the two files faces outward, and the troops look for a place to crash and eat their cans of C rations. I notice a small line of bushes to my right with a good-sized sapling about as big around as my arm in the middle. I look around for trip wires and then step through the bushes so I have a clear view of the area to my right. I put my back against the sapling, glance around on both sides of me again for trip wires, and then slide down the sapling until I'm seated on the ground with my back against the sapling. It's very comfortable, and I can see to my right.

I break out one of my canteens and drink water. I then open a can of pork slices and eat it with crackers. After I've eaten the pork, I drink the salty brine from the can. I drink more water and place my canteen back in its carrier. It feels good to rest with back support.

We are there about fifteen minutes, and then the word is passed down each file that it's time to saddle up and get back on patrol. I've still got all my gear on, so I just have to stand up. I rise to a half-standing position, and for some reason, I glance behind me to the right. I freeze in place. There is a booby trap against my right kidney. It's in a large black cylinder-shaped container that American hand grenades are shipped in. The thing is almost as big as a quart jar. I see wires; how could I have missed seeing it before?

I call for Sergeant Garza in a low voice. He walks over to me, saying, "Fedrick, let's go. We have to move." As he walks up to me, I say, "Sergeant, I'm on a booby trap." His face goes blank, and his jaw tightens. "Where is it?" he asks, and I tell him behind my right kidney. He moves a little to my right and looks behind me. His face turns white, and he says, "Don't move." I say, "Sergeant, I'll retire right here, but I'm not going to move until you tell me."

Sergeant Garza backs up and walks away. He returns in a couple of minutes with Second Lieutenant Fletcher and Corporal Arnold. Some of the other guys try to follow them to get a look. They shout at the other guys to get away from us. Platoon Sergeant John Hall and the other NCOs get the troops away from us and set up platoon security.

Second Lieutenant Fletcher, Sergeant Garza, and Corporal Arnold drop to their knees to my right side and check out the booby trap. I'm still in a half-standing, half-squatting position. Second Lieutenant tells me not to move. I assure him that I'm not going to move. The three of them talk to each other about the booby trap as all four of us sweat. They decide that it's a "pull and release" booby trap, which means that it should go off if it's pulled on or pushed. They ask me how I sat down, and I tell them that I put my back against the sapling and slid down to the ground. Arnold says, "It should have went off when you did that. It may be a dud." Garza says quickly, "Just don't move in case it's live." I tell Garza, "I can stay like this for the next ten months of my tour if you tell me to."

The three of them discuss what to do and decide that they will take the long rope that our platoon carries to cross rivers and tie it to the sapling. They will take up the slack, and a man will get on the other end of the rope and hold it tight. I'm thinking now that the booby trap is a dud and everything will be all right. I don't dare move, though.

They tie the rope to the sapling, and Arnold takes the other end of the rope and walks out as far as the rope will allow him. Garza and Fletcher stay with me and make sure that the rope is tight. Arnold shouts that he's found a depression in the ground near the end of the rope. He lies down in it and is joined by SPC4 Liberato Gonzales. They hold the rope and say they are ready. Fletcher and Garza tell me not to move until they tell me. They then walk away from me. They walk past Arnold and Gonzales and rejoin the platoon about fifty meters away. Arnold and Gonzales are about halfway between me and the platoon.

Garza shouts for me to come off the booby trap and walk to him. I set my jaw, stand up, and come off the sapling. I'm stiff, but I walk past Arnold and Gonzales and up to Garza. I turn and face the booby trap, and Garza shouts, "Arnold, let the rope go." A huge black explosion envelops the sapling and the little stand of bushes by it. It wasn't a dud after all. Arnold walks up rolling the rope up. He says that ten feet are missing off the end of the rope that was next to the booby trap. The smoke thins, and I can see that the sapling and all the bushes near it are gone. If it had gone off against me, they would have had to have a closed coffin funeral.

We line up and move out on patrol. For some reason, I'm not shaking. McVey seems very concerned and asks me if I'm all right. I tell him that I'm fine. It just wasn't my day to die. It's just another day on patrol in Vietnam.

CHAPTER 6

The AWOLs

August 1966

The battalion has pulled into Quan Loi and dug in around the air strip. Quan Loi is the headquarters of a large rubber plantation with a big French house and a swimming pool. Americans are not allowed around the French residence or pool. There is a village for the rubber workers, but it is outside the perimeter. There is a large building that houses a bar at the edge of the village about 150 meters down from Second Squad's foxholes. No one is supposed to frequent this bar between the hours of 8:00 p.m. and 5:00 a.m. That is when the curfew is in effect. Everyone is supposed to be inside a building except soldiers on operations. Anyone who breaks the curfew can be shot without warning.

It's just gotten dark, and it's the rainy season. I hope we don't have to jump in our foxholes, because they are completely full of water from all the rain. These foxholes each have a tiny "hooch" behind them with a grass roof. It gives us partial shelter from the rain. It's a little better than two ponchos snapped together.

The rain has slacked off, and we sit in the dark and look out into the darkness. Then we hear firing from the other side of the perimeter. Sergeant Garza says that the enemy is probing one of the other companies. It's not heavy firing, and then it dies out. Suddenly, one of the guys from Bravo Company's headquarters section runs up to our hooch. He tells Sergeant Garza that an old sergeant E-5 and three other guys from Bravo's headquarters section have slipped down to the bar to our front and they did not take their rifles with them. I'm shocked. Those guys must be crazy. They are outside the perimeter after dark and unarmed! They could be killed or captured by the enemy or shot by our own troops.

Garza tells me to grab my rifle that we are going after the idiots. I start to grab my gear, and Garza says no web gear or helmet that we are going "light" with just our rifles. I grab my rifle and a bandoleer with seven magazines in it. I'm not going to be out "there" with just twenty rounds for my rifle.

Garza and I walk over to the foxhole line and are met by CPL George Arnold and the other guys. Garza tells Arnold that he and I are going after the idiots and to make sure that no one in First or Third Squads shoot us and to not let the officers find out what's happening.

I pull one magazine out of my bandoleer and hand it to Garza telling him that he needs a backup magazine. He puts it in his pocket and thanks me. He then runs down the little trail toward the bar with me running behind him. We have our rifles at the ready and are looking left and right as we run. I'm very afraid, just two of us and lightly armed.

We reach the bar and catch our breath for a second and then open the door and walk in with our rifles at the ready. The lights are bright inside. The jukebox is playing, and the old sergeant is on the dance floor dancing alone. He seems very drunk. The other three guys are sitting at a table talking with a big, young Vietnamese man with a close haircut. A couple of Vietnamese young women are also sitting at the table wearing miniskirts. Three other women in miniskirts are around the room, and there is an older male behind the bar.

Garza shouts, "Sergeant, the gooks are probing the perimeter." The old sergeant stands up straight and seems to be instantly sober. He doesn't say a word but just runs past us out into the dark. The larger American at the table is sitting beside the male Vietnamese. He says, "Garza, this gook speaks English." I step forward one step toward the Vietnamese man and flip the safety off my rifle and holding it waist high. I point it at the man's face and say to him, "Gook, if you move, I'm going to kill you and tell these other gooks if they move I'm going to kill you." He sits rock still and says something in Vietnamese to the other people. They all freeze in place. I then tell the three Americans to get out the door. They get up from the table and run for the door. I become very frightened. Could I be in here alone? I back up to the door, keeping my rifle level and never taking my eyes off the people in the bar. I reach the door and find that Garza is there covering me. Why would I have doubted it?

We step outside and close the door. Garza tells me to run up the trail toward the perimeter and if I see any Vietnamese with weapons to shoot them. I tell him that's what I intend to do. He says that he'll be right behind me and to call out to Arnold when I get near the perimeter.

I run up the trail with my head and my weapon moving right and left looking for enemy soldiers. I look behind me and see Garza is behind me running backward watching our backs. I get near the perimeter and drop to one knee. Garza stops with me. He's still watching behind us. I call in a low voice for Arnold, and he answers. He tells us to come on in. We move inside the perimeter, and Garza asks Arnold if the old sergeant and the other three guys made it in. Arnold says they did. Garza seems relieved and tells me to go back to my foxhole with Ramirez and Bicket. Before I go, I ask him for my magazine back. He laughs and hands it to me.

I move to my position, and Ramirez and Bicket ask me how it went. I play the role and tell them that it was a piece of cake for Garza and me. Ramirez then tells me that I have first watch and he and Bicket are going to sleep. I hope the guys could not tell that I was still shaking.

CHAPTER 7

The Hunter

Late August 1966

I've been in Vietnam a little over two months with Second Platoon, Bravo Company. My team leader is SPC4 Dimas Ramirez, my squad leader is SGT Ben Garza, the platoon sergeant is John Hall, and the platoon leader is 2LT Charles Fletcher. I'm nineteen years old and just over a year out of high school. I feel very confident with the people I work for and with.

We are working day patrols outside of Base Camp Bearcat. The platoon gears up just after daylight to head out when Sergeant Garza walks up to me and says, "Fedrick, you are running point today." My stomach turns over, and my guts freeze. I've never run point before. It's the most dangerous job in the platoon. The point man is the first man up. The point man is the one who trips booby traps, steps on a mine, or takes the first fire if we run into enemy soldiers. I say, "Sergeant, I've never run point before." Garza replies, "I know that. It's time that you learned." I taste copper in my mouth and shake my head yes because I can't speak.

We start out with Garza about ten feet behind me. He has the compass and the map. About every thirty feet, I stop and drop to one knee just like I've seen real point men do. At that time, Garza drops to one knee with me and points where he wants me to go. I proceed with the platoon following behind.

The area is single-canopy jungle with very thick underbrush. It's impossible to see more than ten feet ahead and usually less than that. I move very slowly looking for trip wires, mines, and trails. We've been on patrol about three hours when Garza directs me toward a very large black tree. I reach it and move around it looking for trip wires.

I hear a small tree limb break in front of me and only a few feet away. I drop to one knee and flick the safety off my rifle. Then something lurches up from the ground just in front of me with a crash of brush. I fire back and forth, left and right just as fast as I can pull the trigger. They run away, and I drop to my stomach and slam a fresh magazine into my rifle. Sergeant Garza crawls up beside me and asks, "How many of them were there?" I say, "I'm not sure. I didn't see them only heard them, but it sounded like two pair of feet that ran off." Garza asks, "Did they fire at you?" I reply, "I think I was the only one that fired. I think that they were lying on the ground sleeping."

Garza calls the team leaders, CPL George Arnold and SPC4 Dimas Ramirez, to get the rest of the ten-man squad on line. We then all move forward and find a thick trail of blood leading away. Corporal Arnold gets excited and says, "Damn, Fedrick, you hit at least one of them." A strange feeling spreads over me, and I shake a little. It could have been me who was hit.

We follow the heavy blood trail, being extremely careful. A wounded man can be even more dangerous than a nonwounded one. The rest of the platoon follows us. Everyone is on edge. The blood trail may be taking us to an enemy base camp with bunkers and machine guns.

The Second Squad is still abreast moving very slowing through the thick underbrush when we come to a very small creek. Corporal Arnold calls from the left, "Here he is." Sergeant Garza calls back, "Is he dead?" Arnold says, "Dead as hell." A strange feeling flushes through my body as I move to the left to see what I have done. Garza and Arnold are standing in the brush by the creek looking down at their feet. I walk up to them and see what they are looking at. A large doe deer is lying on her left side, dead. She has been shot in the right hip and shoulder and the right side of her neck. I am overcome with embarrassment. Garza and Arnold are smiling. Arnold says, "You did the right thing. If this had been enemy soldiers, you would have survived." Garza says, "You did really good."

Second Lieutenant Fletcher arrives on the scene, and he gets a laugh as well. He reports to the captain by radio what has happened. No one is laughing at me, and I begin to feel better about the incident. PFC Charles Bickett and a couple of other deer hunters walk up pull out their knives and began carving choice cuts off the deer. The platoon leader tells them to hurry up, that we have to finish our patrol and we are behind time how.

We patrol the rest of the day and find nothing. I run point all day, and as we pull back into the perimeter late in the afternoon, I am feeling like a real point man. Bickett and some of the other guys start a fire and cook the deer meat over it before it gets dark. It tastes good and is a welcome relief from canned C rations. My buddies eat deer meat and tell me how well I've done that day. I feel good about the day and my actions. I feel accepted by the older members of the platoon. Just nine months and three weeks left on my first tour of duty in Vietnam.

A few days later, we are "dug in" in a rubber plantation. The rows of big rubber trees go on for miles. There's one about every twenty feet and in perfect rows. They remind me a little of pecan orchards in the south. There's also a layer of dead leaves on the ground. Second Platoon has a "place guard." We, with help from some of the mortar platoon, are holding down the company foxholes in the perimeter. First and Third Platoons have multiple squad patrols out among the rubber trees. It's an easy day with two men to each foxhole. One has to be watching out, but the other soldier can nap.

Suddenly, we hear rifle fire not too far out in the "rubber." We are all quickly alert and trying to see through the trees toward the firing. About three hundred or more meters, we see movement among the trees. It looks like Americans moving and firing. We hear M-16s firing along with the occasional thump from an M-79. We also hear the steady pow-pow of enemy carbines firing. Sergeant Garza shouts for us to saddle up. A squad from First Platoon is in trouble. We gear up, and Garza tells CPL George Arnold to take the radio with his fire team and the machine gun crew and swing around to the right while he, Garza, will take Ramirez's team, including me, and swing to the left. He quickly tells us that First Platoon's Squad had jumped three VC soldiers and the enemy had ducked into a small bunker and put out a lot of fire. First Platoon's Squad contained eight men, seven armed with M-16s, and one with an M-79. Six of their M-16s have jammed, and they have no jam rods. They are, therefore, falling back toward the company perimeter. I think, *No jam rods, are they crazy?*

We move quickly among the rubber trees attempting to flank the enemy before they get away. We slow down and start moving from tree to tree. I'm glad Sergeant Garza knows where we are going because I sure don't. Then I see it! A small bump among the leaves with a small entrance hole in the back. It's almost invisible. I look to my right and see Arnold and the rest of the squad on line coming through the rubber trees. Arnold is talking on the radio as they approach. About thirty yards from the bunker Arnold and the rest of the squad drop down on their bellies with all their weapons pointed at the bunker. The assistant machine gunner is linking extra belts into the gun. I'm breathing through my mouth.

Garza tells Bicket and Scott to cover our back and the flank. He tells Ramirez and me to move with him as we approach the bunker from the flank. He tells us to cover him. Ramirez and I point our rifles at the bunker entrance. Garza takes a hand grenade off his belt with his left hand and pulls the pin while keeping the "spoon" depressed. Then with his rifle in his right hand, he ducks toward the bunker and throws the grenade into the entrance of the bunker. He dives away, and the grenade explodes. He rushes back to the bunker and goes in. He's out in a second telling us the three enemy soldiers are gone. I notice that the firing port for the bunker was facing Arnold. It's about two feet long and three inches high. We search the area but find nothing. We form up and move back to the perimeter.

We arrive back at the perimeter and drop our gear. Gonzales is very angry. He's saying why that other squad didn't stay there firing their one M-16 and the M-79, keeping the enemy trapped in the bunker until we arrived. Garza tells us that would have been too dangerous. If the enemy had received reinforcements, then the First Platoon's Squad would have been in major trouble. I ask why they did not have jamming rods. Garza admits that there is no excuse for them not having jamming rods for these very unreliable M-16s.

Arnold questions why that squad did not have a machine gun with them. Garza tells us that not having a machine gun was not the squad's fault but that was up to their platoon leader and platoon sergeant. The bottom line is we are all disappointed that we did not get to engage the enemy team. We've got a number of jam rods and two M-79s. We also almost always have a machine gun with us. The enemy team is very lucky that they did not engage our squad, or they would all three be dead now.

CHAPTER 8

L-Shaped Ambush

September 9, 1966

I've been in-country for two-and-a-half months on my first tour with B-2-18. I'm nineteen years old and think I'm starting to get the hang of this infantry combat. I feel like I'm starting to pull my own weight.

Second Platoon is going to conduct a daytime patrol out of Base Camp Bearcat in primarily rubber plantations. This is not a free-fire zone. There are many civilians and rubber workers in the area. We will be checking ID cards looking for enemy soldiers attempting to blend into the population. In South Vietnam, all citizens fourteen and older have an ID card covered in plastic. They are required to have this card with them at all times. We cannot fire at people in this area unless they run from us or they are carrying weapons.

We start out, and the platoon is running in an arrow formation. Second Squad (us) is the right wing of the arrow, and Third Squad is the left wing. First Squad is the shaft of the arrow, and in that position, First Squad can maneuver to assist either of the other squads. The two machine gun crews are with Second and Third Squads.

There's a light rain falling, and we cross a field of short dry stalks. I don't know what crop this was, but it reminds me a little of dry cotton stalks, but it's not. I wonder if I'll recall this field when I'm an old man—if I live to be an old man. Today I'm just trying to get out of my teens which will be over five months from now.

We move into the rubber. The trees are planted in rows about twenty feet apart. The rubber trees go on for miles. There's some tall grass and a few bushes among the trees, but it's basically cleared. These rubber plantations remind me of pecan orchards in the south.

We start coming across rubber workers gathering rubber sap from the trees. The sap collects in small bowls attached to the tree. I've heard that these workers make about fifty cents a day. So far, every worker we have come across has his ID card.

We come to a dirt road running between the trees. The platoon sets up a checkpoint. Second and Third Squads will secure the checkpoint out into the rubber trees. Each of these squads will have a machine gun crew with them. First Squad, along with the LT Charles Fletcher and PSG John Hall will man the checkpoint and check ID cards on all who pass.

The foot traffic picks up on the road. We even start getting a few ox carts coming by. I find it all very interesting watching the First Squad check ID cards as I lean against a rubber tree. I see my squad leader, SGT Ben Garza, walking over to me. He stops next to me, and in a very low voice, he tells me that I need to be looking out for enemy soldiers not watching the checkpoint. I am terribly embarrassed and face out and do my job. I'll not make this mistake again. I'm thankful that Sergeant Garza didn't shout at me and belittle me in front of the squad. Most squad leaders would have done that.

In an hour or so, the platoon forms up, and we start the patrol again. We are still working the arrow formation as we move through the rubber trees. I feel good about being a member of this platoon. It seems to do everything very professionally.

I hear someone say, "Look." I look to my left and see Leo Franovich, a tall dark-haired guy from Connecticut, pointing to his front with a surprised look on his face. I then hear Sergeant Garza shout, "Gooks, left front." He then starts to fire. I look to my front and see nothing. I then shift my gaze to my left front, and I see them. There are two male Vietnamese in black clothing and carrying rifles running away from us at an angle to our left front. I throw my M-16 to my shoulder, and as my front sight passes the two running men, I fire as fast as I can pull the trigger. I fire four quick shots, and then my rifle *stops*. *Jam, jam*. Damn, a jammed rifle. I drop to one knee and pull out the .22-caliber cleaning rod that my mother sent me and screw it together. I then shove it down the muzzle of my rifle and dislodge the jammed shell in the chamber of my rifle. I reseat my magazine, stand up, and bring my rifle back to my shoulder. But it's over. The two enemy soldiers are out of sight.

Someone is shouting that we hit one of the VCs and that he fell but got back up and kept running. We move toward the area where the enemy had been. Some of the NCOs are saying, "Watch out. These gooks may be leading us into a trap."

We arrive in the area, and I see an army web belt lying on the ground. There's one ammo pouch and one canteen on the belt. I kneel and open the ammo pouch. There's two fifteen-round M-1 carbine magazines in the pouch. I then take out the canteen from its holder. It feels full. I unscrew the cap and smell the contents. It smells sour and like rice. I think that its rice wine. I turn it upside down and pour all the contents out on the ground. Jim "the Swede" Norberg asks me what it was, and I tell him it was rice wine. He chastises me for wasting it. I tell him that it might have been poison. He laughs, shakes his head, and walks on by. Someone else picks up the web belt, and we continue our patrol.

We work the rubber for another hour, and then the word comes down to set up a perimeter and face out that we are going to chow down. I place my back against a rubber tree and face out. I break out a can of beefsteak and potatoes. I eat it with some canned crackers and finish up with a small canned pecan roll. I drink some water and am feeling pretty good. We've had a good day. We've jumped two enemy soldiers and wounded one of them while recovering his ammo and wine. It seems to me to have been a pretty good day.

We saddle up and resume our patrol. In about twenty minutes, one of the guys carrying ammo for one of the machine guns suddenly announces that he's left a two-hundred-round can of machine gun ammo where we took our chow break. The lieutenant, platoon sergeant, and squad leader all chew him out. The lieutenant then directs

Sergeant Garza to take Second Squad back to get the ammo. The rest of the platoon will crash and wait on us. Extra work for Second Squad. They send the ammo bearer with us, and we head back. We are moving a little faster than usual and trying to look for an enemy ambush at the same time. The ammo bearer is terribly upset with himself. He should be. He's put us all in danger and caused extra work for Second Squad.

We reach the area of our chow break, and Sergeant Garza has us to spread out even more as we move in. We find the can of ammo. We are a little surprised that the enemy didn't find it first and take it. Garza checks the can to make sure it hasn't been booby trapped. He tells the ammo bearer to pick it up. We then head back to the platoon.

We reach the platoon and form up again into the arrow formation. The rest of the platoon is rested. Second Squad is tired and sweat soaked. We move out through the rubber trees, keeping a sharp lookout.

We approach an area where the jungle is on our left and also toward our front. There is a small grass hooch not far from the wood line to our front. We see a Vietnamese man in black clothing and wearing a conical-shaped straw hat walking from the hooch toward the wood line to our front. He is over one hundred meters to our front and is looking over his right shoulder at us. He is keeping his left arm and hand out of our sight to his front as if he's carrying something. This doesn't look right at all. Our trouble antennas go up big-time.

The platoon stops, and Lieutenant Fletcher tells Sergeant Garza to send one of his fire teams up to check that man out. Garza tells CPL George Arnold to take his fire team up and check out the man. I'm in Ramirez's team, so I'm not involved. Arnold moves forward with Nunnery, Sanders, and Gonzalez. As they move forward, the Vietnamese man disappears into the jungle. The rest of the platoon wait where we are and cover them.

Arnold's team keeps advancing slowly and well spread out. Arnold is on the left with Gonzalez next to him then Sanders and Nunnery on the right. They are about fifty feet from the wood line to the front when a heavy volume of rifle fire opens up from the wood lines to the front and the left. The four of them hit the ground each behind a rubber tree. I see a VC in the wood line to my front on the other side of Arnold. The VC is standing waist deep in bushes, and he is firing an M-1 carbine as fast as he can pull the trigger. He's about 120 meters from me. I brace against a rubber tree and put my rifle sights on him. I'm about to pull the trigger when Arnold pops up into my sight picture, fires some quick shots, and drops back down. I regain my sight picture on the VC and am about to pull the trigger again when Arnold again pops into my sight picture again, fires a couple of quick shots, and drops back down.

I'm so frustrated. I can see the enemy soldier but can't shoot him, because Arnold is in the way. I shout for Arnold to stay down, but with all the firing, he can't hear me. I look over at Sergeant Garza and shout to him that I'm going to help Arnold. He replies that he's going with me.

I break into a galloping run toward Arnold. I'm weaving in and out among the rubber trees. I hear a bullet break the sound barrier going by my right ear. Just as I pass a rubber tree, a round hits it, blowing tree bark and white rubber sap into the air. I fall beside Arnold shouting there's one right in front of him. Arnold is kicking at me with both feet, shouting for me to get away from him that I'm drawing all the enemy fire. I roll over and over to my left until I reach the next tree to Arnold's left. I am lying flat on the ground with my rifle pointed at the wood line to the front, and I can't see a thing.

I stand up behind my rubber tree, and I see the enemy soldier directly in front of me fifty feet away. He's still firing away with his carbine. He switches his fire to me just as I open up on him firing as fast as I can pull the trigger. The VC's fire is hitting the tree I'm partially behind; tree bark and white rubber sap are flying. Suddenly, the VC spins all the way around. I've hit him! But he comes right back on me firing away. I feel something hit my right thigh. Am I hit, or is it flying bark from the tree? I keep firing at the VC, and he goes down. I change magazines and glance down at my right leg as I do so. I see nothing amiss. The VC is back up and attempting to stagger away into the jungle. I've got my rifle on him firing as fast as I can, and he goes down again. *Then* my rifle jams! I jerk out my .22-caliber cleaning rod, quickly screw it together, shove it down the barrel of my rifle, and un-jam it. As I do this, I see that my entire right pants leg is crimson in color. That wasn't flying tree bark that hit my leg.

Arnold on my right is screaming for a jamming rod. I toss him mine just as a bullet from my right front hits my rubber tree at an angle and goes all the way through it. Carbine rounds have not been going through this tree. I shift to my right front just as a bullet hits my gas mask riding on my left hip in its carrier. I look into the wood line to my right front, and I see a VC in a conical-shaped straw firing a full-sized M-1 rifle at me. It may be the same VC that tried to lead us into this L-shaped ambush. It was that big .30-06 round that went completely through my rubber tree and then through my gas mask like a freight train. I throw my front sight on the VC in the straw hat and fire away going through half a magazine, and the VC falls back into the bushes. I keep firing where the VC has disappeared. On the last round in the magazine, my rifle jams again. I look right to Arnold and scream, "Jam rod, jam rod." Arnold throws me my rod back, and as he does, I see that Sanders is throwing his stiff jamming wire to Nunnery so he can un-jam his M-16. Gonzales is popping the little shells from his M-79 into the wood line.

I seat another magazine, look to my left, and see another VC firing a carbine toward soldiers on my left. I open fire on him, and he ducks away into the brush. I empty my rifle into the brush where he has disappeared. *Suddenly*, someone grabs my web belt in the back and starts jerking me to the ground. I hear Garza say, "Get your big butt down." Then he's beside me on the ground on my right firing at a VC that is running along the wood line from our right to our left. Then I'm firing with him. He's changing magazines when he asks me if I'm all right. I tell him no, that I'm hit. He asks where I'm hit, and I tell him in my right leg.

He looks over his left shoulder and shouts, "Medic, medic, this *man* is hit." My throat almost closes with pride. This is the first time anyone has called me a man and really meant it. I look over my right shoulder as I change magazines, and I see Doc Parks a hundred meters away break from behind a rubber tree and start his run toward me. He's a small light-skinned Black soldier from Philadelphia with crooked front teeth. I'm amazed at his run. I've never seen an NFL running back make a run like this. He's holding his medic bag high in the air with his right hand. In his left hand, he's holding his .45-caliber pistol by the barrel, and it's high in the air as well. His legs are moving so fast you can hardly see them.

Doc Parks reaches me, drops beside me, and cuts my pants leg away. Garza and I are still firing at enemy soldiers in the wood line. I change magazines, look at Doc Parks, and ask him, "Doc, is my 'equipment' all right?" Rounds are hitting around us, but Parks and Garza break into gales of laughter. Parks looks at me; and with tears of glee running down his cheeks, he says, "Yes, Fedrick, they are all right, but two inches higher and you would have had to settle for nephews and nieces." I then break into laughter with them. Doc places a large field dressing on my thigh and says I'll be fine.

I face back to the front and put out more fire with Garza. I notice that the rest of Second Squad has pulled up even with us on the left and they are also putting heavy fire into the wood line. We're seeing more VC jumping up. Some are running left, some to the right, while others are scattering away. Are they starting to pull out?

Firing is dying down. The VCs are pulling out big-time now. Lieutenant Fletcher runs over to me and asks how I am. I tell him I'm great. The lieutenant then tells Garza to saddle up Second Squad, that he's leaving Third Squad, to get me back about five hundred meters to a clearing, to medevac me out to the hospital, and the rest of the platoon are going to chase the VCs hoping with them carrying their causalities that Second Platoon can over take them. Garza tells him that his M-16s bolt has broken. I hand Garza my rifle and tell him to take mine.

I find out later that the understrength VC platoon had set up an L-shaped ambush for us. They had two squads in the wood line to our front and one squad in the wood line to our left. They had started digging foxholes but had only gotten about two inches deep when we arrived. They had tried to suck the entire platoon in with the guy in the straw hat who was walking away from us into the wood line. Our leadership had been too smart for them and had just sent a fire team up to check him out.

I learn that Third Squad and one machine gun have just remained in place and put out heavy fire at the wood line to their left and also the one to the front. The remainder of Second Squad, along with the other machine gun, have pulled up with Arnold's team and smoked the wood line to our front. Sergeant Calvino's First Squad, along with PSG John Hall, had pulled around to the left and hit the enemy squad in the wood line to our left and began rolling them up. The firing was a continuous roar.

Before Garza departs, he tells me that when he said we were going to help Arnold, he meant one tree at a time while giving each other cover fire. He says you do not run a hundred meters with an entire enemy platoon firing at you. He says his main point is *you do not stand up in a firefight*. I meekly say, "Yes, Sergeant." The platoon then pulls out as Travis Nunnery passes me he asks if I'm okay. I tell him that I am, and he follows Garza on into the wood line. I'll never see him again.

Third Squad is around me now. Doug McVey and Ed Shaffer are kneeling beside me, checking me out. Shaffer says, "Nine bullets have hit this tree that Fedrick was behind." McVey then states, "There's nine empty magazines lying here on the ground under Fedrick." Sergeant Wilson tells Shaffer and McVey to pick me up and they will move out. Shaffer is stunned. He tells Sergeant Wilson that he can't be serious, that I weigh over 250 pounds, and it would take the entire squad to carry me. I laugh and tell the guys that I can walk but just help me onto my feet.

McVey and Shaffer help me up, and I put an arm around each of them, and we start walking. Third Squad is spread out around us as we head in the direction of the landing zone. I'm still on an adrenaline high and am talking away about the firefight and the enemy soldiers I have shot. McVey and Shaffer are getting a kick out of my endless talking. I find that I'm walking better than I thought I could. I tell Shaffer not to help me and just leave McVey on my bad side— after all, one grenade could get us all. For some reason, this cracks them both up, and they laugh even more. I'm wondering why I'm the only GI to be hit in the firefight. McVey replies that I was the only one dumb enough to stand up. We all three break into laughter.

We see Third Platoon coming though the rubber trees in the distance at a jog, Lieutenant Patrick and Platoon Sergeant Locket in the lead. I also see Company First Sergeant Perry and his two radio men with them. Third Platoon pass us continuing on to back up Second Platoon. First Sergeant Perry and his radio men drop out with us and accompany us toward the LZ. I burn Top Perry's ears about the firefight as we walk along. He's beginning to laugh as much as McVey and Shaffer. Top Perry asks me if I hit any of the enemy, and I tell him I sure did and if I had a rifle that didn't jam I might have got the whole enemy platoon. The guys are laughing harder than ever.

We reach the LZ, and Top Perry tells Third Squad to secure around the LZ and he will get me on the chopper. Top and I talk as we stand and wait for the chopper. I'm having a really big time, and my leg is just hurting like a toothache. This isn't bad at all.

The chopper comes in, and Top throws smoke. The chopper starts to settle into the LZ, and Top takes me by the right arm with his left hand, and we start walking toward the chopper. The tall grass pulls at my bad leg. This makes small spasms of pain shoot though my leg, but I don't quit grinning. I wouldn't want Top or the guys to think that I'm a wimp. Top helps me onto the chopper, and the medic grabs me, and the chopper starts up into the air very fast. I'm on my way to the Third Surgical Hospital.

CHAPTER 9

Third Surgical Hospital

September 9, 1966

I've been in Vietnam for two and a half months and have just received a gunshot wound to my right thigh. I'm on a dust-off helicopter en route to the Third Surgical Hospital. I'm still on an adrenaline high from the firefight and feel like my performance was acceptable despite a number of mistakes I made. I don't think that I let the squad down.

The helicopter lands on the chopper pad at the hospital, and a number of medics meet me with a gurney. I tell them that I can walk, but they insist that I lie down. They roll me into the operating room and cut my uniform off. A doctor asks me what I was hit with, and I tell him an M-1 carbine. He then asks me when I ate last. I tell him a C ration meal of beefsteak and potatoes with crackers and a small pecan roll just two hours before. He then tells me that they cannot put me to sleep, because it has not been long enough since I ate to put me to sleep. He says that they will have to deaden my thigh and operate. He says that I have very thick thighs so I will have to tell them when the pain gets more than I can handle and they will give more lidocaine in my thigh to deaden it.

They began working on my leg, and in a while, I'm getting sharp pain there. I tell them, and they give me more shots in my thigh. It's all right for a while, and then it hurts again. They give me more shots. We do this a couple more times, and after a few hours, they finish. I've got a bandage from my groin to my knee.

They wheel me into a ward full of wounded Americans and help me into a hospital bed. A nurse comes by and attempts to give me an IV. She tries five times in my right arm and four times in my left and cannot get a vein. I've never had this problem before. Apparently, I've lost a lot of blood for my veins to be so flat. She tries in the back of my right hand and misses again. This is getting very painful. I tell the nurse that she has one more chance, the pain is much worse than being shot. She tries the eleventh time and gets a vein. She starts giving me a blood transfusion. I'm relieved.

Then they bring me hot chow to my bed. This is the life! A soft bed, clean sheets, and hot chow, this is great! I go to sleep and wake in the middle of the night. They are bringing more wounded troops into the ward. They place a Black soldier with a head wound into the bed next to me. His wound starts just below his cheekbone goes back through his ear and out the back of his head. It looks like a long deep trough, but I think that it's not serious. He's awake, and I ask him what outfit he's with and what happened. He says he's with the 173rd Airborne Brigade and they are involved in a large battle with a lot of causalities on both sides. Well, at least it's not my outfit or guys I know.

This goes on for days with them bringing in wounded guys from the 173rd Brigade. The hospital staff are very busy. I get fed and am able to hobble to the latrine on my own. They've not checked my wound or changed my bandage since I've been here. I start smelling my leg, and that concerns me. I try to get the attention of a couple of medics, but they are moving fast, and I can't get their attention.

Finally, as a medic walks by, I reach out and grab him by the arm. He tries to get loose, and I hold on tight. He asks me what's wrong, and I tell him that I smell my leg. He settles down and asks me when I came into the hospital, and I tell him on the Ninth. He asks when they last changed my bandage. I tell him that they never have. He says, "You came in on the Ninth, and they have not changed your bandage ever?" I agree with him. He tells me if I'll let him go, he'll get someone to check my wound. I let him go and he leaves.

He's back in a few minutes with a gurney. He helps me onto the gurney and wheels me to the operating room. There are three doctors waiting on me. They cut off my bandage, and the smell is terrible. They talk it over, and one wants to just cut off my leg. A second one doesn't care, and the Third one wants to try to debride the wound each day and see what happens. I say that I vote with that guy. They tell me to be quiet, that they are officers talking. I say no more but promise myself that if they decide to take my leg, it will take four men to hold me when they put me under. They finally decide to debride and ask me when I ate last. It hasn't been long, so they cannot put me to sleep. More pain! After an hour, they bandage my leg and send me back to the ward. They tell me that every morning they will work on my leg in hopes of saving it.

I'm able to move around and go to the mess hall and the small PX. Like all the other wounded, I'm in pale-blue pajamas and cloth house shoes. I'm getting to know the nurses and medics. Two of the nurses are Lieutenants Simmons. LT Grace Simmons has blonde hair and a mole on her right cheek. LT Gail Simmons is a redhead. Both of them are old, maybe twenty-four or twenty-five. The major in charge of the nurses is a small redhead. She is very old, maybe forty or more, way older than my mother. They are all very nice to us, and they are officers and ladies, so we call all of them by their rank or other terms of respect. They look sharp in their jungle fatigues. Theirs fit. They are also starched and pressed. They also have their rank and name sewn on their uniforms.

There is a medic named Chrisodolou. He's a big Hawaiian in his twenties. He is a great guy and treats us right. Another medic is an old bald specialist 5 in his forties. He's kind of a sour guy, but he's good to us. All of them are calling me Chester because I walk like Chester on *Gunsmoke*.

The big draw back for me is that every morning at 1000 hours, the doctors come to my bed. They have me take off my pants, and they put a plastic sheet under me. They then remove my bandage and pour peroxide on my wound. Then they spend thirty to forty minutes scraping my entire wound with a sharp instrument. I lie on my stomach, holding onto my bedstead with both hands and a pillow shoved into my mouth so I will not scream and embarrass myself in front of all the guys. After they are done, they rebandage me and leave with the plastic sheet. I then put my pants on, and the rest of the day is great. I can read, limp around, or even help the medics.

When dust-off choppers bring in wounded, I limp down to the chopper pad if I'm awake to see if it's anyone I know. So far I see no one I know. I worry about the guys in the squad and the platoon. I'm not there to carry my weight, and the guys have the same mission despite being shorthanded.

On October 1, 1966, it's a quiet early afternoon, and I'm in my bunk reading a good western novel. I hear the dust-off choppers coming in, but I'm comfortable, and I've never seen any wounded come in that I know. I just lie there and read.

In a couple of hours, they wheel two wounded soldiers in at the other end of the ward and place them in beds. I read without my glasses, so by glancing, I can only tell that they both have dark hair.

In a few minutes, I finish my book. I get up, put my glasses on, and limp toward the other end of the ward. I'm planning on going to the post exchange. I reach the other end of the ward, and someone says, "Fedrick." I look to my right, and SGT Ben Garza is lying in the bunk in bandages. I rush over to him and see his right wrist and his left hip are covered in thick bandages. I say, "Garza, what happened?" He tells me that they had hit some bad stuff. He then looks at me with tears in his eyes and tells me that Nunnery and Frasier are dead. I say that, no, they can't be. He says they are and that Raminez is terribly wounded and he was taken to another hospital. He then points with his left hand across the aisle and tells me that Calvino is right over there. I look, and SGT Juan Calvino from First Squad is lying there with a big bandage on his stomach waving at me.

It's hard to take in. My squad leader and team leader and the First Squad leader wounded and Travis Nunnery and Leroy Frasier dead. I stagger around from Garza to Calvino and back attempting to process the terrible news. Garza gives me the run down, and it just gets worse and worse. I ask where they have taken Travis and

Leroy. Garza tells me that they came in on the chopper with him and Calvino.

I break away from Garza and Calvino and head down to the morgue. I walk in, and a Staff Sergeant Medic is working. I ask him if he has Travis Nunnery and Leroy Frasier. He quits smiling and tells me that he does. I ask to see them. He says, "No, Chester, I'm not going to let you see them. Just remember them like you saw them last."

I return to the ward and attempt to help Garza and Calvino all I can. I hear people coming into the ward and turn and look. It's Lieutenant Fletcher and Corporal Arnold. Fletcher's face is white as a sheet, but Arnold is hanging tough. He speaks to Calvino and calls him John. Fletcher is beside Garza talking to him. Arnold goes over to Ben and asks him how he is doing. Both of them also speak to me. Fletcher then tells Garza that he and Sergeant Arnold have been to the morgue and identified Nunnery and Frazier. He said "Sergeant Arnold". I look, and Arnold is wearing three stripes. I tell him congratulations. He tells me that Ramirez and Mulchaney also made sergeant. Garza, Calvino, and Wilson all made staff sergeants the week before. Fletcher has also made first lieutenant. Geez, there's been a lot of promotions in the three weeks since I got hit. Lieutenant Fletcher and Sergeant Arnold then leave. They have to get back to the platoon.

The next few days go by with me helping Garza and Calvino walk to the latrine and around the ward. It's tough, but the three of us are dealing with the deaths of our friends. I tell LT Grace Simmons what has happened and that I feel bad because I wasn't there to help. She tells me that I was seriously wounded in another fight and it wasn't my fault that I wasn't there for the guys. This makes me feel somewhat better.

The major in charge of the nurses gets very excited. Her husband is a helicopter pilot and is "in country." The two of them have swung a three-day pass at Vau Tau, an R&R center on the coast. They haven't seen each other in some months. She tells us all good-bye and leaves. One of the older guys on the ward makes a crude remark that the only thing wrong with the major is that she has been going "without." I'm shocked. I say, "What do you mean?" You know that forty-year-old people don't still have sex. The entire ward breaks into gales of laughter. I'm terribly embarrassed. I'm only nineteen years old, and I had assumed that by forty, your sex life was over.

There are two other medics who work the ward. They are Maroon and Green (not their real names). They are best friends but are as different as daylight and dark. Maroon is a slender guy with a great personality. He is also very caring of his patients. Green, on the other hand, is fat and slow moving with very little personality. We wonder why they are friends.

One morning numerous military police jeeps pull into the hospital compound. Numerous MPs descend on the hospital, and very quickly they have Maroon and Green in handcuffs. They load the two medics in jeeps, and then they are all gone in a cloud of dust.

Then we are told what happened. The afternoon before, Maroon and Green had the day off and went to town in a jeep. They had their M-14 rifles for protection. Apparently, they got drunk in town, and on the way back, they saw farmers working in the rice paddies. They stopped the jeep and calmly shot five of the farmers to death.

We are all shocked. It's the only time that I knew anyone that committed a "war crime," and they are not even infantryman in the field. They are two rear echelon soldiers that have never been to the field. Garza is really upset. He says he understands how Green could have done such a terrible thing but cannot understand how a nice guy like Maroon could have committed murder. All the wounded in the hospital are infantryman, and they are all upset. Well, Maroon and Green will probably spend the rest of their lives in Leavenworth Federal Prison, as they should.

They are still working on my leg every morning, and Garza is shocked by how bad my leg looks. They then move Garza and Calvino to another hospital. It's lonely without them with me. I just limp around and help the medics all I can. Then they tell me that they think that they have removed all the crud from my leg and they are going to transfer me to the Ninety-Third Hospital at Long Binh. They load me on an ambulance and drive me to the new hospital. I'm leaving a lot of friends.

I arrive with my boots and helmet in hand. They take these from me and say they will be in the supply room. I'm placed in a ward and find out that it's not air-conditioned like the last hospital. The ward is also much larger, and there's not as much personal care. I'm homesick for the platoon and for the last hospital I was in.

Then I recall that Ramirez was taken to this hospital. He could still be here. I check and find out that he is still here. He's in a ward about two hundred meters from mine. I limp over there in the hot sun and walk to the nurses' station. It's being manned by a stunningly beautiful blonde second lieutenant. I ask her if Dimas Ramirez is on this ward. She says he's five beds down on the left and he's very weak, not to talk to him too long. I move down to the fifth bed, and I don't know this man. He looks seventy years old, and his body is gray in color, and he is covered in stitches. He's also got tubes running into every opening in his body. I look at the name on the end of the bed, and it is him. His eyes are closed, and I'm glad that he did not see how shocked I was.

I call his name, and he opens his eyes. He seems glad to see me. I find that he has to put a finger over a hole in his throat to talk, so I do most of the talking. I hear people speaking Spanish behind me. I look around and see First Sergeant Perry along with Jose Martinez and Chico Ruiz. The two Puerto Ricans are Ramirez's two best friends in the company. I shake both their hands as I walk by them and then shake First Sergeant Perry's hand. He and I stand and talk while Jose and Chico carry on a loud conversation with Dimas in Spanish. Top Perry and the other two soldiers leave, and I head back to my ward.

I visit Dimas every day, and he seems to like my visits. One day, I go to visit him, and the beautiful nurse tells me to have a good visit that they are flying Dimas out tonight to an army hospital in Japan. I talk to him longer than usually and tell him I'm glad he was my team leader. I leave his ward and now really feel alone.

One morning, a specialist 5 medic comes in and tells me that I'm going to paint the ward. I tell him I'm wounded that I'm not going to paint. He tells me that it's an order and that I will. I tell him that I have to go to the latrine first. He tells me not to take long.

I leave and limp to the supply room. There are new jungle uniforms there along with socks and my helmet and boots. I quickly dress and head toward the front gate. I feel like a thief leaving the scene of a crime. I walk out onto the highway and stick my thumb up. A truck stops with two GIs in the cab. They ask where I'm going, and I tell them Di An. They say that's where they are going, and I hop in. I tell them I'm leaving the hospital and going to B-2-18. The driver says he knows just where they are located, and we take off. I'm glad he knows their location. The unit has moved to Di An from Bearcat while I was in the hospital.

I tell them all about the day I got hit as we drive. They seem very interested. Before I know it, we arrive at Bravo Company's area. I thank the two guys and get out of the truck.

I find Bravo's headquarters tent. I take a deep breath and walk in. I see Lieutenant Leary sitting at a desk. I walk up to the desk, salute, and say, "Private First Class Fedrick reporting for duty, sir." Lieutenant Leary jumps up and shouts, "Fedrick." He runs around the desk and hugs me. He tells me that he's glad to see me back. I tell him that I've gone AWOL from the hospital. He gets serious and asks me when I did that. I tell him just this morning. He laughs and says that's no problem, that he will just pick me up on the morning report the next day.

Lieutenant Leary then takes me to the battalion doctor. The doctor looks at my leg and puts me on light duty for the time being. The lieutenant then walks me back to the company area and puts me on a tiny switch board. It only connects with the orderly room, supply room, and mess hall. There's not a lot of calls, and it's an easy job.

I get off the switchboard, and someone points out Second Squad, Second Platoon's tent. I walk into the tent and see canvass cots with duffle bags lying on them. I check and find my duffle bag is on one of the cots. The guys have not forgotten me! I feel warm all over. It's great to be a part of something so important.

It's time for the evening meal. I go to chow and run into Staff Sergeant Garza, Staff Sergeant Calvino, and Sergeant First Class Locket from the Third Platoon. They are all back from the hospital and like me are on light duty. They don't have to worry, because no one puts E-6s and E-7s on details. The four of us buddy around, but they tell me that when we go back with the platoon that our relationship will change. I tell them that I understand that.

Staff Sergeant Slayton from Third Platoon comes in from the field. His tour is done, and he's going home. He and Garza are very tight. Slayton was Garza's squad leader in Germany. Slayton tells Garza that he, Garza, only has six weeks left on his tour and he can "sham" in the rear area with his wounds until his time to leave. Garza tells him "no" that when the company comes in, he'll be going back to the field with them. I'm impressed with Garza's character. He's been seriously wounded and been decorated a number of times, but he's going to let himself get shot at for the next six weeks just to be with the guys.

The next day, Lieutenant Leary passes the word that the company will be back in the next day. I tell Lieutenant Leary that I want to go to full duty and go back out with the company. He walks me over to the doctor's tent, and the doctor checks me out. He says I still have some drainage and I need at least two or three more weeks before I'm fit for full duty. I tell him that, with all due respect for his rank, I'm either going out with the company or going to the Long Binh Jail. Lieutenant Leary calls the doctor over to a corner, and they have a whispering officers' conference. The doctor comes back to me and asks me if I can keep my wound dry. What is he thinking? It's the rainy season. I look him right in the eye and say, "Yes, sir." He says that he's putting me back on full duty. My guts turn over. Well, this is what I wanted. The lieutenant and I walk back to the company area, and I wonder if I have given myself a death sentence.

CHAPTER 10

Operation Attleboro

November 5, 1966, four and a half months in Vietnam

I've just returned to the unit at its new base camp at Di An after spending thirty-seven days in the Third Surgical Hospital on the Bien Hue Air Base and the Ninety-Third Evacuation Hospital at Long Binh. I had suffered a very serious gunshot wound to my right leg in an ambush on September 9, while Second Platoon was on patrol in a rubber plantation. I've spent a few days on light duty with the unit rear at Di An, and just today the doctor has put me back on full duty.

The company flies in from the field that morning from an operation that I have missed because of my wound. I meet the guys at the helipad. They dismount the helicopters and spread out as they walk toward the tents. They are still in full combat mode as their eyes dart back and forth looking for an enemy that is not there. They are filthy dirty with torn uniforms and heavy loads on their backs. They have been in the jungle five weeks and smell like long-dead roadkill. I'm clean, having had a shower just that morning. I feel self-conscious that I'm not like them, and I've missed an entire operation on which the platoon and company have suffered casualties. A buddy of mine from Tennessee had been killed along with another soldier from Second Platoon. Five other members of the platoon were wounded, including my team leader, Dimas Ramirez. He was so badly wounded that he was shipped back to the States.

My squad leader, SSG Ben Garza, was also wounded in that action, having been hit in the left hip and right wrist. Garza has been with me in the rear the last few days waiting on the company to come in from the field. He has also been cleared for full duty.

The first of the guys to recognize me is my buddy from Mississippi, Doug McVey. He lights up when he sees me, and we slap each other on the back as he asks about my leg. My God, he stinks, but I'm sure glad to see him. Gonzales and Arnold, who is now a sergeant, give me quick hugs.

The guys head into the tents and clean their weapons. They then strip naked, put their filthy uniforms in a pile, and hit the cold outside showers. When they exit the showers, there is a pile of clean uniforms and socks for them to pick from. Most of the uniforms are the same size, medium. It matters not if you are six feet three and 250 pounds like me or four feet ten and 90 pounds like Chico Ruiz. When I wear the medium-size uniforms, I feel like I have been stuffed into them. The shirt I can get by with, it's just tight, and the sleeves are short. The pants are another matter. We do not wear underwear, because it would gall us in the heat. Usually, the second or third day out on an operation the stride in my pants tear out, leaving me very exposed. We have a few green towels, so sometimes I'm able to use the towel and a couple of safety pins to fashion myself a kind of diaper. This protects me from thorns and briers. Sometimes, this may go on for weeks or even months, and it gets very uncomfortable.

After the guys are clean, we go to chow. I find out there are many changes in the platoon. Now that Arnold is a sergeant, he has been moved from senior team leader in Second Squad to Third Squad leader because SSG Wilson has rotated stateside. Garza is now a staff sergeant E-6 and still has Second Squad. SSG Juan Clavino has First Squad and Staff Sergeant Bass has the machine gun squad. The platoon sergeant is still John Hall, and the platoon leader is still Charles Fletcher, now a first lieutenant the platoon has a number of brand-new men and some other wounded back from the hospital like Garza and me. We are nearly up to full strength. We have three rifle squads with ten men each, an eleven-man weapons' squad, which really only consists of two three-man machine gun crews and a squad leader who is also the assistant platoon sergeant. The table of organization calls for two two-man rocket teams in weapons squad, but we don't use the huge 3.5 rocket launchers. Each squad has a couple of M-72 laws, which is a one-shot throwaway rocket. This is much lighter and good for enemy bunkers since we are not faced with enemy tanks.

I also find out that each four of a five-man fire team will be issued an automatic M-14. The M-14 weighs ten pounds, and each twenty-round magazine weighs one and a half pounds. Therefore, the M-14 with twenty magazines and weighs forty pounds. The M-16 weighs seven pounds, and each twenty-round magazine weighs a half pound. Thus, an M-16 and twenty magazines weighs seventeen pounds. The difference is that the M-16 jams every few rounds that you fire, and if you fire it on automatic, it jams in the first couple of bursts. When the M-16 jams, it takes a cleaning rod down the muzzle to un-jam it. There are very few cleaning rods in the platoon. My mother had sent me a .22-caliber cleaning rod so I could un-jam my M-16. Also, it's company SOP not to fire the M-16 on automatic due to the jamming. The bullet from an M-16 is 5.56 mm or .223 cal. and weighs fifty-five grains, not much bigger than a .22 rifle. The M-14 fires the same round as the M-60 machine gun. It is 7.62 mm or .308 cal. and weighs 168 grains or three times larger than an M-16 round. The enemy soldiers are small people, about five feet tall and one hundred pounds, and you still have to hit them in the right place to knock them down with one round from an M-16. The M-14 or M-60 round will knock them down like a freight train. You can also fire the M-14 all day long on automatic, and it will not jam.

I tell Staff Sergeant Garza that I badly want one of the M-14s. He tells me to go draw one from the arms' room but I'll get no extra consideration for carrying the extra weight. I tell him that's fine, I just want a weapon that works.

I go to the arms' room and draw an M-14 with twenty magazines. I return to my tent and set up my gear. My waist is much larger than most of the guys, so I can carry four ammo pouches on the front of my web gear, instead of two. That will carry eight magazines and one in my rifle. I carry seven more in a claymore bag hanging from my left shoulder and the last four in my pack. I also have four hand grenades hanging on my web gear. I have four canteens and an entrenching tool on my back. I also have four army socks tied on my back, each with nine cans of C rations. My helmet or "steel pot" weighs nearly ten pounds as well. I have my poncho liner, which is really just a green nylon blanket, in my pack. My poncho is rolled and tied on the bottom of my pack. I also have a large M-14 bayonet in its sheath hanging on my web belt. I get my gear all squared away; and then McVey, Gonzales, and I go to chow. It's good being back with my friends. We finish chow and return to our squad tent. We sit around on canvas cots and shoot the bull. We talk about the world and our past lives and our hopes for the future. McVey starts talking with our "new guys." He's trying to give them a thumbnail sketch on how we operate and what to expect in the field. Mac then begins telling them how scared they will be and that's natural. We are all very afraid. One of the new guys starts saying that he knows what it's like being afraid. He starts telling about a brawl after a football game when he was in high school. Mac comes unglued. He starts shouting at the new guy. Mac tells him that he's not talking about a fist fight in high school. He's talking about large numbers of enemy soldiers attempting to take your life with automatic weapons. The new guy shuts his mouth and hangs his head.

Suddenly, Staff Sergeant Garza runs into the tent telling us to saddle up and head down to the helipads. We are shocked. We've never moved by helicopter at night. We grab our gear and do as we are told. When we arrive at the helipad, our NCOs begin getting us into "sticks" of seven men. A Huey helicopter has a pilot, copilot, crew chief, and machine gunner. It will also hold seven combat loaded infantrymen.

The "choppers" come in, and we load up. I'm on the chopper with Staff Sergeant Garza, Gonzales, McVey, and three others. Each chopper has a flashing red light on it. When we take off, our chopper comes within inches of striking the chopper that carried Sergeant Arnold and six other guys. The incident takes our breath.

They tell us later that this is the first mass movement of troops by helicopters at night in a combat zone in history.

We fly high in the night air, and it's almost cold. Staff Sergeant Garza tells us above the roar of the chopper engine what has happened. Seventy miles north, above Tay Ninh, near the Cambodian border, the 196 Light Infantry Brigade has made contact with a regiment from the enemy Ninth Division. The 196th is a green unit that has just arrived in Vietnam, and they are in serious trouble. A couple of battalions from the US 25th Infantry Division have attempted to help the 196th and have run into even more enemy soldiers. It sounds like a really big fight, and between the night air and my fear, I turn cold as ice.

We land at Tay Ninh and our NCOs tell us that we are going to have to secure part of the perimeter that night and tomorrow we will move by chopper to help the 196th. Staff Sergeant Garza takes us along the bunker line and assigns us to one of three bunkers that Second Squad has to man. SPC4 Louis Sanders, SPC4 Liberato Gonzales, and I are placed in one of the bunkers. It is not a good bunker. It has not been dug into the ground but has been built up with sandbags from the ground up. It's about five feet high, a perfect target for an enemy shoulder-fired RPG rocket. The sandbags are old, and the scent of mildew is strong, but it seems to have a good roof, and it's about to rain. The bunker is about ten feet square and has a one-foot firing slot all the way across the front. The floor is dirt, and there is one partially broken canvas cot and one folding metal chair. Sanders tells me that I've got first watch. He then spreads his lanky six-foot-four frame on the broken cot, covers with his poncho liner, and starts to snore. Gonzales roles up in his poncho liner and goes to sleep on the ground.

I find that I can sit in the folding chair and see out the firing slot, but all I can see is the blackness of the night. I hear squeaking in the bunker and realize we have rats. I place my bayonet on the end of my rifle and run the rats out the door. I sit back on the broken chair and watch out the slot into blackness. It starts to rain hard. I'm so glad we are in the bunker, and I find out that the roof doesn't leak. The hard-cold rain falling is making it almost cold. I wrap my poncho liner around my shoulders and stare out at nothing. Then I hear the rats come back into the bunker. If they leave us alone, I'll leave them alone. I have the only watch for the three of us. It belongs to Sanders. When my time is up, I wake Sanders. He gets up, drinks some water, and takes my place on the chair. I take his place on the cot, cover up, and go right to sleep with the cold rain beating on the roof.

When I wake, it's gray light outside. Sanders is sleeping on the floor, and Gonzales is standing at the firing port, looking out. The rain has stopped. Sanders wakes, and the three of us eat cold C rations and drink water from our canteens. Staff Sergeant Garza comes by and tells us to saddle up and head down to the chopper pad.

We gear up and walk down. I'm starting to get knots in my stomach. Our cannon on the other side of the base camp has fired all night, and I assume it's in support of the 196th.

We reach the chopper pad and break into sticks of seven. First Lieutenant Fletcher then briefs us. The 196th is dug into the edge of a wood line, and the gooks have hit them all night. We will air assault into a huge landing zone of maybe thirty acres with four-foot-high elephant grass just outside the wood line where the 196th are located.

We wait half the day, and then the choppers arrive. We load up and head out. The sky is full of choppers. My stomach is in knots, but I keep my "hard face" on. As we approach the landing zone, I see jets and helicopter gunships making runs on the wood line where the 196th is located. I see green enemy tracer rounds coming up at the planes from the jungle. Then I see puffs of black smoke in the air. It's a 20 mm enemy antiaircraft gun firing at the jets. It's the only time I will ever see this type of weapon used.

We land and spread out. The choppers leave, and we set up in the elephant grass. We are still about two hundred meters from the wood line. We are getting a few sniper rounds in but nothing heavy. We get down in the grass and wait for orders. A couple of hours pass, and then we move toward the wood line. We enter the wood line with our weapons at the ready and bump into 196th Company and Platoon command post foxholes. We get down and our leaders talk.

Staff Sergeant Garza comes over to the squad and tells us that he's going to put us into position and the 196th is going to pull out. We scurry along the line of foxholes, keeping low. The jungle in front of the foxhole line is thick. Garza drops three of the squad off at one foxhole. The next foxhole, he drops off two of the guys and says that he will also be in this position. He then takes Sanders, Gonzales, and me to the next hole and tells us that will be ours.

There are three troops from the 196th at this hole. Two are alive, and the third is dead. He is a young soldier with curly auburn hair and freckles. I notice the size on the bottom of his boots. They are size 10. The foxhole is terrible. It's not much bigger or deeper than a bathtub. There is no way three troops can get into it. The two troops tell us that the gooks came at them all night and the enemy main line is less than forty meters to our front with logs and four or five feet of dirt on top of each bunker.

The two 196th troops pick up their dead buddy and head back toward their command post. Sanders opens his entrenching tool and tells Gonzales and me to put out our one claymore mine and one trip flare. He then starts digging fast. Gonzales is armed with the M-79 grenade launcher. It is a single-shot weapon that looks like a sawed-off shotgun with the barrel nearly two inches in diameter. The M-79 fires a shell that is about half as powerful as an American hand grenade. The shell, before it's fired, is about four inches long and nearly two inches in diameter and weighs nearly a half-pound. The weapon has the disadvantage of the shell having to travel twenty-nine feet, after being fired, before it will explode. This protects the shooter. Also, this weapon has no muzzle flash at night and a range of 375 meters. It cannot be used in thick jungle, so the M-79 man has been issued a .45-caliber pistol to protect himself at close range. Just before we left on this operation. the M-79 men have each been issued a half a dozen canister rounds. We are told that this is like a giant shotgun round and will clear an area at close range, but none of our men have ever fired one.

Gonzales takes his .45-caliber pistol, and our trip flare. I take my M-14 and our claymore mine. The claymore mine is encased in green plastic and is about nine inches long and five inches high. It contains 720 steel ball bearings backed by about an inch of C-4 explosive. It sits on two small bipods that can be pushed into the ground. There is a port at the top where an explosive cap can be screwed in. A rubber coated wire runs back one hundred feet and is plugged into a small hand detonator. When the detonator is pressed, the claymore fires and sprays 720 steel pellets to the front.

I place the claymore behind a small tree pointed toward the enemy. The tree will stop the back blast, which can be deadly to the shooter. Gonzales sets up the trip flare from the tree by the claymore to another tree about five feet away. He ties the flare to the second tree and sets the flare. If an enemy soldier trips the wire, it will cause a huge burst of light that lasts about ten seconds. We crawl back to Sanders, and he's still throwing dirt, but it will soon be dark, and our SOP is that we don't dig after dark. It makes it too easy for the enemy to find us. This hole is only going to be deep enough for the three of us to be in on our knees. Then we'll barely be able to get our heads below the lip of the hole. We are used to foxholes that come up to our shoulders. These 196th troops sure don't know how to dig a foxhole.

It's getting toward dusk dark, and Staff Sergeant Garza works his way down the line. He tells us that the platoon has to put a listening post (LP) out in front of the platoon. My blood turns to ice. The way we work it is one man from each of the three rifle squads takes their weapons, and a radio and one of the squad leaders take them out in front of the platoon anywhere from a few meters to a couple hundred meters.

The LP is then set up for the night, and they become the platoon's early warning system. It's usually a very scary job, but tonight it will be near suicide because the enemy is in those big bunkers just to our front in the jungle. I pray that it's not my night to go on LP. Garza then tells us that he has Sam Collins from First Squad. Collins is a slim Black guy from Florida with a great personality. He has been in country about as long as I have. He also has Phil Cisero from our squad. Phil is a new guy, an Italian from Connecticut. He is an average-sized guy who is a carpenter in civilian life. I like the way Phil handles himself. I think he's going to make a good troop. Sanders asks Garza how he's going to put out an LP with the gooks right in front of us. Garza says he's only going to put it forty or fifty feet in front of his foxhole so he can get to them if need be.

Garza moves down the line to get a man from Sergeant Arnold in Third Squad. He returns in a few minutes with Willie Johnson, a heavyset Black guy from New York. Johnson has been in country about nine months and knows what he's doing. Johnson is very dark, and it's almost night when he and Garza crawl past us, but Johnson's face looks white. They reach Garza's hole, and Garza and the three "lucky" guys crawl out into the brush. A few minutes later, Garza crawls back.

It's full dark now. We can't see Garza's foxhole to our left or Mulchaney's foxhole from Third Squad to our right. I take stock of what we have. Sanders is on the left of the hole. He's a tall thin Black guy with eight months "in country." He's a solid guy to have with you. Sanders has an M-16 with sixteen magazines and four hand grenades. Gonzales is in the middle of the hole. He has an M-79 with forty high-explosive (HE) rounds and a half dozen of the new canister rounds. He has two hand grenades and his .45-caliber pistol with three magazines. He also has eight months in country and is a great guy to dig in with. I'm on the right with the big M-14 and twenty magazines and four hand grenades. I have over four months in country and am, by now, somewhat "seasoned." I am very jealous of Sanders and Gonzales. They are both twenty years old, and I'm only nineteen and will never be twenty, because I *know* that the gooks will over run us tonight and kill all three of us.

Suddenly, there's a shout to our left front in the jungle. Then the sound of excited gooks shouting. It sounds just like excited turkeys. There's AK-47s firing, people running, shouts in English, "LP coming in, LP coming in." Suddenly, the shouts and the firing stop. The three of us have our weapons trained on the black jungle in front of us with just our helmets and eyes above the lip of the foxhole. It gets very quiet.

In a few minutes, I hear some crawling toward us from Garza's hole. I turn and train my rifle on a dark form crawling in on us. I think it's a GI, but why take a chance? The form then whispers, "It's Johnson." I whisper back, "Come on in, John." He crawls to the back of our hole, and I ask him what happened out there. He tells me that he and Collins and Cisero had the LP set up in the brush when a patrol of about eight enemy soldiers walked up on them. They then broke and ran for the foxholes with the gooks shooting at them. I ask him if anyone was hit. He tells me no, but he threw the twenty-five-pound radio as he came into the First Squad foxholes and hit Tom Davis with it and knocked Tom out. He says he thinks Tom will be okay. I remind him that the next hole is Mulchaney's and be sure and call out. He then crawls off into the darkness.

Our artillery begins firing high-explosive rounds to our front and firing flares above us. The flares give us some flickering light through the leaves on the trees. When a flare goes out within a few seconds, another is fired above us. It's a little better than complete darkness but not much.

Suddenly, our trip flare goes off with a blinding flash. Sanders and I each throw a hand grenade. They go off only a second apart and throw dirt back on us. The gooks throw three or four of their grenades back at us. They are only about half as powerful as ours, and we duck below the lip of our hole as they go off.

Somewhere down the line, another trip flare goes off, and there is an exchange of grenades at that location as well.

Sanders has both ears infected, and he has trouble hearing, but Gonzales and I can hear well. We hear gooks whispering to our front. They have to be within twenty or twenty-five feet from us. Gonzales throws a grenade, and we hear the gooks jump away from it. The grenade goes off, and we get two enemy grenades thrown back at us. They are all over us up and down the line probing us, trying to find the location of our foxholes. I hear them crawling and whispering to our front and throw a grenade. I hear my grenade hit a tree with a loud *whack*. I panic. We don't know where my grenade has rolled. I say, "Duck," and the three of us get as low as we can in this shallow foxhole. My grenade goes off with a roar, and one side of our hole caves in. Our ears are ringing. That was close. The enemy throws a couple more grenades toward us.

We hear people crawling toward from the direction of Garza's hole. I put my rifle on them as they crawl in, whispering in English. It's 1SGT Bill Perry and a man I don't know. Top Perry is almost as big as me and tough as a nickel steak. He's a veteran of the Korean

War and has been known to really mix it up in a firefight. He's seems to have no fear. I wouldn't get out of this foxhole for all the gold in Fort Knox. Top whispers to us and tries to pump up our morale. I tell him that the gooks are all over us. Even in the dark and flickering flare light, I see him smile. He pats me on the shoulder, and he and the other man crawl off toward Third Squad. In about thirty minutes, he and the other man crawl back by. I guess that they have checked all of our platoon as well as Third Platoon to our right.

The same pattern continues into the night. The flickering flares, hearing the enemy crawl or whisper, the exchange of grenades. It's after three o'clock in the morning, and we are down to two grenades. Gonzales and I start to notice something to our right front at about twenty feet out. When an artillery flare is about to go out, it appears that a man wearing a conical straw hat stands up and begins looking around. He's looking for us, but he's looking past us. He doesn't realize that we are as close to him as we are. Sanders can't hear, so Gonzales and I whisper. We are down to two grenades and don't want to use them. I ask Gonzales if we can use his M-79 with one of the new canister rounds—after all, the HE rounds have no muzzle flash to give away our location, so these shouldn't either. He says that's a good idea. I'm on the right and have a better angle, so I ask him if I can shoot the gook with his M-79. He says it's okay with him. I take his weapon and load a canister round in it and sight in where the gook has been popping up. The flare is about to flicker out, and the enemy soldier stands, and I fire the M-79. A two-foot tongue of flame licks out the muzzle of the M-79. A half a dozen enemy rifles open up on me, kicking dirt around the foxhole. I duck down as I see Sanders and Gonzales heave our last two grenades at the muzzle flashes. They then duck down, and the grenades go off. It's deathly quiet, and then we hear something being dragged away to our front. We are out of grenades, so I place my bayonet on my rifle, and Sanders follows suit. Gonzales loads another canister round into his M-79 and pulls his pistol. We still have our claymore mine that we are saving for the big rush. We crouch there and wait for the enemy to overrun and kill us. I pray silently for God to take my soul when I die. Gonzales whispers jokes as we wait. Sanders looks over his rifle sights into the jungle. Someone is quietly crying. Is it me or one of the others?

It seems that I can see a little better. I think, good, I'll be able to see them when they rush us. Then I realize that it's getting light. We have made it through the night and are alive. I feel weak as water. We hold our position until it's fully light. Garza calls to us to check our front. We move out of our hole, keeping low, and crawling to our front. I check the claymore. It's still there, but the cord from the claymore and the detonator has been cut during the night by either one of our grenades or one of the enemies. So we didn't have our claymore as a last resort. I'm so glad we didn't know that.

We get a resupply of grenades, claymores, and water. We then gear up and attempt to advance on the enemy bunker line. We take heavy fire and fall back to our foxholes. We wait in our holes for a couple of hours, and then Garza brings us the word. Another battalion will be moving in. We will adjust around and dig in. The holes will be closer to each other, and we will get a heavy resupply of grenades and claymores. We are trying to keep the enemy trapped in his base camp until we can destroy him with artillery and air strikes.

We move a couple hundred meters and dig in. This time we have half a day and dig them deep. On the ends of the floor of the hole, it's just right for Sanders and me, up to our shoulders. Sanders ears are better. They are no longer draining, and he can hear better. In the middle of the floor of the hole is a tall hump because Gonzales is a foot shorter than we are. This time we put out *three* claymores and *two* trip flares. We also have more than twenty hand grenades. The foxholes are only about fifteen feet apart, instead of thirty. We can even whisper to Garza on our left and Mulchaney on our right.

Night falls, and it's a rerun of the night before, except we do not feel alone and throw grenades at will. Some of the guys even set off a claymore because we have so many. I feel sure that I'll live through this night and am even having a good time. We get a few enemy grenades in but not as many as the night before. Daylight comes as I expected it this time.

We saddle up and advance into the enemy base camp. We take no fire. They have all slipped out through us or been killed by artillery or air strikes. We find quite a lot of supplies and ammunition. We call in the engineers, and they blow the enemy bunkers and supplies.

Garza fills us in. Helicopters will pick us up and take us to Tay Ninh. Operation Attleboro is not over. We are still trying to block the enemy's Ninth Division and the NVA 101st Regiment from escaping into Cambodia. We will get some hot chow and sleep before we air assault into some other LZ, attempting to block the enemy's escape.

CHAPTER 11

Hot Landing Zone

We climb on helicopters to travel back to Tay Ninh after a three-day fight at an enemy base camp after relieving the 196th Light Infantry Brigade. We have not slept during that time. We have fought off enemy probes all night each night. This morning, we had finally taken the base camp and blown up the enemy bunkers and supplies. Staff Sergeant Garza tells us that they will have hot chow waiting on us. That sounds great, but I can hardly hold my eyes open.

We land at the chopper pad at Tay Ninh and are directed away from the bunker line to a small grassy field where they have a chow line set up. They issue us heavy paper plates, and we move through the chow line getting meat, potatoes, beans, fruit, and bread. We also get cold Kool-Aid in our canteen cups. I am very hungry and eat mine quickly, hoping that they call out that they have seconds, but they don't.

First Lieutenant Fletcher, Platoon Sergeant Hall, and the squad leaders have a meeting and then give us the word. We do not have to stand bunker guard tonight. We will clean our weapons and then sleep right where we are. Great, a solid night's sleep with no guard breaks. I clean my rifle and then lay my web gear for my head to rest on. It's the rainy season, and we would usually build small tents out of our ponchos and sleep under these. We are too exhausted to do that. I lay my head on my web gear, hold my rifle close, pull my poncho over me, and go right to sleep.

Sometime during the night, I awaken. I'm very cold, and my bladder is very tight. I realize that I'm lying on my stomach with my face on my web gear. A cold, heavy rain is beating down on my poncho, and I am lying in four inches of cold water. I don't get up. Instead, I urinate through my pants into the cold water. The water turns warm, and I go right back to sleep.

I wake the next morning to a bright and beautiful day. I'm no longer lying in water, but my uniform is still wet. The squad leaders move among us, telling us to saddle up. We move down to the chopper pads, break into sticks of seven for the chopper loads, and then drop our gear.

First Lieutenant Fletcher calls the platoon for a briefing. We leave our gear on the ground in the sticks we have set up and crowd around the platoon leader. First Lieutenant Fletcher advises us that we will be flying into an LZ far on the other side of the Black Virgin Mountain, that we can see in the distance. We are to block the Ninth Enemy Division and the 101st NVA Regiment from escaping into Cambodia. We have fought one of the three regiments of the Ninth Division for the last three days. Other battalions in the First Infantry Division have been fighting the remaining two enemy regiments of the enemy Ninth Division, as well as the 101st NVA during the same time period.

Fletcher also advises that the LZ will only hold five choppers at a time, so the choppers will be in sticks of five. We only have choppers to lift one company at a time. Charlie Company will go in first, and then the choppers will return to get us, Bravo Company. After dropping us in the LZ, they will return to Tay Ninh a third time and pick up Alpha Company.

Charlie Company moves up to the edge off the pads in sticks of seven, ready to go. We return to our gear. I lie down with my head on my gear planning to take a nap. Some of the guys start playing a card game called whisk. They are usually very loud when they play, so I doubt I'll get my nap.

The choppers come in five at a time and pick up Charlie Company. We watch them fly into the distance until they look like tiny mosquitoes. Then five at a time, they disappear around the Black

Virgin Mountain. The word is passed—when we see the first stick of choppers appear back around the mountain, we are to saddle up and take our places by the helicopter pads. I watch the guys play cards and dry out in the sun for about twenty minutes. I have decided that we've had our big fight on Operation Attleboro and the rest of this month will probably be a walk in the sun.

Someone calls out, "Here they come." I stand up and put my gear on looking toward the mountain. I see the first stick of choppers far in the distance. Four are together, and the fifth is falling behind the others. As we move to the pad, some of the guys are saying that the fifth chopper must have engine trouble. Then the second stick comes around the mountain. There are only *four* choppers in this stick. Everyone gets real quiet. Then the third stick appears. There are only three choppers in it. Some of the guys break into oaths and cursing. Fear engulfs my body. The lieutenant and the NCOs run up to us shouting that the LZ is red-hot and to get ready to board the choppers. Charlie Company is pinned down on the LZ and taking casualties. They need our help.

My body turns hard as wood, and I breathe through my mouth. I feel like I am going to vomit. Lord, please don't let me do that in front of the other guys. The choppers begin coming in, and I see bullet holes in their windshields. Six of the guys and I run to the nearest chopper and load up. One of the chopper gunners shouts that the LZ is "hot as hell." I see three bullet holes in the windshield of our chopper, and then we take off, gaining altitude quickly. We head toward the mountain with cold air whipping into the chopper. Four of us sit on the canvas bench seat, and the other three sit on the floor. The chopper gunners are breaking out more belts of ammo.

We pass around the mountain, and in the far distance, I see where we are going. Lots of smoke is rising from the jungle, and I see helicopter gunships and jets make gun runs on the area. I feel vomit come up into my mouth, but I swallow it back. I look next to me at Scott, a small Black soldier from SC. He's usually a joke-a-minute guy, but he says nothing now. He has a very dark complexion, but now his face is a gray as ashes in a campfire.

The pilot passes the word to us that we will not land on the LZ, only "pause" a few feet off the ground and then we are to jump. The helicopters drop down just above the tree tops and speed up. We must be going well over a hundred miles an hour and be over a hundred feet in the air. I know I'm going to throw up. Suddenly, a big troop sitting on the floor lurches up and shouts, "I'm not going to go. I'm getting out." He heads toward the open doorway. Scott grabs him, but Scott is small, and the big man is about to pull both of them out of the chopper. I reach and grab the web gear of both men and lean back.

Suddenly, we are over the last line of trees. Both chopper gunners open fire on the wood lines with belt long bursts of fire. I see muzzle flashes come from the tree lines and green tracers coming up meeting our gunners red tracers. I see Charlie Company down in the four-or five-foot elephant grass firing into the wood lines and on the far end of the LZ I see the three shot-down helicopters. Hell must look a lot like this.

Our chopper is taking hits from the fire from the wood line. It sounds like we are being hit by baseball bats. The chopper almost stops just above the elephant grass, and the pilots and gunners are screaming for us to jump. Four of the guys are falling out the left side of the chopper. Scott and the big guy fall out the right side. I vomit on the floor of the chopper and then dive out after Scott as the chopper takes off.

I fall forever and then hit the ground on my side knocking out my breath. I find that the grass is nearly five feet high and there's two inches of water on the ground. I catch my breath and face the wood line where the enemy is. Staff Sergeant Garza is everywhere getting us set up. I pull out my entrenching tool and start to dig; but he tells me to hold off, we don't know where we are going to set up yet. I feel naked out here in this grass. Grass will not stop bullets.

I see the three shot-down choppers about two hundred meters to my front. One is on its nose, and the other two are just sitting there as if they've landed. They are very close to the wood line. I see Americans moving around the choppers; some are firing machine guns into the wood line. Enemy green tracers are coming back at them. I guess it's the chopper crews firing into the wood line. I'm so glad I'm not that close to the wood line.

First Lieutenant Fletcher runs up to Staff Sergeant Garza and tells him to get Second Squad on line, that we will assault across the elephant grass to the choppers and rescue the chopper crews. He also says half the crews are wounded. My guts turn to ice. I'm not going to live through this day. Fletcher shouts that the rest of the platoon will cover us and that he and his radioman will go with us.

Garza gets us on line in the grass. I'm the last man on the left. No one is at my left elbow. I'm terrified. Garza advises that we will walk across the field, firing as we go. I've pulled my spare four magazines out of my pack so I can get to all twenty of them. Fletcher gives the order, and we all stand and start walking toward the choppers. Every time my left foot hits the ground, I fire a short three-round burst at the wood line, just like I've been trained. The enemy sees us and is firing at us. I hear bullets going by and see some hit the ground around us, making a little splash in the two inches of water. I feel in control, as long as I'm firing, but when I have to change magazines, I feel helpless. I'm dropping my empty magazines into the cargo pockets of my pants as I reload. Suddenly, a green enemy tracer round goes by my left ear. Two inches to the left and I would be dead. I fire back where I think the tracer came from, empty my weapon, and then began to reload.

While we are firing, the rest of the platoon is firing cover for us. The chopper crews are firing machine guns into the wood line. The rest of Bravo Company is firing, and Charlie Company is firing. Helicopter gunships are firing, jets are firing, and a wood line full of enemy is firing back at all of us. The roar of the fire is unbelievable. You couldn't hear the crack of doom above this terrible noise. Then above it all, I hear my name called. I look to my right and see Garza in the middle of the file. He's shouting for me to move up. I realize that I've fallen two steps behind the file. Shame floods my body. I'm so embarrassed. I've not paid attention and have fallen two steps behind the others. I feel I have let Garza and the other guys down. I will carry the guilt with me the rest of my days. I lurch forward and pull even with the rest of the guys. I'm firing into the wood line to my front and left.

We reach the chopper that is sitting on its nose. One of the pilots is still strapped in his seat. He's lost his helmet and has blond hair and blue eyes along with a golden tan. He looks down at us, but he doesn't see us. An enemy .51-caliber round has come through his windshield; hit him in the steel plate on his chest; punched through it; and went into his chest, out his back, and through his seat. He's dead, but it hasn't been for long, because he hasn't turned gray yet. The other eleven members of the three crews are lying online just past the other two choppers. They have taken the machine guns off the choppers and are putting a blistering fire into the wood line, which is only about forty feet from them.

We drop down with them firing into the wood line. We notice then that at least five of them are wounded but still functioning. We fire up the wood line for a couple of minutes, and then First Lieutenant Fletcher tells the chopper crews to gather their wounded and head toward our lines two hundred meters away. I'm uneasy. I was getting very comfortable lying here with all of these machine guns firing into the wood line, and now they are going away.

The chopper crews get their wounded up and head back toward our lines as we smoke the wood line with fire covering them. Then First Lieutenant Fletcher drops beside Staff Sergeant Garza and tells him to pick one man to go with the lieutenant, his radioman, and Garza to cover the rest of the squad as they fall back to our lines. Garza shouts, "Fedrick, on me." I know I'm not getting out of this alive.

The rest of the squad falls back as the four of us fire cover. The big M-14 is kicking my shoulder like a mule. The lieutenant then says, "Let's get this dead pilot and get out of here." I had not realized that the chopper crews did not get their man. I speak up. "Sir, there's only four of us, and that's a big man. Let's get back to the platoon. We can cover these choppers, and the gooks can't get to that pilot. We've got all day to get control and get back to him." The lieutenant thinks for a second and then says, "I guess you're right. You and Garza cover us." The lieutenant and his radioman fall back, and Garza and I fire into the wood line. I *know* now that I'll not live through the day.

The lieutenant and his RTO only fall back about fifty feet and stop and fire cover as Garza and I fall back with them. As I go by one of the choppers, I grab a two-hundred-round can of machine gun ammo. It fits my M-14, and I know I'm running low on ammo. The two of us then leapfrog backfiring cover for each other until we reach our lines. I flop down in the two inches of water completely exhausted and drink half a canteen of water. I then check my twenty magazines and find that only five are still loaded. I've fired three hundred rounds in that short action. Blood is seeping through my shirt at my right shoulder. I pull my shirt back and look and see my right shoulder is turning purple, and there are a number of small cuts there, and some are seeping blood. Firing three hundred rounds on automatic with that M-14 and that steel butt plate beating into your shoulder will do that.

I break open the two-hundred-round can of machine gun ammo and start breaking it down, loading my empty magazines. I finish and have fifteen loaded and five empty, but I'm in better shape than I would have been if I hadn't grabbed that can of ammo. The other guys are digging in, and I break out my entrenching tool and start throwing mud along with them.

The choppers return with Alpha Company, and we fire cover when they come in. The jets and helicopter gunships are still working over the wood line. We are also getting a lot of support from our artillery. The big cannon shells are tearing up the wood line on one side of the LZ. We start getting medevac choppers in taking out our wounded. We then get resupply choppers in with more ammo and water. I'm reminded of that Rudyard Kipling quote, "When it comes to slaughter, you do your work on water."

I grab enough M-60 ammo to fill all my magazines, with two hundred loose rounds extra. I put these loose rounds in an empty claymore bag that will hang from my shoulder. That will give me six hundred rounds. We are in some serious stuff here, and I don't plan to run out of ammo.

By midafternoon, we seem to have gained control of the area. We are only getting a few sniper rounds in now, and we have our foxholes dug. I'm dug in with Gonzales. He's a foot shorter than me, and the lip of our hole comes up to our arm pits; therefore, the floor on his side of the hole is a foot higher than on my side. This means that I'm standing in six inches of water and his feet are dry. There are advantages in being short.

I overhear First Lieutenant Fletcher talking with CPT Ben Dishman, Bravo Company commander. They are wondering if we have fought an enemy battalion or regiment all day. They think that if it's a battalion, like us, that we've fought all day, the enemy will pull out after dark, just leaving a few squads to harass us. If it's a regiment, which contains three battalions, then the enemy will probably attempt to overrun us tonight. Gosh, it just gets better and better. I'm glad I have this deep hole and a good man like Gonzales with me.

Staff Sergeant Garza and Scott dig in on one side of us. My buddy McVey, a good hand with an M-14, and Shafter, who are both from Third Squad, dig in the hole on the other side in the edge of the bushes. We also have only elephant grass in front of us, a lot of which we've beaten down. We've got lots of claymore mines out, and I'm feeling pretty secure, if we do get hit.

We have so much control now that the pathfinders come in with their black baseball caps on and start work on getting the three shot-down choppers out. These pathfinder guys usually work in teams of two or three men with a radio deep in enemy territory scouting for us. It's not a job I would want. I like having at least ten or twelve guys with me at all times. That way if someone or even two get wounded, there's someone to carry them out.

The pathfinders recover the dead pilot's body, and a dust-off chopper comes in and takes him away. I watch the pathfinders attach long cables to the top of the helicopters. I notice a smaller blond-haired pathfinder who looks about fourteen years old. He moves quickly and seems to know his job. The cloth name patch above his right pocket says "Vickers." I remember the name because it reminds me of the famous Vickers machine gun. I will work with this man thirty years later. It's a small world! The big Chinook helicopter comes in and takes the damaged helicopters back to Tay Ninh, one at a time.

The call goes out for the squad leaders to report to the platoon command post, also known as First Lieutenant Fletcher and Platoon Sergeant Hall's foxholes. Staff Sergeant Garza returns in a few minutes and calls us over to his foxhole. He's got his map out and looks serious. Garza says, "Men, we've got night ambush tonight." There go all my secure thoughts. We are going out in that wood line tonight. I know I will not live till morning.

We get our gear together and wait for dark. We have seen a lot of action in the last week, and Second Squad is down to six men, instead of ten. We will have Norberg and his machine gun with us, but Norberg, "the Swede from Minnesota," is the only man on his gun. There is supposed to be three men on the gun, but he has no assistant gunner or ammo bearer. That makes seven of us going out tonight. There should be thirteen of us.

Garza shows us on the map that there is a faint trail about three hundred meters into the wood line. We are to ambush this trail. In reality, if the gooks come against the battalion in force, we will be an early warning system. I guess it could be worst. It's not real far into the jungle. If we do get hit in force, two or three of us might make it back to our perimeter.

Garza tells us that Scott will carry the radio. Sanders and I are looking at each other. We are thinking the same thing. Scott has the radio, Norberg the machine gun, Gonzales and Cisero both carry M-79s. That means that none of them can run "point," so it's me or Sanders. It's usually the point man, then the squad leader, and then the radioman when we head out. Sanders is looking as scared as I feel. If we run into gooks on the way out in any number, then the point man is dead for sure and probably the second man in the file as well. I will not see the sunrise tomorrow.

That is when we all get a lesson in leadership. Garza tells us the order of march. He says, "He, Garza, will run point. Fedrick will be second, then Scott with the radio, Norberg with the machine gun. Cisero, Gonzales, and Sanders bring up the rear watching our backs." I feel a little better about not running point, but I still don't think this will end well. It's getting dark, and a cold hard rain begins to fall. We are all loaded down with extra ammo for the machine gun because Norberg has no one to carry it. I also have all my extra ammo. All this weight makes it hard for me to walk. I'm glad we're only going three hundred meters. We enter the jungle and find that it's very hard to walk and impossible to see. We each have to hold onto the web gear of the man in front of us. We are making a lot of noise in the thick brush, but the heavy rain covers our noise. My teeth are chattering badly. Is it the cold rain or my great fear?

We move very slowly for about an hour. Then Garza stops and has us all come forward. We crouch down in a circle, and he tells us in a whisper that apparently the trail we were hunting has become overgrown since the map was made. He tells us we have gone as far as we were supposed to and a little more. He says we will set up here in the brush in a "wagon wheel" formation and face out in seven directions. We set up, and the rain never stops. I have Cisero on one side of me and Norberg on the other. I can't see my hand in front of my face, and the rain never slows down. My teeth chatter so badly that I have to hold my jaw closed with one hand all night. Garza has told us that if the enemy comes against us in force for each of us to empty a magazine and then run for the perimeter shouting, "Ambush coming in." I pray that it doesn't come to that.

Morning finally breaks; the enemy did not come. I guess there was just one battalion that we fought the day before. I feel a great deal of relief with the morning breaking. Second Squad saddles up, and Garza tells me to run point going back into the perimeter. Some fear returns; there might be enemy scouts between us and the perimeter. We start out with Staff Sergeant Garza right behind me. I go very slowly and take my time checking for trip wires and enemy soldiers. Garza has called in on the radio and advised First Lieutenant Fletcher that we were coming in, but there's always some GI that doesn't get the word. It is always a very tense moment when you approach a perimeter with very frightened and armed nineteen-year-olds at the perimeter. As I move through the heavy brush, I realize that I'm getting close to the perimeter. I start giving low, short whistles. It's something that we've always done when we're coming in.

I haven't seen the perimeter yet in the thick brush and grass when Doug McVey says, "Fedrick, if you will quit whistling, I'll tell you to come on in." I laugh and walk up to McVey and Ed Shafter's foxhole in Third Squad.

We file in all soaking wet and go to our foxholes. The men from First and Third Squads that have held down our positions during the night go back to their own positions.

Word is passed to any Protestant interested: there will be a quick service at company headquarters foxholes in five minutes. I clear it with Garza, grab my rifle, and head that way. Doug McVey drops in step with me as we head that way. He asks how the night before went; and I tell him it was cold, wet, and scary. We arrive at the Company CP and find about thirty guys gathered. Chaplain Wes Geary is waiting on us. He's a six-and-a-half-foot Black chaplain from Texas and is loved by the entire battalion, even the Catholics. He hugs me and McVey and tells us he's glad to see us. We are glad to see him as well. I think that this is ironic, two White boys from Mississippi being this tight with a Black guy from Texas. After all this is 1966. Combat will do that to you—make you judge each man by his worth, not his color. We all sit on the ground, and Chaplain Geary gives us a quick ten-minute sermon. I find it very comforting. We all hug the chaplain and head back to our foxholes.

When I get back, Garza tells me to fill my foxhole. The entire battalion is heading out after the enemy unit that we fought the day before. I quickly shovel the loose dirt back in my hole. We do that to keep the enemy from using our old foxholes.

I work in a crouch with my little shovel filling up my foxhole that I have not been able to use due to the ambush Second Squad had pulled the night before. I mutter curses under my breath as I work. *Suddenly*, a giant hand grabs my right ear and twists. I drop to my knees, and there is Chaplin Geary in front of me still holding on to my ear and shaking the index finger of his other hand in my face, saying, "Young soldier, tell God that you are sorry for using such language." I gasp. "God, I'm sorry, and, Chaplain, I'm sorry." The chaplain lets go of my ear and helps me to my feet. He says, "I love you, young soldier." I say to him, "I love you, Chaplain." He walks away, and I finish filling my foxhole. We then gear up and prepare to move.

The entire battalion, all five hundred of us, head out into the jungle. I'm glad that Bravo Company is not on point. As we patrol, we notice a helicopter very high in the air above us. The word is passed that it is a medical evacuation helicopter on standby in case we make contact with the enemy and have men wounded. This way, the chopper does not have to come from a long distance to pick up our wounded. They can swoop in and get them right away and get them back to the hospital much quicker. The brass does this quite often. It gives us grunts on the ground a much more secure feeling about having a better chance of surviving if we are wounded.

We walk all day and find nothing. We stop before dark and dig in, just like the night before; part of the foxholes are in the open and some in the jungle. Ours are in the open, and I'm glad. As it approaches dark, word is passed that tonight our Third Squad has ambush along with De Jesus's machine gun. I feel for my buddies in Third Squad, but I'm glad it's not me. The rest of the platoon is to adjust to cover Third Squad's foxholes. It makes us very thin, and a couple of holes in the platoon area are left unmanned. I'm even more glad that we have an open field in front of us.

Sergeant Arnold heads out with his squad as it gets dark. McVey runs point, with Arnold second, then the radioman, and then De Jesus with the machine gun. There are nine of them. McVey is a very good point man, and he's carrying that big M-14. He was in Second Squad at one time, and I hated to see him be sent to Third Squad. He was a good man to dig in with in a foxhole. I still get to pull LP with him on occasion, and it's always good to have him with me. It gets fully dark, and I'm in a hole with Cisero, the new guy in the squad. He seems to be working out well, and I like working with him. It's tough in a two-man position, very little sleep. Staff Sergeant Garza and Scott are next to us and Sanders and Gonzales in the hole on the other side of them.

Suddenly, far out in the jungle, I hear a long burst of automatic fire. It's either an M-60 or an M-14. They fire the same round and sound much the same. That burst is followed by the heavy beating sound of M-16s, M-60, M-14s, and AK-47s. It's a terrible unbroken roar of sound. Third Squad has blown their ambush on enemy soldiers.

We have three radios in the platoon. Arnold has one out on the ambush, the second is at the platoon CP, and the third one is at Garza's hole. I can hear Garza's radio: First Lieutenant Fletcher is attempting to raise Sergeant Arnold with no success. The heavy firing goes on for perhaps a minute. A soldier in close contact can fire over half of his basic load of ammo in that period of time. McVey and Craft firing M-14s on auto, De Jesus burning belts through the M-60, Hankins and Weaver putting out the shells from the M-79s, and Sergeant Arnold and the other three guys firing M-16s on semi-auto as fast as they can put out a heavy volume of fire. The enemy firing AK-47s on auto and carbines on semi makes a terrible roar. Sergeant Arnold also carries a twelve-gauge pump shotgun with just a pistol gripe, and the barrel sawed off just in front of the tube, but he just uses the shotgun in very thick brush. I don't hear the shotgun tonight. On patrol, he always has one weapon at the ready and the other slung upside down on his back.

The firing drops off, and Sergeant Arnold comes on the radio. He's out of breath and tells the lieutenant that a file of enemy soldiers walked into one of his positions and some were shot down. Arnold had artillery flares coming in now and is about to take his squad and sweep the kill zone. There has been no mention of any of our guys being hit. I'm relieved about that.

A few minutes pass, and another short, heavy burst of fire breaks out. I hear no AK-47s being fired in this burst. That's a good sign. The enemy is not firing. This fire is over quickly, and then nothing for a couple more minutes. Arnold then comes on the radio even more out of breath. They have found two enemy hand grenades lying in the kill zone. They have bullet holes in them. Third Squad has shot them off enemy soldiers' web gear. There are no bodies found, just pools of blood. The enemy is so good at getting his dead and wounded off the battlefield. Third Squad had a glimpse of a couple of enemy soldiers running into a wood line while they searched the kill zone. That was the reason for the second burst of fire. I'm disappointed. All that fire at close range and no enemy bodies.

The flares go out, and Sergeant Arnold moves his squad to a secondary ambush site for the rest of the night. We settle in on the perimeter for the night. I tell Cisero that I will take first watch because I'm too excited to sleep after Third Squad's action. He goes to sleep right away. It begins to rain, but we have set up a tiny tent made from our two ponchos just behind our foxhole. It keeps half the rain off us. My two hours pass, and I wake him up for his turn. I then sleep. We each have one more two-hour watch, and then it's daylight. We've each gotten four hours of sleep in two-hour increments.

As day breaks, Garza then passes the word that Third Squad is coming. McVey breaks from the wood line, followed by Arnold and the rest on the squad. They look worn out, wet, and haggard. They file into the perimeter, and Sergeant Arnold is showing the two enemy grenades. They are made from gray sheet metal with wooden handles. The grenade part is not much bigger than a tomato paste can. One has a bullet hole in the metal "can," and the other grenade's handle has been splintered by a bullet. They were shot right off the gooks' gear. The other guys and I press Third Squad for the story of what happened.

McVey, Beatha, and Willie Johnson made up one of Third Squad's positions. A file of a dozen or more enemy soldiers walked up the trail and right into them. McVey fired a twenty-round burst into them at very close range with his big M-14, and three of them fell. The others got down as the whole squad opened fire. The enemy returned fire for about a minute, and it was wild and crazy. The enemy soldiers then fell back, and Third Squad swept the kill zone, finding the two grenades and pools of blood where McVey had shot the three gooks down. The enemy is so good at getting their dead and wounded off the battlefield after a fight. Then Craft got a glimpse of a couple of the enemy running for the wood line, and the squad fired at them but apparently hit nothing.

I'm pumped about Third Squad's close contact even if they didn't get a body count. I tell McVey what a good job he did, but he seems a little strained and not as much into it as I am. He seems just glad to be alive. Sergeant Arnold is "pumped," though, and can't quit talking about firing up the gooks at such close range.

The word comes down. First and Third Platoons will each send out three squad patrols. Second Platoon, with help from some of the mortar platoon, will secure the company's perimeter. This is great. A day of kicking back and watching the wood line. No walking and no chance of making contact with the enemy. We spread out leaving every other foxhole vacant. Cisero and I are in one hole, then a vacant one, then Staff Sergeant Garza and Scott, then a vacant hole, and then Sanders and Gonzales. We kick back with one man watching the wood line and the other napping.

I watch the other two platoons break up into three squads and head out. There are only two machine guns in each platoon, so only two of the squads have a machine gun. The Third Squad has no machine gun. We are taking over Third Platoon's holes. I watch them go with Jim Swick's machine gun with one squad and Bingle's machine gun with the second squad. The last squad has no gun and that scares me. I'm sure I'm not as frightened as the members of that squad. I can't imagine going on a squad patrol with no machine gun.

We crash and rest with most of us getting some naps as long as one man in each position watches the wood line. About noon, we hear heavy firing coming from far into the jungle. It sounds like an M-60 is beating out six-or seven-round bursts just as regular as if he was on a firing range. There are many other weapons firing, including the enemies weapons.

Garza passes the word that a squad from Third Platoon is in heavy contact. That M-60 keeps beating out a tune. I wonder if it's Jim Swick's gun or Bingle's. The fight goes on forever, but I'm sure it's less than two minutes; then it ends. Garza tells us that Third Platoon had walked into an enemy base camp and stumbled into an enemy platoon. The gooks have pulled out, and there is no one hit in Third Platoon. I'm relieved that all my friends are okay.

A few hours later, the three Third Platoon squads break from the wood line and head toward us. As they take their foxholes back from us, I try to find out which machine gun did such a good job that day. I'm told the squad that made the contact was the squad with no machine gun. I'm shocked. I ask what was that firing I heard. The Third Platoon tells me it was George Witham's M-14. George is a small guy with a big grin from Maine. I'm told that they found a great deal of blood on the ground and some enemy equipment but no enemy bodies. I tell George what a great job he did and that I was sure I was hearing an M-60 firing. George is tired looking but grinning and thanks me for my words.

The next day, Second Platoon is ordered to make a full platoon sweep during the day. I assume that after the squad from Third Platoon's fight the day before the brass wants us in platoon-sized groups today.

We form up and head into the jungle with Second Squad (us) in the left file, Third Squad in the right file, and First Squad broken in half and tacked on the end of each of the other squads. We move a few hundred meters and stop. It's time to do cloverleaf patrols of two men to each side of our unit. Staff Sergeant Garza taps me to go on cloverleaf with him. Garza runs point with me behind him. We move in a circle to our left and are out about fifty meters when Garza drops to his knee with his rifle at his shoulder. I move up beside him with my rifle pointed where his is pointed.

He touches his lips with his left index finger, then points at his own eyes, and then points out into the jungle. I look hard out into all the thick greenery, and then I see two flickers of movement out about twenty-five meters. Whatever it is, it's going back toward our perimeter. Garza then motions for me to follow him, and we move back toward the platoon.

We reach the platoon, all lying down and facing out. Garza moves over to Lieutenant Fletcher and tells him that we saw two gooks moving back toward our perimeter but the gooks did not see us. Then lieutenant reports the movement to higher on the radio and then sends two men from Third Squad on a cloverleaf to our right. Garza and I drop down with the rest of the squad to get a couple of minutes' rest until the two men from the Third Squad returns. I tell Garza that I don't think I would have spotted the two enemy soldiers if he had not seen them. I then ask him why we didn't light the two enemy soldiers up. He tells me that he doubts that his M-16 would have penetrated all the under growth and reached the enemy. He says that my M-14 might have. He also tells me that the enemy would have then known where we were located. They were scouts looking for us.

The two Third Squad men return, and the platoon continues the patrol. We change directions a couple of times and run more cloverleaf patrols. Suddenly, from near the front of the right file, I hear Sergeant Arnold hiss, "Claymore." Terror floods into me as we all crouch down. Garza hisses to us to all move left or right and watch out for trip wires. I move to the left in a crouch with my heart in my throat and my rifle ready. I then move forward from the left. Then I see the claymore. I have never seen a claymore mine this big. It looks like it is three feet in diameter. I have seen a lot of enemy claymores. Most are round and about a foot in diameter. This mine is a monster. It looks waist high standing there on its metal legs and looking at us. Sergeant Arnold moves in on the claymore from the right, steps behind the claymore, and cuts the claymore wire with his knife. What a relief! We form on line and move forward hitting a bunker line not far behind the claymore. We move forward and check each bunker, but no one is home. We find that it is a company-sized base camp. Someone measures the claymore and says that it is thirty inches in diameter. It sure looked bigger to me. If the enemy had been home and set off the claymore on us, it would have killed or wounded over half the platoon. Then the enemy would have overran the rest of us. We secure the base camp and wait on the engineers. They arrive and blow up the bunkers and the giant claymore. We then continue our patrol. We were so close to death.

We dig in that night in sparse jungle. We can even see a short distance into the trees and bushes. I'm digging in with Phil Cisero. We snap our two ponchos together and prop them up just behind our foxhole with two three-foot sticks we have cut. We dig a small trench around our "tent" to keep the rain from coming inside with us. This never fully works. In the wet season, the rain will be so heavy our little ditch cannot handle the volume of water. Sometime during the night, we will get water running in on us. Also, our poncho tent is fully open at each end, so if we have rain blowing in from the front or the back, we will already be wet.

We will each pull two, two-hour stints of guard duty until daylight if nothing happens. We've put out our trip flare and claymore mine. I've got first watch. I'm sitting inside the tent cross-legged with my rifle across my knees. Rain is beating down on the ponchos just a couple of inches from my head. Cisero is asleep beside me. *Suddenly*, about forty feet into the jungle, our trip flare goes off with a blinding burst of light. I see a man's figure in the light darting away. I throw my rifle to my shoulder, but the enemy soldier is gone before I can fire. There's no need in just firing blindly and letting the enemy know our exact location. Lieutenant Fletcher crawls up to my position and asks me what happened. I tell him that a gook tripped our trip flare, but by the time I threw my rifle to my shoulder, he was gone. The lieutenant asks if I'm sure that I saw a man's figure out there. I tell him sure as cancer. He tells me to keep a sharp lookout and he'll report the sighting to higher. He moves back to his position. Cisero is still asleep by my side. The rain is still beating down, and water starts coming in on us. Cisero just rolls over and continues to sleep in the water.

We work the area for another week, moving closer and closer to the Cambodian border. We get mortared a number of times and make more small contacts with small groups of enemy soldiers. Apparently, the enemy has broken his units into small groups that are trying to reach Cambodia.

We dig in one evening in thick jungle. I know that I will have LP that night and just hope that I get two good men to go with me. Staff Sergeant Garza will take the LP out tonight, and he and I report to the platoon CP to get our orders. Sam Collins and his M-79 come from First Squad and Burner Craft with his M-14 from Third Squad. Collins is a slender Black guy from Florida. Craft is a tall brown-haired soldier from St. Mary's, Ohio. I was hoping to get McVey from Third Squad, but Craft is a very solid guy, and he has the second M-14 in Third Squad. We gather around First Lieutenant Fletcher and Platoon Sergeant Hall. The lieutenant has his map spread out. He points to where we are digging in and where the listening post will be. I'm shocked. It's 1,500 meters from the perimeter to the LP position. That's a solid mile. We have been fighting large and small enemy units for weeks. We know they are all around us. I was expecting the LP to be two hundred meters out, three hundred at the most. This is crazy. I know it's not the LT's idea. He has too much sense. Some idiot at battalion level has dreamed up this idea. I go off. I rage and voice my views. First Lieutenant Fletcher says to Staff Sergeant Garza, "Shut that man up." Garza gets in my face and quietly says, "Be at ease, Soldier." I shut up immediately and come to parade rest. The lieutenant finishes his briefing, and we all return to our squads. When I get back to my foxhole, I start raging again. Garza, in a low voice, tells me to quiet down, and of course I do. After all, this is Ben Garza.

It gets a little darker, and Garza and the LP are called to the platoon CP. Usually on an LP, a man carries his weapon with six or seven magazines, a couple of hand grenades, and a canteen of water because we're not going far from the perimeter. I carry all my gear up to the CP. Craft asks me why I'm carrying all my gear, and I tell him that this is not an LP, it's a three-man ambush. I see First Lieutenant Fletcher give me a dark look, but he says nothing.

We start out with me running point, then Garza, then Craft with the radio, and then Collins. We move slowly through the thick jungle for about an hour. It's black dark when Garza stops us. We have come to a trail with a large stand of bamboo beside it. Garza tells us to set up under the bamboo and just observe and report. He tells Craft that he is in charge, and then Garza turns and is gone in the darkness. My blood freezes. Garza is going back 1,500 meters in the dark, alone with no radio. I can't imagine the fear I would have if it was me. I think if I was the NCO, I would call back and report that I had "movement" out here and that I would set up with the LP tonight. Ben Garza has so much character and is too good of an NCO to pull that.

We crawl under the bamboo that bends almost to the ground. Craft says to me, "Listen, you aggressive SOB, we are not firing on any enemy unless they spot us." I tell him that I understand. Gee, I guess I've really been angry. I start calming down. We set up our watches for the night, and it starts to rain. The bamboo keeps part of the rain off us. Craft has first watch, and I go right to sleep. Much later that night, Collins wakes me up and tells me it's my turn. He gives me the watch, and he lies down and goes right to sleep. I sit there a while and listen to the rain. Then I hear someone coming down the trail, moving fast. I point my rifle in that direction, and the person is by me moving fast on the trail in the rain. Is he a scout for a larger unit? I wait a few minutes and hear nothing else. I think, "Should I wake the guys or inform the perimeter on the radio?" The guy is past us and is not moving toward the perimeter, so I decide not to bother anyone. I'll tell them in the morning unless we get more activity.

Morning comes, and I wake Craft and Collins. I tell them about the guy who came by during the night. They're not worried about it. We gear up and head back toward the perimeter with me running point, then Craft with the radio, and Collins brings up the rear.

Craft is talking to them on the radio as I keep my eyes peeled for any gooks that may have gotten between us and the perimeter. We approach the perimeter, and I whistle. Jerry Sweatt tells me to "Come on in." We enter the perimeter, and I report the one enemy that passed us moving toward Cambodia. We then head to our foxholes. When I reach my foxhole, Garza tells me we'll be heading to Di An in a couple of days. The brass has decided that the enemies that are alive have made it into Cambodia. That's great. We'll be back for Thanksgiving and off Operation Attleboro.

CHAPTER 12

The Rung Sac

The last of November, we are in the rear at Di An. We came off Operation Attleboro in time to make it home for Thanksgiving. The cooks really did a great job, and we have eaten well. We've gotten cold showers for the first time in over month, haircuts and clean clothes. We have even been able to go to the village and party. I don't drink at this point in my life, but I've had fun with my friends who do.

We know we've got another operation coming up, so I'm not surprised when the platoon leaders and platoon sergeants are called for a meeting with Captain Dishman and First Sergeant Perry. We hang around the tents, some playing cards, others like me napping. It is best to get some sleep when you can.

First Lieutenant Fletcher and Platoon Sergeant Hall return from their meeting and call a platoon meeting. We find that we will be flying out the next morning to Vung Tau. I am surprised. That is an R&R center and a big party town. We will be staying in tents on the beach with canvas cots to sleep on. Sounds great.

Then we get the bad news. We will be working the Rung Sac Special Zone. It is a large area of salt marshes between Vung Tau and Saigon. The enemy has a very large supply network based there. The Rung Sac has no dry ground. The tide from the South China Sea comes in every evening and is four-or five-feet deep. It goes out in the morning, leaving thigh-deep stinking mud everywhere. The only dry ground is where the enemy has built the mud up to above tide level.

They use these "islands" for base camps and workshops. They do all their traveling by small sampans. We can only stay in the swamp for three days at a time, or the salt will break down our skin. Then we will spend two days on the beach in the tents. One of those days, we will be a ready reaction force in case a unit in the Rung Sac gets in trouble. The other day on the beach, we will be off and get to go into Vung Tau and party.

The briefing continues, and we find that we have to go light, or we will not be able to travel in the mud all day. They tell us we will leave our ten-pound steel helmets in our duffle bags here at Di An. We will all be issued army baseball caps. There will only be two entrenching tools carried per squad. We will be issued black nylon hammocks to string in the trees for sleep at night. We will be ambushing river and creek junctions at night and patrol for enemy base camps during the day.

I start getting my gear ready. I place my helmet, entrenching tool, and four of my twenty magazines in my duffle bag on my cot. I take my four socks of C rations that I carry tied on my back. Each contains nine cans. I place two in my bag and then take three cans out of each of the other two and store them away. That leaves me with twelve cans of C rations, instead of thirty-six. I take the light-weight black hammock and place it in my pack. I also pack away my gas mask. We will not carry those in the Rung Sac. They would be soaked the first day and useless. I believe I have dropped about twenty-five pounds. It only leaves me sixteen magazines for the big M-14, instead of twenty, or 320 rounds instead of 400; but I am not leaving the perimeter with less than sixteen magazines.

The next morning, we get a hot breakfast and then grab our weapons and gear then move down to the helicopter pads. The NCOs break us into sticks of seven for the helicopters. I notice that Sergeant Arnold is not with us and the other NCOs are nervous about him not being there. Staff Sergeant Garza has one stick with only six men in it, hoping that Arnold makes the flight. Missing a military movement is a major no-no. Arnold may lose his new stripes. I hear someone cheer, and I look and see Arnold running toward us with his web gear over his shoulder, his rifle in one hand,

and his cap and sawed-off shotgun in the other. First Sergeant Perry hollers at him as he runs up that he better be glad he made it or he would have gone to the Long Binh Jail. Then the helicopters start coming in to pick us up.

We arrive in Vung Tau later that day. The tents are great, just like ours at Di An. Most of us strip down and wade into the ocean for a few minutes. Then it is chow time. Hot chow on paper plates. This is the life.

This is a secure area, so we only have one man per squad on watch at a time. We can even have a bonfire. We sit around the fire for an hour or so and sing songs. SSG Paul Evans, who has just joined us to replace Staff Sergeant Bass as weapons squad leader, has a good tenor voice and sings some Hank Williams songs. Niquest, the Norwegian, has found an old guitar somewhere and plays it well. This is like a beach party.

The next morning comes, and they load us on a Navy Ship. It looks like the type of boats that the Marines hit the beach in during WWII but much larger. They will land us on a riverbank about two hours away. I get seasick, and the only reason I do not throw up is because I am able to go to sleep.

Gonzales wakes me. We have arrived. I see a muddy bank with about fifty feet or more of mud until you reach the tree line. The Navy drops the ramp, and we walk off onto the riverbank. I go more than knee deep in the mud with the first step. It is hard work pulling your foot out for the next step, and by the time I reach the wood line, I am exhausted. I am covered with mud nearly to my waist and am breathing through my mouth. I have got three more days of this until we are pulled out. This is going to be a nightmare.

Our sister battalion, the first of the eighteenth, usually works the Rung Sac; and we are giving them a break for a month. I see why they are called swamp rats.

The Rung Sac is covered with large cypress trees and ragged underbrush. It is crisscrossed with rivers and creeks and mud, mud, mud. We use our long platoon rope to cross a couple of smaller rivers. We are moving so slowly. I feel like a turtle.

It is getting close to dark, and I'm exhausted. The tide has already started in and is nearly a foot deep. We arrive at the intersection of a large creek and a river. This is where we will set up our ambush. We place our hammocks up in the trees and climb into them. I tied my web gear to the tree near my head so I can reach my magazines and grenades. I place my rifle sling around my neck. I then break out a can of C rations and eat. I then relieve myself into the tide under me. It must be three-feet deep now and still rising.

We set up our watches as best we can by running a light cord from hammock to hammock. I hope I don't fall out of my hammock in my sleep. That water looks four-feet deep now. I hear a large splash about fifty feet into the brush. They have told us that saltwater crocodiles are in this area and they come in with the tide. I do not believe them. I will find out much later that they were telling us the truth. I decide that the splash was a big fish and go to sleep.

Morning comes, and I eat my rations and take down my hammock while standing knee deep in mud. We move out and stumble through the mud with the heat becoming almost unbearable.

About midday, we spot what looks like a small island in all the mud. We move to it and spot a sampan pulled up into the bushes. Fear floods my system, and my stomach knots up. We move up onto the island with our weapons at the ready. We spot a small bunker and move toward it. My heart beats like a drum. We find it empty. We spread out still searching. I fear mines and booby traps. I'm really on edge.

We discover that the built-up island is only about sixty feet across. It's got six small bunkers on the edges of the island. There are two very small thatched hooches in the middle. There's thick brush overhead, so they cannot be seen from the air. Most of us are placed around the edge of the island in case the enemy comes home.

Someone finds what appears to be a grave, and First Lieutenant Fletcher radios the info back to the higher-ups. They instruct him to dig it up and count the bodies. Body count is a big thing. That is one reason the enemy tries so hard to remove his dead from the battlefield. A detail of troops starts digging. I am glad I am not on the detail. They start hitting something after a couple of feet. The smell is terrible. There is no stench like a dead body. I notice some of the guys are doing a lot of spitting.

It is noontime, so I open a can of pork slices and begin eating them with crackers. I hear something and see that a couple of the guys are throwing up. Staff Sergeant Garza walks over to me, and in a stern voice, he says, "You did that on purpose." I say, "Sergeant, I was hungry." He shakes his head and walks on checking the other guys.

The lieutenant calls back and tells the higher-ups that there are four bodies in the grave. The detail began throwing the dirt back in the hole. They look a little green. When they are done, Willie Johnson walks by me headed for Third Squad. I say, "John, what killed those gooks?" He replies, "Looks like artillery."

A helicopter brings in a team of engineers with explosives. They are going to blow the bunkers. Damn, I was hoping we would set up an ambush on this solid ground and wait for the gooks to come home tonight. No such luck. They set their charges, and the helicopter returns and picks up the engineers. We move out after chopping a large hole in the sampan.

We have moved for about fifteen minutes when the charges go off in the bunkers. We are still close enough to see dirt fly in the air. We struggle in the mud and the heat. I can barely pull my boots out of the mud with each step. Finally, we reach our objective. A river and creek junction. It is a repeat of the night before—hammocks tied up in the trees, climb up and tie your gear, put on lots of mosquito repellent, because they are out in clouds. We do not have to worry about leeches here. They cannot live in the saltwater. Thank God for small favors.

Two days later, choppers come and pick us up. It's wonderful being out of the mud. They fly us back to the beach and drop us near our tents. They have set up a cold-water shower, and we all drop our muddy uniforms and socks in a pile. We take our boots into the shower with us and clean up and shave with the one razor that our squad has. The razor is carried by Sanders and Gonzales carries the small mirror. We then pick out a shirt, pants, and socks from a big pile of clean clothing. They will send our dirty clothes to be washed.

We move to the tents and put on our shirt and pants. We hold off on the socks until our boots are dry. We either go barefoot in the sand or wear shower shoes. I crash on my cot and go to sleep. Phil Cisero wakes me up for evening chow. It is fried chicken, and I get a breast and a wing. It's great with mashed potatoes, green beans, and peaches. We sing again that evening, and some of the guys sneak a beer even though they are supposed to be sober while we are on standby.

The next day, we get to go to downtown Vung Tau to party. Staff Sergeant Garza tells us that Second Squad will stick together. Sergeant Valaire is now in Second Squad. He is an old guy, maybe thirty-six or thirty-seven. He's a Korean War veteran and a former POW of the Chinese. He is a big Black soldier from the gulf coast where Texas and Louisiana meet. He has been in the Army eighteen years, owns five bars in Germany, is married to a German woman, and has five sons. He plans to retire in Germany when he gets his twenty years in and run his bars. He had been wounded earlier in the year and has just returned to full duty. He seems like a nice guy, and I think they are planning on him taking over Second Squad when Garza rotates home, which will be in a couple of weeks. It scares me to think of not having Garza as my squad leader. He is the only one I've had in Vietnam, and he's great in every way.

We bar hop in Vung Tau with everyone drinking but me. No one gets drunk, however, and we return to the pickup point for the truck to take us back to the tents. It has been fun with the guys and now hot chow and sleep.

The next morning, we are waiting on the choppers at daylight. It is another three days in the mud and heat. We drop in and go nearly crotch deep in mud. Second Squad has Second Platoon's extra radio this trip, and Garza has picked me to carry it. I hate the radio. It weighs twenty pounds and makes you clumsier. Worst yet, you cannot shoot a radio. I don't like to carry anything that you can't shoot. It makes me sink even deeper in the mud. When I asked for the big M-14, Garza advised me that I would get no consideration for carrying the extra weight, so I say nothing about carrying the M-14 and the radio. I was warned.

We struggle all day, crossing a number of small rivers. It's getting to the point that the only way I have the strength to pull myself out of the mud is with my arms by pulling on bushes and small trees. I almost feel like I'm going to pass out. I keep drinking my water so I do not get heat stroke. Garza encourages me by saying that I was the only man in the platoon who could carry so much weight.

Finally, we reach the river-creek junction where we are supposed to set up our ambush for the night. It is about an hour till full dark, so we have time to set up in the light.

I've got my back to the river while I break out my hammock. I'm looking at Tom Davis in First Squad. Tom's a tall White guy with curly hair from North Carolina. He also has a bad scar on the right side of his face. It runs from just below his right eye, down his check, across his jawline, and into his throat. The scar is as wide as my little finger. It is usually white in color; but as I look at Tom, the scar turns red, and his eyes get big.

Someone shouts, "Sampan." I turn and see a sampan coming down the river with three enemy troops in it. I'm bringing my M-14 to my shoulder when Davis fires the M-79. The shell hits the bow of the boat, splinters fly in the air, and the gook in the bow falls back. Then all thirty of us are firing. I rip out my twenty rounds and shove a second magazine in my rifle and empty my magazine a second time into the sinking sampan. Everyone has fired. Gonzales is shaking his head and tells me my ejected brass has hit him in the back of the head.

A helicopter is overhead in a couple of minutes as the sampan sinks. The chopper pilot radios down and tells Fletcher that there are three enemy bodies floating down the river, all riddled with our fire.

We are all pumped and shouting. All this mud wading has produced some good results. Then we have to saddle up and move to a secondary ambush position because the first one is now compromised.

It takes us nearly an hour to get to our second location. The water is already two feet deep. That and two feet of mud makes the tide come up to my lower chest. It is up to Gonzales's neck and Ruiz's chin.

I get my hammock tied up in the trees and tie the radio to the tree by my head along with my web gear. I am almost unable to climb into the hammock, because of my fatigue. I finally get in the hammock and am barely able to eat my C rations. I then fall into a deep sleep.

I wake to the radio chattering and Gonzales asking me something in Spanish. He then switches to English and asks me what is happening. I can hear heavy firing in the distance. Both First and Third Platoons are out here with us but about a mile on each side of us. The firing is coming from the direction of the Third Platoon.

I listen to the radio and find that Third Platoon has ambushed four enemy soldiers in a sampan awfully close to the riverbank. They have killed all four gooks and recovered their bodies and a couple of weapons. The Third Platoon also has a slightly wounded soldier. By his radio call sign, I know that it is Staff Sergeant Sayers. He is a big beefy White guy who has been in the Army over seven years. He is very well-liked by the guys in Third Platoon. As I listen longer, I find out that it is just minor shrapnel wounds to his arm. He will not require a medevac helicopter.

I pass the info to the other guys, and they are all glad for Third Platoon's success but sorry that they are one up on us on body count. It is my turn at watch, and I sit up in my hammock and look out into blackness until it's time to wake Gonzales.

The next couple of days pass with no more contact, and we find no enemy stashes or base camps. The choppers then pick us up, and it's back to the tents. We shower and put on clean clothing. Staff Sergeant Garza then approaches the squad and shakes each man's hand. A chopper is coming to take him back to Di An. His tour is done. He is going home. We are all glad to see him making it out but sorry to see him go. Sergeant Valaire is now Second Squad leader.

We party the next day and have a good time even though it seems like there's a hole in the squad without Garza. That night we party and sing, and the guys drink some beer. The next day, we will be on standby at the tents in case some unit out in the swamp gets in trouble.

I am awakened the next morning by Sergeant Valaire shouting for us to saddle up. He shouts for us to get our gear and head for the chopper pad. I grab my gear and run to that location. I'm one of the first ones there and relieve my bladder by the pads.

We are all in sticks waiting on the choppers when First Lieutenant Fletcher comes and gives us the word. Three Navy SEALs are out there in the swamp and have discovered an enemy base camp with a platoon of twenty to twenty-five gooks in it. They are lying low and attempting to wait on us before they open fire. They do not think the three of them can hold the enemy platoon by fire until we arrive. My gut tightens up. This is serious. A platoon of enemy and a platoon of us. I've no doubt that we can take them, but they will hurt us while they die. I also wonder why just three Navy SEALs are out on patrol.

The choppers come in, and we load on. We take off and climb high in the air. It's sure cooler up here, but I'm just as scared. Then we get the word that the Seals are in contact. The gooks have spotted them, and the firefight is on. I hope we can get there before they overrun the SEALs.

The choppers head down, and I see grape colored smoke from the SEALs. We jump out in the mud and try to move to cover. Then we see the three SEALs. They are coming over to us. The one in charge says, "They spotted us, and just three of us couldn't pin them down." He then begins talking to First Lieutenant Fletcher. The other two SEALs are standing between Fletcher and me. One of them seems very upset. He is loud as he tells his buddy, "The damn Army took their time, and the gooks got away." Anger sweeps over me, and I shout, "Swabbie, you can go to hell. We got here as fast as we could, and I'm muddy a day early because of you." The SEAL explodes and lunges toward me. I head toward him as his buddy grabs him. Sergeant Valaire jumps in front of me and puts his nose against mine and says, "Young soldier, you be at ease." I come to a halfway parade rest and shut my mouth. They then get the SEAL and me further apart.

The choppers then return, and we load up and return to the tents and showers. We will be clean till in the morning. After returning to the tents, I find out that Platoon Sergeant Hall has also departed for Di An. His tour is up as well. They have moved Staff Sergeant Sayers over from Third Platoon to be our platoon sergeant. I also find out he has just gotten his promotion orders and is now a Sergeant First class (E7). Gee, things happen fast in the Army. The Third Platoon hates to lose Sayers, but their loss is our gain.

I walk to chow and take a shortcut through a Third Platoon tent. When I walk in, I see the Third Platoon leader, First Lieutenant Patrick, in a fight with a Third Platoon staff sergeant. They are down on the ground fighting like dogs. This is a real no-no—an officer and an NCO fighting. I do an about-face and walk back out of the tent. I walk around the tent and go to chow. I do not think that either the lieutenant or the staff sergeant saw me, and I sure don't want to have to testify at anyone's court-martial. I never hear anything about the fight, so apparently no one else saw the fight, and neither of the combatants ever said anything.

The next day, we are out in the Rung Sac again. It is more of the same. The second day, we find an enemy base camp. We search it and find that it is a small claymore mine factory. The gooks are making claymores out of sheet metal, explosives, nuts, and bolts. We call in the engineers, and they blow it up.

Sergeant First Class Sayers is doing a good job as platoon sergeant, and Sergeant Valaire is doing great as Second Squad leader. I'm feeling better about Staff Sergeant Garza and Sergeant First Class Hall going home now that I see the platoon and squad working well.

We are at the tents during one cycle, and we get the word that a man in Charlie Company has drowned. We don't hear his name, and I don't want to know it. I have many friends in Charlie Company whom I went through AIT with at Fort Polk. It is sad, but the Rung Sac is a very dangerous place and not all from enemy soldiers.

Finally, we come in from the Rung Sac for the last time. We clean up, and it is Christmas Eve. They tell us tomorrow we'll head back to Di An on Christmas Day. We also find out that the day after Christmas, the Bob Hope show is going to be at Di An and we will get to see it. I'm thrilled.

CHAPTER 13

Bob Hope

I have been in Vietnam for over six months now and was wounded back in September. I am still nineteen years old. SSG Ben Garza has just rotated home; his tour is done. Second Squad leader is now SGT Maurice Valerie. He is a big Black soldier with eighteen years in the army. He is a Korean War veteran and a former POW of the Chinese. He seems like a nice guy and a good squad leader. He went into the army when I was a year old and was a POW for two and a half years before I started first grade.

Our platoon sergeant, John Hall, has also rotated home and has been replaced by newly promoted Sergeant First Class Sayers from Third Platoon. He is a big White soldier with about eight years in the Army. He is friendly for an E-7 and seems to know his job. I think we are going to be all right despite losing two such fine NCOs. I am just glad that they both survived.

We are flying back to our base camp at Di An on Christmas Day by helicopter. We have just spent four weeks working the Rung Sac Special Zone, a stretch of mangrove swamp between Vung Tau and Siagon. The enemy has a supply system in the Rung Sac. We found a number of small base camps and one small claymore mine factory during those four weeks. We destroyed these enemy camps. We have had no big fights during those weeks, but Second Platoon has killed three enemy soldiers. Our Third Platoon has killed four enemy soldiers and had one of their own wounded during this same period.

We arrive back at Di An, in midafternoon and square out gear away and clean our weapons. We get the word that the next morning the Bob Hope show will be at Di An and we are all getting to go. After the show, we will return to the company area for Christmas dinner a day late. I am very excited. I have seen all the old films of Bob Hope entertaining the troops in WWII and Korea. I will be honored to be in the audience. Unfortunately for them, one platoon from Charlie Company will be on patrol outside Di An to keep the enemy out of mortar range of the show. Well, better them than us.

The next morning, we fall into formation and march to the site of the show. They have set up benches, and our platoon will be only about ten rows from the stage. This is going to be great. I notice that they have about twenty wounded soldiers in blue hospital pajamas in the front row. Those guys deserve it.

Bob comes on stage, and the hundreds of us break into laughter at his jokes and one-liners. He has also Joey Heatherton dancing and Phillis Diller cracking jokes and Vic Damone singing. The girl from India Miss World and the trio the Korean Kittens are also on stage. This goes on for over an hour, and it is great. I have not laughed this much since I arrived in Vietnam.

Too soon it is over, and we form up and march back to the company area. They have Christmas dinner waiting on us, and we all dig in. It's a great meal, the best I've had in Vietnam. We are almost finished when in the far distance we hear heavy gunfire. Our leaders begin shouting for us to saddle up. Charlie Company's platoon that was on patrol has been attacked by a large enemy force.

I grab an apple and an orange with one hand and a handful of turkey and dressing with the other and run for the tent to grab my gear. We quickly form up Second Platoon, and Lieutenant Fletcher leads us out of the base camp headed toward the sound of the gunfire.

We are spread out in combat formation as we enter the jungle, but the enemy knew that someone would be coming to help Charlie Company. The enemy unit has set up for us booby traps and the whole nine yards. We run into a meat grinder. Something hits me in the head just above my left ear. It feels like a wasp sting. I jerk around and put my hand to my head, and it comes back covered with blood. A short way away in the jungle, I hear what I think is a pig squealing at the top of its lungs. How did a pig get here, I wonder? Second Squad is down in the brush on line, facing out. It is all so confusing. I hear voices screaming for a medic, hollering and weapons firing. It appears that our squad has the flank secured. I pass the word down the line that I need Sergeant Valaire. In a couple of minutes, he crawls over to me asking what I have got. I tell him that I am hit. By this time, my shirt is soaked in my blood. Sergeant Valaire sees me, and his face turns gray. I quickly tell him that I am not hit bad, it is just that head wounds bleed a lot. He checks me and places a field bandage around my head. The bleeding stops.

Second Squad then gets the call to pull over with the rest of the platoon a few meters away in the jungle. We arrive and find that Sergeant First Class Sayers is torn almost to pieces. It was him screaming that I thought was a pig. The medic has given him a shot for pain and placed numerous bandages on him. He's still awake, but his pain is less. Private Schuster has his right knee completely torn away and is lying quietly breathing through his mouth. Lieutenant Fletcher is hit in the right thigh, but it's been bandaged, and he's still functioning and leading the platoon. A couple of other guys have assorted wounds but have been bandaged and are quiet.

Lieutenant Fletcher tells Sergeant Valaire to take Second Squad and secure this area that he is going to take the rest of the platoon and the wounded to an opening a short distance away and dust off the wounded by helicopter. The Lieutenant then tells me to fall in with the other wounded to be dusted off. I say, "Sir, with all due respect to your rank, I'm staying with the platoon. All I've got is a cut on the head, and it's not bleeding anymore." He grins and tells me okay.

Second Squad secures the area until the rest of the platoon gets the wounded out by helicopter. They then return, and Lieutenant Fletcher is still leading them. I did not think that he would leave. His leg wound is not bad. We form up in a combat formation and start moving toward the sound of the guns. That sound has not slacked off at all, and I am worried that Charlie Company's platoon will be overrun before we arrive to help them.

We arrive near our sister platoon and form up on line and push forward. Apparently, the enemy has been badly hurt because they are unable to stand against us. We push them away from one side of Charlie Company's defensive perimeter and fall in with our brother soldiers.

I drop behind a huge fallen log with a tall blond soldier whom I knew from AIT at Fort Polk. The soldier had a deep tan, but today he is as white as a sheet. He looks at me and panics at my blood-soaked shirt. He says, "My God, Fedrick, how bad are you hit?" I assure him that it is just a scalp wound. I then notice that there are twenty-seven empty magazines lying around him. I say, "Damn, man, you've fired twenty-seven magazines?" He tells me that he has and that he has thrown all his hand grenades. He then looks at me with his white face and says, "Fedrick, for a while, the gooks were on the other side of this log."

We push the enemy away, and it looks like they have quite a few casualities of their own to carry away. We then begin helping the Charlie Company platoon gather their casualities for dust off. They have four men dead, and nearly half the platoon is wounded. We secure a perimeter around an opening in the jungle; and helicopters come in for a while, taking out the dead and wounded.

We get all the dead and wounded evacuated out by helicopter and are about to form up to head back to Di An. Then the brigade commander, Colonel Grimsley, calls Lieutenant Fletcher on the radio. The Colonel is overhead in his command helicopter. He asks the Lieutenant if all the dead and wounded have been taken out. The Lieutenant tells him that all are out except a slightly wounded rifleman and Lieutenant Fletcher. The Colonel replies that all the dust-off choppers are tied up so he will bring his chopper in to take Lieutenant Fletcher and me to the hospital. The Lieutenant turns command of the platoon over to SSG Paul Evans, and he and I get ready to board the Colonel's chopper.

The helicopter comes in, and the Lieutenant and I scramble aboard. I am sitting on the floor, dirty and blood soaked. The Colonel and everyone else on the chopper have starched jungle fatigues and spit-shined boots, and they all smell of aftershave lotion. I have never been this close to a full colonel before. He leans over, pats my shoulder, and asks me how I am doing. I tell him that I am doing fine after coming to "attention" while sitting.

We arrive at the hospital, and Lieutenant Fletcher and I dismount, and we are escorted into surgery by medics. They clean us up and check us over. It turns out that I need ten stitches in my head and Lieutenant Fletcher needs eight stitches in his leg. They give each of us a couple of shots and bandage us up. If my wound had been just an inch or so to the left, I might not have survived, but it wasn't, so I'm doing fine even on some kind of "high."

A jeep arrives at the hospital from the company at Di An and takes us back to the company area before dark. I hit the rack and get a full night's sleep. The next morning, the company saddles up and heads to the field on another operation. We will be searching the Di An area for the enemy unit that attacked the Charlie Company platoon. Lieutenant Fletcher and I go with them despite our minor wounds. We search until the first of the year but are unable to locate the enemy unit. Possibly, they were hurt so badly in the fight on December 26 that they have pulled out of the area.

CHAPTER 14

The Paymaster

Early January 1967

Ｗe are back "in" at Di An preparing for another big operation up north near the Cambodian border. I've been in my tent getting my gear ready for the big operation when a runner comes into the tent and tells me that the commanding officer, executive officer, first sergeant, my platoon leader, and my platoon sergeant want me to report to the mess hall. I wonder what I have done wrong and ask the company runner what it's about. He tells me it's something about how unreliable the M-16 is. My guts knot up. I have written my congressman and both senators regarding the terrible problems with the M-16. This might be my letters coming home to roost.

I walk to the mess hall and walk in. There's the commanding officer, executive officer, First Sergeant Perry, Lieutenant Fletcher, and Staff Sergeant Evans. They are standing and talking with four chief warrant officers 4s. The CWOs are the same pay grade as a Major, but they are not commissioned officers; they are warrant officers in a technical branch. The four CWOs are all in their late thirties or forties. It turns out that they are from the ordinance section in the States and they are here on temporary duty investigating the problems with the M-16.

Staff Sergeant Evans introduces me to the CWOs by telling them my name and rank and referring to me as a "good troop" who has killed several enemy soldiers. I'm embarrassed by the praise and try not to blush.

The CWOs ask me what is wrong with the M-16. I tell them that most of them jam every magazine or two and some jam every shot or two. That rounds jam in the chamber and have to be "muzzle loaded" out, that if you attempt to fire the weapon on fully automatic two rounds, try to get into the chamber at the same time. I also tell them that the chamber pits easily and the weapon is hard to clean.

They ask me how often soldiers clean their rifles, and I tell them every day but it's hard to do with no cleaning kits. The CWOs are shocked. They ask why we have no cleaning kits, and I tell them that I have no idea but that I've never seen an M-16 cleaning kit. They ask how soldiers clean them, and I tell them they use stiff sections of wire with about a third of an M-14 rifle patch, and as far as the chamber, they try to use toothbrushes. I then tell them that it's battalion SOP not to ever fire the M-16 on fully automatic, because it would jam in the first magazine, instead of the second, like it usually does on semiautomatic.

The CWOs are in shock and ask me if my M-16 is as bad as the others. I tell them that I carry an M-14 and would not go to the field with an M-16, that each of our squads have two automatic M-14s to use as the automatic weapons and, with the two M-79s in each squad as well as the two machine guns in each platoon, we have nearly half the guys with a weapon that works. We hope this will keep us from getting overrun.

I tell them about the last time I carried an M-16. It was when I was shot in the leg and the only thing that saved us was I had a .22-caliber cleaning rod that my mother sent me and a couple of the other guys in the squad had stiff pieces of wire that we called jamming rods. Thus, we were able to un-jam the M-16s as they jammed, and mine jammed several times during the firefight.

The CWOs talk among themselves about possibly chroming the chambers and adding heavier buffers in order to slow down the rate of automatic fire and for sure get a cleaning kit for every M-16. The CWOs have no more questions for me. I salute, turn, and leave the mess hall. Apparently, no one knew that I had written those letters after all.

January 13, 1967, we have been on Operation Cedar Falls for a week and a half. We are in the Iron Triangle attempting to break up an enemy sanctuary. We have some bulldozers tearing out strips of jungle for future landing zones. I am still nineteen years old and have seven months in-country.

I'm amazed that I've been here for seven months, been wounded twice, and am still alive. Sergeant Valaire is still running Second Squad and doing a good job of it. They've moved "Country" Mike Wallace from First Squad to Second to give us some seasoning. Mike has been in-country for ten months and been wounded once. He's a short stocky White guy from South Carolina. He is a good soldier, and I like having him for a team leader.

We've been searching the Iron Triangle and finding enemy base camps. The enemy seems to have been ducking our battalion so far. We've only had some sniper fire and booby traps.

This day has been a hot patrol through the thick jungle. About noon, we come to a trail about four-feet wide with signs of heavy traffic. The jungle canopy covers the trail from the air. It's time for noon break, so we set up with the trail running left and right across our front. The First Squad and a machine gun set up on the trail to our right in four positions. Country Mike Wallace, Raul Sepulvedo, and I are in the first position of Second Squad on the trail. Then there's a machine gun and two more Second Squad positions along the trial to our left. The Third Squad sets up three positions in the jungle to our rear. All this security to just eat chow. It's why we take so few casualties.

There is a large termite hill where Mike, Raul, and I have set up. We are very close to the trail. I have noticed that First Squad's positions are further back from the trail than ours are. We have lots of shade because of the thick overhead jungle. We eat our C rations and then relax. I think we are very secure. The enemy does not travel in the jungle. They run the trails. I can't see how the enemy can get to us. Mike and I tell Raul to watch the front. He's a new guy from San Diego and speaks very little English, but he's shaping up well.

Mike puts his back to the termite hill and starts reading an army *Times* newspaper. I sit cross-legged facing the trail with my big M-14 across my lap. I've got my magazines loaded with duplex ammo. It's a "piggyback" round, one on top of the other. Ever fifth round is a red tracer round, so in a twenty-round magazine, I have thirty-six projectiles. I only have my first ten magazines loaded with duplex because they are hard to find. If we make contact, I'll use those ten magazines first.

I reach inside my helmet liner, get a letter from my mother, and begin to reread it. It's so quiet and not too hot in the shade. Sepulvedo taps me on my left shoulder. I look to my left at him and quietly ask, "What is it?" He points to the trail five feet in front of us and in Spanish asks, "What people are these?" I look to the trail and see one gook dressed in black with a bush hat and armed with a carbine who has just walked by us. A second gook is standing over me. He looks like he's in his late thirties, dressed in black and carrying a brown leather briefcase and a small red bag. A third man is in a long-sleeved white shirt and black shorts. He's carrying a long bolt action rifle. The rest of the trail is full of gooks dressed in green uniforms and carrying heavy packs.

The second gook in the file is barefoot. He's taking a step, and the toes on his right foot are just touching the ground. His jaw is dropping, and he is reaching for a Chicom pistol hanging at his side by a cord as he looks down at me. I rock back and forth left to right and right to left firing my M-14 on auto and kill the first two men in the file. The magazine is emptied in less than two seconds. As I fire, I hear what sounds like tree branches breaking. I then dive over on top of Wallace, shouting, "Gooks on the trail." Sepulvedo falls on top of the two of us.

I see the third man in the file run up to the second man and grab the brown briefcase and turn and run down the trail. I've been trying to jam another magazine into my M-14. I get it seated and fire a second twenty-round burst down the trail. Wallace is firing his M-16 from the right side of the termite hill. I'm firing my M-14 left-handed from the left side of the hill. Everyone is shouting and firing. First Lieutenant Fletcher runs up with his radioman and asks what has happened. We shout, "Gooks on the trail," and I point at the two dead bodies just feet in front of us. I notice then that my muzzle flash has started the second gook's clothes smoldering. The Lieutenant grabs the radio and calls Captain Dishman. The Lieutenant says into the radio, "I've got two dead gooks on my hands and a bunch more running from my location." The Lieutenant then calls in artillery so close to our location that we get huge pieces of metal fragments impacting around us.

In a few minutes, things quiet down, and we have control of the area. We move forward to check the dead gooks on the trail. I cover down the trial, and Sergeant Arnold from Third Squad searches the gook who was in front of me. He digs into the red bag and says, "Hey, there's money and records here." First Lieutenant Fletcher tells him to get it all to First Sergeant Perry. I see now why I thought I heard tree branches breaking. The second gook in the file is lying on his back with his right leg crushed under him. Only his foot is protruding. The rounds from my big M-14 have broken his hips and leg. His shirt has popped open, and his chest and stomach are full of bullet holes.

We sweep the area, but the large group of enemy troops is gone. I ask First Squad why they let the enemy walk past them. They tell me that they believed them to be South Vietnamese soldiers. I tell them that any time that friendly troops are working the areas near us, we are told about it. One of the First Squad guys asks me what I would have done if they had been friendly troops. I tell him in that case I would have apologized.

We work the area for a couple more days, and then one evening, I'm called to the Company CP. I report and am told by First Sergeant Perry that the South Vietnamese money has been checked and it is real. Some of the money has my bullet holes in it, but they are still good to spend. He tells me that I'm being given the money because it's not American or North Vietnamese. It's more than a thousand dollars. The records recovered are pay records. The older enemy soldier was a paymaster. We wonder how much money was in the briefcase that the enemy soldier in the white shirt got away with. They also give me the paymaster's pistol. I will eventually give this pistol to

Lieutenant Fletcher. I think it would be easier for him to get it back to the States when he rotates home.

I'm surprised about the thousand dollars. I have it sent back to Di An to be placed in the company safe. The next time we are in the rear, I buy a large quantity of beer and whiskey and throw a party for the platoon. I send $200 home to be placed in the bank. The rest I use on R&R in Japan for a week in February.

We are still on Operation Cedar Falls and working the Iron Triangle. We have made contact with the enemy a number of times since I killed the paymaster a couple weeks before. Our First Platoon has had four soldiers badly wounded by machine gun fire just a few days before. They are so seriously wounded that we doubt that any of them will ever return to the company. We are digging in in the jungle late in the afternoon when we hear a huge explosion from First Platoon's area. Then many voices are shouting for medics. All our medics rush to the First Platoon area. I turn and watch the jungle with a sick feeling in my stomach. Soon we get in a dust-off helicopter, and I hear guys carrying people to the dust-off. The chopper leaves, and things settle down. The Second Platoon medic returns to our area covered with blood. I ask him what happened. He tells me that McCann and Sergeant Ski in First Platoon stumbled into some ground explosives, and they went off. McCann is dead, and Sergeant Ski is very badly wounded. Sergeant Ski is a blond-haired very handsome NCO in his early twenties with over three years in the Army. McCann was a big burly older soldier in his midtwenties with brown hair and the map of Ireland on his face. He had served a four-year stint in one of the other military services and then got out. But the Vietnam War heated up, and he could not stand not being a part of it. He joined the Army for the infantry and Vietnam. It is a sad ending, one patriot dead and another possibly crippled.

A few days later, they fly us into Loc Khe to relieve another battalion that is holding down the perimeter. We arrive and take over their bunkers. They file down to the landing strip and set up in groups of seven and drop their gear waiting on helicopters to pick them up and take them somewhere out into the jungle. As I watch, one of the groups of seven are enveloped in dust and an explosion.

All the medics in both battalions rush down to help. I turn and watch the wood line. This would be a good time for the enemy to move on us with all the attention on the tragedy. I know what has happened. A hand grenade has exploded on one of the soldiers' web belt. You have to keep the pin bent on those grenades when they are on your belt.

Dust-off helicopters come in and take the wounded away. Our platoon medic returns once again covered in blood. I ask him what happened. He tells me what I already knew—a grenade went off on a soldier's belt, killing him and wounding his six buddies. In a few minutes, large numbers of helicopters come in and take the other battalion away to work the jungle. After all, the war must go on.

We continue to work the Iron Triangle and make a lot of light contact but get in no big fights. The bulldozers tear up large areas so in the future we can get in the helicopters. We destroy enemy bunkers and tunnel complexes with the help from the engineers.

One day, we are on a squad patrol in the jungle attempting to locate the enemy and also keep them away from the engineers. We have a light observation helicopter hovering over our heads, just above the treetops, also looking for enemy movement. Suddenly, a long burst of AK-47 fire rings out only about thirty meters to our front, and the helicopter zooms away. We all hit the ground with our weapons to our shoulders. We lay there for a couple of minutes realizing that the fire was not at us but at the helicopter. We then form up on line and move forward expecting to come under enemy fire at any minute. We move forward about one hundred meters and see or hear nothing. Apparently, it was an enemy scout or small team that fired at the helicopter. They then pulled out either not knowing our squad was here or not being strong enough to take on a full squad with a machine gun.

We get the word that we will be air assaulting closer to the Cambodian border. We are still trying to keep the enemy from escaping into their sanctuary base camps in Cambodia. It is a crazy war that they can fight from Cambodia and hit us with mortars and rocket fire from with in Cambodia, and we cannot fire back or go into Cambodia.

We find a large landing zone and gear up for the air assault. The choppers will be in five chopper sticks, and as usual, we will have seven infantrymen on each chopper. I find that I will be on the first lift and there will be some company radiomen on the chopper with me. There is a small sergeant E-5 in his forties with over twenty years in the Army. This is his third war, and apparently, he is a real hell-raiser for him to only be a sergeant E-5 after being in the Army for longer than I have been alive. He and another company radioman will be on the chopper with me and four other guys from Second Platoon.

The choppers come in and pick us up, and we head toward our LZ. We will be the first lift in, and there has been no indication that there are any enemy troops in the area. Therefore, the LZ has not been "prepped" by artillery or gunships. We plan on being on the ground before the enemy realize what is going on.

I've always been afraid of heights, but I have been in-country for seven months and made many air assaults. I have become hard. I'm sitting on the left side of the bench seat in the chopper, and when we start descending, I grab a strap hanging from the ceiling of the chopper with my right hand. I then step out on the chopper's skid while holding my rifle in my left hand. I've done this a couple of times before and think that it really looks cool and makes me feel like a hard-core troop.

We are the second chopper in the stick, and the first chopper is "flaring" to sit down, and our chopper is right behind them and only a little higher. *Suddenly*, heavy fire breaks out from each side of the LZ. I hear rounds hitting our chopper, and the pilot takes the chopper straight up as fast as he can. My feet slip off the skid, and I'm hanging by one hand and lose my helmet. The small sergeant reaches out and grabs me in my web gear and shouts, "I've got you, boy." I reach up with my rifle, and someone grabs it. All the guys are crowding over on the left side of the chopper, and the crew are all shouting for us to spread out, that we are becoming overbalanced to the left.

I see the first chopper smoking badly and attempting to pull away over the treetops. I also see two of the enemy soldiers who are firing at us, but I cannot return fire. We get higher and higher, and the guys finally are able to pull me into the chopper at more than a thousand feet high. I'm breathing heavily and frozen with fear. I had planned on jumping when we were just a little closer to the ground. If I had, I'd be alone down there with the enemy unit. I know one thing. I'll never stand on a skid again. This incident reinforces my fear of heights. Gonzales digs into his pack and hands me an army baseball cap to wear until I can get a replacement for my helmet. We fly to an alternate LZ and land with no opposition. We then begin patrolling looking for the enemy unit that "lit" us up. We patrol all day but are unable to locate the enemy unit. We then dig in in a perimeter and place listening posts out in the jungle and send out ambush squads. It's just another day and night in Vietnam.

The end of January brings the end of Operation Cedar Falls. We fly back into Di An, walk to our hooches, and clean our weapons. We then drop our filthy clothes in a pile and hit the cold outdoor shower, each of us with a tiny bar of soap. We wash a month's worth of dirt and jungle off and also wash our wild hair with the little bar of soap. We also shave the same way.

We exit the showers naked; and there's a pile of shirts, one of pants and one of socks waiting on us. I go through the pants and find a pair of large-size pants. This is one of only two times on my first tour that I'm able to button my pants, because most of the uniforms are medium in size. I pick up a shirt and socks, walk to my hooch, and get dressed. It feels so good to be clean. I dig into my duffle bag and find my Army baseball cap and put it on. It feels good not wearing that heavy helmet. We walk over to the mess hall and have a sit-down meal on trays with a table. It sure feels human.

After chow, most of Second Platoon walk over to the beer tent. We pull three of the little tables together, and eighteen of us sit around the tables. Weaver and I get cokes and the others beer. The beer is either Falstaff or black label. The guys in the rear get all the premium beer. The jukebox is blaring out the good songs from the sixties; and we can shout, laugh, and sing along with the music. We do not have to whisper like we do in the field. It is so good being with our friends and not being afraid.

After an hour or so, most of the guys have had four or five beers and are feeling no pain. The soldier on my right is really feeling his "oats." His name is Buddy (not his real name). He's five feet eight, 160 pounds, well-built and quick moving. He has always bragged about boxing in the golden gloves for a couple of years before he was drafted. He's a very outgoing soldier and well-liked by nearly everyone in the platoon. It's very loud at the table, but Buddy is at my right ear. He asks me, "Big man, do you think that you can whip me?" I'm not surprised by the question. I've always felt that Buddy was sizing me up despite him being very friendly nearly all the time.

I think if I tell Buddy that he can whip me, then he will try to bully me. If I tell him I can whip him, I may have to prove it. I think I can, but it would not be an easy task, and even if I won, Buddy would mark me up. This is a lose-lose event. If I whip Buddy, people will talk me down about how much bigger I am than him. If I lose, they will laugh at me for the same reason. I let my "hard face" come on and put my face an inch from his. I say, "Buddy, you would be hard to handle, but, yes, I can whip you. There's not a hundred-sixty-pound man in this world that can whip me." That's sheer propaganda, but I hope he believes me because I don't want any trouble with another American soldier. I'm sure that there are many 160-pound men in the world who can take me.

Buddy looks me in the eye for a few seconds and then breaks into laughter. He puts his arms around me and shouts, "I love you, big man." I hug him back and laugh with him. He then shouts to the other guys, "I love this big man so much." I tell him, "I love you, too, Buddy." The party continues until about 2200 hours (10:00 p.m.) when they close the beer tent. We then head back to our hooches with some of the guys needing help from others. One soldier has to have two other soldiers help him. We get to the hooch, and the two soldiers helping the very drunk soldier lay him on his cot. He begins snoring right away. I lie on my cot and go right to sleep looking forward to eight hours of unbroken sleep.

About midnight, I'm awakened from a very deep sleep by shouting. The lights come on, and I sit up. Our NCOs are shouting for us to saddle up, that a unit outside Di An is in heavy contact and need our help. Damn! Can't we get a night off? I gear up and look around. Half of the guys are drunk and having trouble getting their gear on. I help a couple of them, and other more sober guys are helping others.

We then find that we can't wake the very drunk soldier. We put his gear on him, and four of us pick him up. He's deadweight and still snoring. The guy weighs about 180 pounds, and then there's his gear. We carry him, and the platoon staggers toward the gate and then out of the perimeter. I'm terrified that we will make contact with the enemy. Two or three of the guys throw up as we move though the dark.

We come to a barbed wire fence, and some of the guys have to have help getting through it. We lay the passed-out soldier next to the fence. We then crawl through the fence and then drag the passed-out soldier under the fence and then pick him up again. I'm exhausted, and so are the other three soldiers helping me carry this drunk. He's a good friend of ours, but is he ever heavy!

Finally, we are told to set up that the enemy is heading our why and we will try to ambush them. The other three guys and I drop the drunk and try to catch our breath. The drunk begins to snore loudly. We roll him over on his stomach, and his snoring lessens. I'm soaked in sweat and breathing through my mouth. I face out along with the other three guys with our weapons at the ready. Down the line, I hear another guy throwing up. How can the enemy not hear all this if they approach us? We lay there until it starts getting gray in the east. Thank God the enemy didn't come our way.

We then get the order to saddle up. We are heading back to the perimeter. The other three guys and I have to carry the drunk back. We enter the perimeter and head to our hooches. We lay the drunk on his bunk, and he's still snoring. I drop my gear and crash on my bunk.

"They" let us sleep about two hours and then wake us up for formation. We are able to get the drunk up for formation, but some of us have to help him stand. The Captain says a few words including the plan for us to leave the next day on another big operation up near the Cambodian border. If it weren't for bad news, we wouldn't have any news at all.

First Sergeant Perry takes over the formation and tells us that we will be trucked to town in a couple of hours to "party." He tells us all to get a haircut, or we will face a fate worse than death. He then tells us that the cooks have a hot breakfast of powdered eggs, creamed beef, and biscuits waiting on us. We fall out of formation, and I head toward the mess hall. About half the guys go with me, and the others head back to their cots to go back to sleep. I reach the mess hall and go through the line. I get powdered eggs, creamed beef, biscuits, and a cup of hot coffee. I sit at a table, put ketchup on my eggs, and chow down. I finish and look toward the chow line. The mess sergeant says, "Fedrick, I know you want seconds, so come get them." I hit the chow line again and get a second full plate. I finish it and get up and walk back to the hooch feeling really good. I lie down and go back to sleep.

In a couple of hours, they get us up to go to town. I'm feeling great. Some of the guys are still hung over. The guy we had to carry the night before is up but holding his head. He's saying that he drank too much. I ask him if he recalls what happened last night. He gives me a blank look. I then tell him that we were called out a couple of clicks outside the perimeter and three others and I had to carry him. He's shocked and embarrassed. He says that he's not going to drink as much the next time we come in.

We load up in trucks and head toward town. We come to a narrow bridge over a creek. The "white mice" (South Vietnamese military police) have a checkpoint set up on the bridge. They are checking ID cards of all Vietnamese moving on the road. This requires our trucks to stop. I see an adult male Vietnamese on a bike coming toward us as he approaches the bridge. He pedals past the white mice as they shout, "Dung lai" (Halt) and "Lai dai" (Come here). The gook on the bike is still pedaling toward us when one of the white mice pulls a .38-caliber revolver from his hostler and fires three quick shots at the bicyclist. The bicyclist falls over on the side of the road and lies still. The ARVN policeman holsters his revolver and starts checking ID cards again. Everyone ignores the dead gook and continues about their business. Then our trucks are allowed across the bridge.

We arrive in town, and the first thing I do is go to a barbershop and get my hair cut. I don't want First Sergeant Perry to be on my case. We are all with other GIs. We know not to be alone; someone might try to rob us. Three hours later, the trucks come to pick us up. Some of the guys have had a few beers, but no one is really messed up. I guess that last night showed some of the guys how bad that can turn out. We truck back toward the headquarters. We come to the bridge, and the white mice are still checking IDs. The dead bicyclist is still lying dead beside the road, but someone has taken his bike. Passersby are ignoring him. My family back in the world would not believe all this death and callousness.

We arrive back at the company area, and First Sergeant Perry holds a formation. He checks all our haircuts, but everyone has gotten one. We then head to our hooches to get our gear ready for the big operation tomorrow.

CHAPTER 15

Village Seal

Late January 1967

De Jesus has rotated home, and I have taken over his M-60 machine gun. Bravo Company has been op-conned (loaned out) to another battalion. This battalion has an operations plan to do a village seal (surround a village) on a large village that is very pro-enemy. Enemy units have been using this village to rest, resupply, and nurse their wounded. A village has been built about twenty miles away in a secure area. The plan is to move all residents of the village to this new village and then bulldoze the old village flat, leaving the enemy no sanctuary in this area.

They have obtained enough helicopters to lift all four companies at once and land us all at one time on the four sides of the village. We will do this before dawn and allow no one to exit the village. After day light ARVN (South Vietnamese Army) will man loud speakers and command all enemy soldiers to surrender. We will then enter the village, search it, and then move the people and their livestock on trucks to the new village.

It's a great plan, but the enemy haven't voted yet. He may have a large unit in the village and no plans to surrender. This could get really hairy, and I'm afraid. We are not working for *our* battalion, but another and I don't know how they work or react. I don't know if I can depend on them.

We load on helicopters in the wee small hours of the morning and lift off. I'm carrying the twenty-three-pound M-60 and four hundred rounds or twenty-four pounds of machine gun ammo. Each one of my two-man gun crew is "humping" five hundred rounds of machine gun ammo and their own personal weapons. I hope it's enough, because we can't carry anymore.

We fly high in the dark night air. It's almost cold this high up, and I'm shaking from the cold and the fear. Then we roar in on all sides of the sleeping village and land. There are dry rice paddies on all sides of the village, and the little dykes make good cover. We run to the nearest one, and I set the gun's bipods on the dyke and face the village. We get a small amount of incoming fire, and I fire a few quick bursts at a muzzle flash. Then it all stops. Second Platoon and the other two rifle platoons are facing the village with our weapons at the ready. Our mortar platoon, without their mortars, are spread out behind us facing the wood line, watching our backs. If we've caught a large enemy unit at "home" in the village, they will try to break through us. My assistant gunner lays out some belts of ammo for the gun. We are ready.

Daylight comes, and the ARVN began calling out to the village on loud speakers. This goes on for a while, and a handful of combat age males walk out and surrender. I guess the enemy had no large units in the village. I'm relieved and a little disappointed.

We have been given the order that no one will leave the village. There is a dirt road coming out of the village and going through our lines about one hundred meters to my left. I see a male Vietnamese on a bicycle riding out of the village on that road. He's just pedaling slowly and coming toward our troops. I'm expecting them to stop him and turn him back into the village. He gets near our troop line and begins to pedal a little faster. I hear the troops down there giving the command, "Dung lai" (Halt). The suspect pedals through the line of troops and keeps going. I hear the troops calling to him "Lai dai" (Come here). He keeps pedaling. I think, are they going to let him escape? I pick up my M-60 and turn it around. Before I can fire, a machine gunner down by the road fires a twenty-round burst at the bicyclist. He falls off his bike into the ditch beside the road and lies still. He should have listened to the orders given to him.

We then move into the village and search it. We find some tunnels and some weapons. Also, a large supply of rice in large burlap sacks and canned fish. We load it all in trunks along with the residents and their chickens and water buffalo. It's a lot of confusion and a lot of trucks. Army engineers come in with their bulldozers and begin leveling the village as the trucks begin departing for the new village. I guess the Army wanted the people to see that there would be no village to return to. The enemy unit working this area is going to be hungry for a while. Before dark, we load back on helicopters and head out, leaving the other battalion to work the area for the enemy unit. They don't need us anymore. They have their three companies and their recon platoon.

We arrive back with our battalion and begin patrols as usual. We are running platoon-size patrols out of a battalion perimeter in the jungle.

Second Platoon is on a day patrol in the jungle when we start seeing signs of an enemy base camp. There's dead brush in a line in the jungle. The enemy does this so if we are moving in on their base camp at night, they will hear the dead brush breaking. Our fear factor goes through the roof. Is the enemy unit at home? Are their booby traps and mines around this base camp?

We move slowly in with our weapons at the ready. We start seeing the small enemy bunkers. We move in among the bunkers, and some of the guys duck their heads inside the bunkers to make sure they are empty. These guys have more guts than I do.

We see grass hooches in the middle of the base camp. The jungle is thick, and you cannot see the hooches from the air. It's a company-sized base camp, and it's empty. I feel so relieved. I would not want to go up against these bunkers if they had enemy troops in them, not with just my shirt between the enemy fire and my body.

Then in the distance, we hear mortar rounds leaving their tubes. Guys are shouting, "Incoming," and guys are scurrying around. The NCOs are shouting for us to take cover in the enemy bunkers and prepare for an enemy ground attack. I run up to a bunker and look at the bunker entrance. There is no way that I could get my large body through that small opening. I flop down behind the bunker and place my M-60 MG on top of the small bunker facing out into the jungle.

The mortar rounds begin impacting around and in the base camp. The enemy had their own base camp zeroed in with their mortars and had waited until we were fully in their base camp and then began dropping mortar rounds onto us. I get as low as I can and try to get under my helmet. The mortar rounds are impacting all round me, and I shake like a leaf expecting one to land on me at any time.

I notice that the LT and the NCOs have their compasses out getting a direction on where the mortars are being fired from. You can also tell how far away they are by how long it takes them to land after they are fired. The lieutenant is calling back to our perimeter for our mortars to fire counterbattery against the enemy mortars. I'm waiting on the enemy troops to come boiling out of the jungle and hit us with a ground attack.

Our mortars are landing out in the jungle and the incoming mortar fire from the enemy stop. I suppose that the enemy have grabbed up their mortar tubes and ran when our mortar fire began impacting on them.

I look around and see some of our troops crawling out of enemy bunkers. The majority of the guys seem to have been able to fit their bodies into the small enemy bunkers. I hear no calls for the medic, and the NCOs are checking to make sure that we have no wounded. We are blessed. No one has been hit. It is also apparent that the enemy is not strong enough to hit a full platoon with a ground attack.

Norberg calls to me and asks why I did not get into a bunker. I ask him how I would have gotten my large body into the small openings in the bunkers. He says that he sees what I mean. We saddle up and resume our patrol after the engineers come in and blow the enemy bunkers. We expect to make contact with the enemy unit that mortared us.

We move slowly through the jungle trying to make as little noise as possible. The point men are not using their machetes so as to be as quiet as possible. The jungle is very thick, and I'm very large and carrying the M-60 and four hundred rounds of ammo. Most of the guys are having no problem slipping between the trees and saplings, but I do. The man in front of me slips between two saplings, and I attempt to do the same thing. I get hung up with all my gear catching on the saplings, and I cannot get free. I whisper to the man in front of me to stop the file, and he stops and passes the word forward. The file stops, and Sergeant Valaire comes back to see what the problem is. He helps the man in front of me and the man behind me in getting me unstuck. I ask Sergeant Valaire to tell the point man to be aware of me when he moves between these saplings. I cannot get through as small an opening as most of the guys. He smiles and says he will take care of it.

We patrol the rest of the day with our nerves on edge, but we make no contact with the enemy. We move back into our perimeter and drop our gear at our foxholes, relieving the men from the "stay behind" platoon that secured the perimeter while we were on patrol. I break out some C rations and begin to eat. Sergeant Valaire comes by and tells me that just after dark that my gun crew will be leaving the perimeter with Second Squad to set up an ambush about three "clicks" into the jungle (about two miles). It's another busy day and night in the jungle, and I only have five more months on this tour.

CHAPTER 16

Danger Zones

February into early March 1967

I'm just turning twenty and have been in Vietnam for eight months on my first tour with Bravo Company, Second Battalion, Eighteenth Infantry Regiment, First Infantry Division. I've been wounded on two occasions, in September and December. I'm one of the two machine gunners in Second Platoon. We are out on Operation Junction City, the largest operation in the Vietnam War. We are working near the Cambodian border about seventy miles northwest of Saigon.

The First Infantry Division, the Twenty-Fifth Infantry Division, the 173rd Airborne Brigade, and the Eleventh Armored Cavalry Regiment are fighting the enemy, Ninth VC Division, 101st NVA Regiment, Eightieth NVA Guards Regiment, and the famed VC Phu Loi Battalion. About forty thousand American soldiers on the ground fighting about twenty-five thousand enemy soldiers in an area about the size of two counties. The fighting has been heavy.

A Company in one of our sister battalions is being overrun and may be wiped out. Bravo Company is moving through the jungle toward the sounds of the guns, attempting to relieve the other company. Our Third Platoon is leading the way with Vern Bramlett running point. He's a medium-sized soldier from northern Georgia. He's been here about three months and has become "seasoned." Artillery is "walking" in front of Bravo Company in order to break up any enemy ambush as we move to help our brothers. From what we hear on the radio, this may be a massacre. Helicopter gunships and jet fighter planes are working in the distance attempting to keep the enemy from completely overrunning the other company.

Vern Bramlett comes across an enemy soldier's foot and his broken rifle. Apparently, the artillery impacting ahead of us of us is doing a good job breaking up any enemy ambush. As we approach one side of the beleaguered company, the air strikes are called off on that side of the friendly perimeter. We push in and start seeing an occasional enemy body. Bravo Company then moves into the perimeter and start seeing many American dead and wounded. Bravo Company then pushes the enemy away from our sister company, and the enemy breaks and begin pulling out big-time, taking as many of their dead and wounded with them that they can.

Bravo Company secures a perimeter around our sister company, and our medics begin working on the other company's wounded. The other company has thirty-two soldiers who have been killed in the fight. The majority of the remainder of the company are wounded. We locate a middle-aged Black Platoon Sergeant, Matthew Leonard, lying dead with five enemy soldiers lying dead around him. His fellow soldiers are saying that he was the mainstay of their defense. (We would later learn that this fine soldier's widow would be awarded his Medal of Honor.)

Large numbers of medical helicopters are coming in, and the wounded are loaded in and taken out. When all the wounded have been taken away, more helicopters come in and take away all the dead. Bravo Company checks the area and find many pools of blood and drag marks. It appears the enemy unit paid dearly in blood for hurting our sister unit as badly as they did. Bravo Company will soon clear the scene and begin searching for the crippled enemy unit that killed so many Americans. We do not find them. They have taken their wounded and most of their dead and escaped.

A few days later, Second-Eighteenth is dug in forming a perimeter in the jungle, and we are running day patrols and night ambushes, attempting to locate enemy units. The Third Squad, Second Platoon has been tapped for a day patrol, and my machine gun crew has been tapped to accompany them. My buddy, Doug McVey, is the Third Squad leader. He's only a Specialist 4 in a Staff Sergeant E-6 slot, but we are very short on NCOs. First Squad is led by Jerry Sweatt, a small guy from Georgia; Second Squad leader is Liberato Gonzales from Taos, New Mexico; and the machine gun squad is led by Jim "the Swede" Norberg from Minnesota. All of these squad leaders are Specialist 4s. An infantry platoon is supposed to have one E-7, four E-6s, and six E-5s. We have no E-7 and no E-5. We have one E-6, SSG Paul Evans, and he is the Platoon Sergeant. First Lieutenant Fletcher is the platoon leader and has been since August. He is a good platoon leader, and I like working for him. All our squad leaders and team leaders are Specialist 4s or PFCs.

Third Squad has seven men, instead of the ten that the TO&E calls for. I have a full gun crew. My assistant gunner is Graves, a Black guy with a bad knee from E. St. Louis, Illinois; and my ammo bearer is Lambrett, a stocky White guy from the Midwest. Each of them carries five hundred rounds for the machine gun, as well as their personal weapons and ammo. A hundred-round belt of MG ammo weighs nearly six pounds. I'm carrying the M-60 MG, which weighs twenty-three pounds empty and four hundred rounds of ammo. Most gun crews only carry nine hundred rounds. Four hundred on each of the crew members and one hundred with the gun. That doesn't cut it with me. I'm a shooter. I put out a large volume of fire, so I am carrying eighteen extra pounds, and each of my crew carries an extra six pounds. This gives us 1,400 rounds for the machine gun. It may make the difference in our unit living or dying.

We begin our patrol with two files of five men each. McVey is the second man in the left file behind the point man. The radioman is behind McVey and then two more soldiers. The point man on the right file is Burner Craft, a tall brown-haired soldier from St. Mary's, Ohio (a good soldier and a good point man). He carries a big M-14 that doesn't jam. I'm second behind Craft with the MG and then my two crew members and one rifleman bringing up the rear. The two files are only fifteen or so feet apart so we can still see each other. This helps us to survive if we are ambushed. The enemy might only see one file, and it's hard to pin down two files.

We move slowly through the thick jungle, stopping often and sending out small two-man cloverleaf patrols to each side when we stop. They are checking for ambushes, sound, and movement around us. McVey is working the compass and the map and keeping us on track. He, like Craft, is carrying an M-14; and Weaver, a short quiet White soldier from the Carolinas, is carrying a single-shot M-79 that fires a small explosive shell. That makes four of us out of the ten with weapons that do not jam. The other six soldiers have the terrible jamming M-16. I'm hoping that the four of us with good weapons can keep the ten of us alive if we make contact with an enemy unit.

We come to a break in the jungle. In front of us is a wide field of elephant grass about three-feet high and over one hundred meters wide, and then the jungle starts again. It's what we call a danger zone. We spread out along the edge of our wood line. We begin watching the wood line across the field from us. Our SOP is that after a good while of watching if we see nothing, we have two of our men sprint across the danger zone and set up in the other wood line while we cover them. Then we move across two at a time.

I'm scanning the other wood line, and I see nothing. Suddenly, McVey whispers, "Gooks in the wood line." Craft whispers back, "Yeah, I see them." I start to panic because I see nothing. I have my eyeglasses on, but I still see nothing. I whisper to McVey, "Mac, I can't see them. Where in the hell are they?" Mac crawls over to me and puts his hand on my shoulder. He tells me that they are spread out across the wood line in front of us, waiting on us to cross the open area toward them. I tell him, "Damn, Mac I can't see them." He tells me to look at the big tree across from us with the black trunk. I tell him that I see the tree. Mac then tells me to look at the base of the tree on our right side. I do and I see him! An enemy soldier in a tan uniform shirt standing in the brush at the base of the tree watching "our" wood line. I become excited and tell Mac that I see the enemy soldier. Mac then tells me the rest of the enemy unit are spread out in the wood line, one every ten or fifteen feet down the wood line on both sides of the man by the big black tree.

I put the sight of the M-60 on the soldier by the big tree and tell Mac I'm ready to open fire any time he says. He tells me to wait until he alerts the perimeter to what we have and gets some cannon shells coming to support us. Mac calls back on the radio and is informed that our executive officer, 1LT Bob Leary, is saddling up the Third Platoon to head our way to support us and soon they will have shells coming in on the other wood line. They advise Mac that they will advise on the radio when the shells are being fired and then we can open fire.

I've got two hundred rounds linked in my M-60 and am holding the sight tight on the man by the big black tree with Graves ready to feed belts into the gun. Mac shouts, "Fire!" I open up, holding my trigger down. I see my red tracer rounds zip across the open area and spear into the chest of the enemy soldier by the big tree. He flips over backward, and his sandals fly up in the air. I keep the trigger down and work the tracer rounds around the base of the tree where the enemy soldier has fallen. Then I remember the other enemy soldiers and spread my fire across the entire opposing wood line. I keep the trigger down until I have run through three hundred rounds without a break.

Our cannon shells start landing, and I drop my fire back to short bursts. We are receiving only light return fire as Lieutenant Leary runs up with Third Platoon. He places them on line to our right, and they open fire on the enemy positions along with us. Lieutenant Leary shouts for everyone to fix bayonets on the end of their rifles, that we are going to charge the enemy position. My guts turn to water with fear. Bayonets do not go on the end of a MG, so I just link three hundred-round belts into my gun and wrap them around my left arm and shoulders. Lieutenant Leary has the artillery fire stopped, and then he shouts, "Charge!" and we start across the open area at a trot, all firing as we go. I pull the trigger back on the M-60 and hold it back, firing an unbroken stream of fire into the enemy positions.

We reach the enemy wood line and charge in. The enemy is gone; they couldn't stand up under our fire. We check the area and find some empty shell casings, and a Third Platoon soldier finds a green baseball cap with a little blood on it. I check by the big Black tree and find a pair of sandals and a small pool of blood. Craft walks up and says, "Fedrick, you killed that gook. I saw your tracer rounds go into his chest." I tell Craft that I agree with him. The enemy is so good at getting their dead and wounded off the field of battle.

We form up with Third Platoon and head back to the perimeter. I check my ammo and find that I only have five hundred rounds left for the gun. I've fired nine hundred rounds in that short fight. It sure goes fast.

We arrive back at the perimeter, and the guys from Second Squad are waiting on us. They have been securing Second Platoon's foxholes while Third Squad and my gun crew were on patrol and First Squad and the other gun crew were on patrol in another direction. Phil Cisero, Liberato Gonzales, Louis Sanders, and Raul Sepulveda crowd around me as I set down the machine gun and my gear. Cisero asks me what happened, and I tell him. He seems surprised. He says, "All that shooting and that's all that happened. It sounded like the Battle of the Bulge." I tell him that it seemed pretty serious to me, and it appeared that we hit at least two of them, and I think I killed one of those. He still doesn't seem impressed. He wasn't there, but I cut him some slack; he's my good friend.

McVey comes around getting an ammo count to replace what we have expended. I tell Mac that I need nine hundred rounds for the machine gun. He seems a little surprised. He says, "You shot up that much ammo." I tell him I sure did. McVey asks how much ammo I had left. I tell him I still had five hundred rounds after the fight. He grins and says, "Damn, Fedrick, you need a mule to carry ammo for you." I agree with him but tell him I don't know how we could get a mule to ride on a helicopter when we air assault. He laughs and moves toward the platoon sergeants' position to turn in his ammo request.

I sit down by my foxhole and open a cold can of C ration ham and lima beans. I take my little plastic spoon, flip the large glob of cold grease off the top of the beans, and throw it on the ground. I reach into my pack, take out my bottle of Louisiana Hot Sauce, and pour some into the can and mix it up with my spoon and begin to eat. I wish I had some raw onion and cornbread to go with it, but I don't.

Jerry Sweatt walks over and tells me that First Squad has ambush tonight and my gun is going with him. I tell him, fine, just let me finish eating and clean my gun. I ask him if he would check with Staff Sergeant Evans on my ammo resupply. I then call out to Graves and Lambrett that we've got ambush tonight so they need to eat and clean their weapons. I think, another night with very little sleep, at least it's not the rainy season, so we will not be soaked tonight. Staff Sergeant Evans calls over to me that my ammo is ready. I tell Graves and Lambrett to pick up the ammo and make sure they get nine hundred rounds. I finish cleaning the gun as Graves and Lambrett bring back the ammo. We distribute the ammo between the three of us and get ready to move out.

First Squad has eight men, so there will be eleven of us tonight. It's getting dark, so we form up. Mike Yaw is point man in the right file. He's only been here a couple of months but is making a very good combat soldier. He is medium sized with light-brown curly hair and blue eyes. He hails from Saginaw, Michigan. The most important thing is he carries one of the two M-14s in First Squad. I'm second in file behind Yaw, then Graves and Lambrett and a rifleman behind Lambrett. The left file includes Jerrigan on point, then Jerry Sweatt (Sweatt carries the second M-14 in First Squad). Sweatt's radioman is next then Sam "Homey" Collins, a slender young Black soldier with a big smile follows the radioman. Homey is from Florida and carries an M-79. Two riflemen follow him.

We move though the dark jungle very slowly, stopping often to listen. The two files are too close together, but it's the only way we can see each other. We are also within arms' reach of the man in front of us. We are heading toward a small footpath that we saw on earlier patrols. The path looked well used, and the only people in this area besides us are either VC or NVA soldiers, and we *never* walk on trails.

After an hour and a half and about a mile, we find the trail. Sweatt sets us up with two positions facing the trail but about ten feet back from it. The third position is in the jungle and watching to the rear. My gun will be set up on the left with Yaw in position with the gun crew. Sweatt will be about thirty feet to my right with

Collins, Jerrigan, and the radioman. The other three riflemen are in the rear position.

We set up with Lambrett on the right, then me and Graves to my left to feed the gun. Yaw will be to the left of Graves. We have two claymore mines to set out. I send Yaw and Lambrett and tell them to put one about thirty feet to our left with a tree between it and our position. I tell them I want it facing the trail in front of us at an angle. The second mine will go about twenty feet further down and will point down the trail away from us.

They crawl off, and Graves and I wait with the gun ready in case the other guys run into something. Soon they both crawled back, and I tell them to make sure they know which detonator is which for the mines. We then wait for enemy foot traffic on the trail. We wait and wait, taking turns two at a time dozing.

It starts to get a little lighter, and Sweatt crab walks over to our position. He tells us to pull in our claymores that we'll be moving out soon. The enemy is lucky they didn't use that trail this night. Lambrett and Yaw move down and police up the mines, roll up their wires, and put them in their cloth bags. We then form up and move back toward the perimeter with Sweatt on the radio advising Lieutenant Fletcher.

We near the perimeter, and it's full daylight. We start calling out with low voices, "Ambush coming in." Gonzales calls out for us to come in, and we walk into the perimeter. We drop our gear, sit down by our foxholes, and open up our C rations. Gonzales walks over and tells me that Second Squad has a patrol today and my gun will be with his squad. I say, "Okay," and tell Graves and Lambrett to get ready, we'll be leaving in five minutes. We form up with Second Squad in two files. Sepulveda is point man in the left file. Gonzales is second and then Sanders with the radio. Three more soldiers follow Sanders. The point man in the right file is Phil Cisero with his M-14, then me with the machine gun. Graves, Lambrett and another rifleman follow them.

It's another day of slow movement, stopping, then sending out two-man cloverleaf patrols. We change directions often. The soldier walking behind Sanders is the count man. He carries a bootlace and has measured his steps, and each time he judges we have moved one hundred meters, he ties a knot in the bootlace.

Late in the afternoon, we arrive back at the perimeter, drop our gear, and crash. Staff Sergeant Evans announces that Second Squad has ambush tonight, *but* the other gun crew will go with them. They move out into the jungle while my gun will secure Second Platoon's section of the perimeter along with First and Third Squads.

A platoon in a perimeter always sets out a Listening Post. We put three men with a radio out in the jungle some distance in front of our foxhole line. They are an early warning system. If the enemy forces mass to overrun us, the LP will warn the perimeter before they die.

First Squad has eight men and Third Squad only seven. So two men will come from First Squad and only one from Third Squad for the LP. As it gets almost dark and Sweatt takes out the LP and soon returns, we set up on the perimeter. Usually, a "full" platoon will have eleven foxholes on the line. Second Platoon is understrength, so we have only nine. I'm the only machine gun on the platoon line, so I take the middle hole. Third Squad to my right and First Squad to my left. Each squad now has only six men, and each has four holes to cover. They each break into three two-man teams, and each squad occupies three of the four holes on each side. That leaves one hole on each side without troops, so they pull four men from the small mortar platoon. They will hold down a hole in the Third Squad area and another in the First Squad area. The lieutenant, platoon sergeant, and their radioman are in a foxhole to my rear. The depleted mortar platoon is set up behind us with their three 81 mm mortars dug in and ready for action.

I'm sitting behind my gun in the dark with my crew asleep on the ground behind me. McVey crawls over to me and tells me that the lieutenant says the Second Squad is not answering their radio. Mac is very worried. He, Gonzales, and I are very tight. I tell Mac not to worry that they are alive, or we would have heard a lot of shooting. I tell him that my guess is that their radio is on the blink. He seems somewhat relieved and crawls back to his position.

In a few minutes, far in the distance, on the other side of the perimeter, I hear heavy firing. It must be an ambush squad from either Alpha or Charlie Companies. I am glad that it's not our Second Squad. I hope all the Americans come out okay.

When morning comes, Second Squad walks into the perimeter. The lieutenant and Staff Sergeant Evans meet them, chewing them out about losing communications. Gonzales and Sanders explain that the radio handset went bad. They then turn their chewing on the senior radioman for not having two handsets with each radio.

Staff Sergeant Evans then walks over to my position and tells me that my gun will go on day patrol with First Squad and the entire platoon today. I ask Graves and Lambrett if we are having fun yet.

Lieutenant Fletcher and Staff Sergeant Evans then held a quick meeting with just ten of us in the platoon—McVey, Sweatt, Norberg, Craft, Collins, Franovich, Bicket, Taylor, Beathea, and me. They tell us that the battalion is starting up a battalion security platoon. They will handle security back at Di An. Each of the line companies—Alpha, Bravo, and Charlie—are required to man machine gun bunkers on the perimeter at Di An. Each company has to man two gun bunkers in the daylight and three bunkers at night. So each company has to have four men on the bunker line during the day and six at night. Thus, the battalion requires twelve men in the day and eighteen at night. The companies have been using new guys just coming in-country who have not gone to the field yet, short-timers who are about to go home, wounded men who have come back to the company from the hospital but have not been cleared for field duty, cooks, and clerks. It has become a real strain on the companies being able to supply the man power to accomplish this mission.

The battalion commander has decided to take two men from each platoon in the battalion. There are four platoons in each company and the battalion recon platoon for a total of twenty-six men. These men would form a security platoon in the rear to handle this detail as well as run an occasional short patrol near the perimeter. This new security platoon could also run a small ambush just into the tree line just outside the barbed wire. The requirement for this platoon is that a man has to have at least six months in-country and have more than three months remaining before they are due to rotate home.

There are ten of us in Second Platoon qualified to be considered for this assignment. The other twenty-something guys in the platoon have either not been here six months or less than three months before they rotate home. Staff Sergeant Evans says he will write all ten of our names on small pieces of paper; place them in a helmet, mix them up, and hold them high in the air; and Lieutenant Fletcher will reach up and take two names from the helmet; and these two guys will be assigned to the security platoon. Some of the guys get very excited. This is pretty much a rear job with very little danger.

I think about it. If I got this assignment, I would wonder every day what the guys in the field were doing and if they were in battle. I would be checking each day about where they were and what they were doing. I would spend most of my time sitting in a bunker with another soldier looking out at the wood line past the barbed wire. I think the time would just drag, and I would be bored to tears. That's one thing about the field in a combat zone. It's not boring, and time passes fast.

I walk over to Staff Sergeant Evans, and in a low voice, I tell him not to put my name in the helmet. He looks surprised and asks me if I'm sure. I tell him that I am, that time will pass a lot faster in the field. Doug McVey and Bobby Beathea are standing close enough to hear what I have said to Evans. Mac gives me a strange look and walks away. Beathea says to me, "Damn, Killer, are you not going to be in the drawing?" I say no, I'm not, and Beathea says, "You are a crazy SOB, but you just made my chances better."

Staff Sergeant Evans puts the nine names in a helmet and lifts it high in the air. Lieutenant Fletcher reaches up and draws a name. It's Nelson Taylor, a good soldier who was being groomed to take over Second Squad someday. Taylor's knees seem to go weak, and he starts thanking God for saving his life. He then says if he ever won anything in his life, he would want it to be this. The lieutenant then draws a second name. It's Bobby Beathea. Bobby is a joke-a-min-ute guy and well-liked by the men in the platoon. They have been grooming him to take over Third Squad someday. But today he is a happy camper. He dances and sings about being "in the rear with the gear" and out of the field forever. Some of the guys are happy for him and congratulate them. Other guys turn away to hide their disappointment. I congratulate Taylor and shake his hand, and he thanks me. I turn to do the same for Beathea; but he laughs, hugs me, and says, "Thank you, you crazy SOB."

Taylor and Beathea will leave on the resupply helicopter today. I walk over to Graves and Lambrett and tell them to saddle up we have a day patrol.

Today the entire platoon will be on patrol together. The Brass must expect us to run into something heavy. I'm scared, but then I always am. We move out in a direction that approaches a non-free-fire zone. This means that there are civilians in this area, so we can only fire on people if they have weapons or run from us. Also, this area is not solid jungle. There are strips of jungle and open areas like pasture. We see some cattle with kids herding them. My gun is in the left file, and Norberg's gun is in the right file.

We enter an area that is open with jungle to our left and our right. About four hundred meters to our front is some underbrush and a large tree without leaves. Suddenly, we start taking semiautomatic fire from our front in the distance. Our left file breaks left, and the right file breaks right. One 60 mm mortar round is fired from our very distant front and lands between our two files, and we all hit the dirt. The NCOs start shouting for us not to move into the wood line, there may be booby traps set up there, and the enemy may be trying to force us to run into them.

Then we receive more semiautomatic rifle fire from the front, but it doesn't seem to be hitting near us. Then the guys up front spot the sniper. He is high up in the big dead tree with bare branches four hundred meters to our front. Just a little too far for M-16s to place effective fire and just out of range of the M-79s. Lieutenant Fletcher calls for Norberg's machine gun crew to come to the front along with McVey with his M-14. I feel a pang of jealousy that they called for Norberg's gun instead of mine, but he's been on the gun longer than me. McVey and Norberg move up to the Lieutenant, and he points out the sniper far in the distance. The Lieutenant then tells McVey and Norberg that when he gives the order, he wants them to kill the sniper.

We are all belly down with weapons pointed in every direction. This is just not feeling right. I am thinking that this is a setup. I feel that the enemy is trying to suck us into an ambush.

Lieutenant Fletcher then gives the order to fire. Norberg and McVey open fire on the tree with Norberg firing about thirty rounds from the machine gun and McVey firing a full twenty-round magazine in short bursts from his M-14. The enemy soldier and his rifle fall from the tree into the bushes below. I'm thinking that we will patrol over and search for the enemy soldier's body. But Lieutenant Fletcher and the NCOs agree that is what the enemy want us to do so they can ambush us. The Lieutenant orders us to turn around and go back the way we came for about two hundred meters and then we move to the left and continue the patrol. We get no more incoming fire.

We patrol the rest of the day, changing directions often. The plan is for us to set up a platoon-size ambush after dark. At about 1900 hours (7:00 p.m.), we reach our ambush location in an area that is pretty much open pastureland with a few trees scattered about and some small clumps of brush. We began setting up our ambush, and then someone spots two male Vietnamese sitting by a big tree about 250 meters from us. I immediately place the sights of my machine gun on the two Vietnamese by the tree as I lay in the prone position. I tell the Lieutenant that I am on them and ready to open fire at any time. The Lieutenant says that we can't fire until 2000 hours (8:00 p.m.) as we cannot tell if the two men are armed or not. I keep my gun trained on the two guys in the distance while the Lieutenant and NCOs set up our ambush. They also tell the guys to all pretend that we have not spotted the two suspects. It gets completely dark at about 1930 hours, and we hold in place. The Lieutenant passes the word that at 2000 hours we will very quietly move the platoon to a secondary ambush location and hope that the Vietnamese will think we are still in the first location in case they are planning to hit us during the night.

We move very slowly in the dark for about an hour. We then set up a second ambush site and stay very alert all night expecting an attack that never comes. When morning comes, we are moving back to the perimeter.

While we patrol, I have the gun hanging from my right shoulder on a strap. It's hanging horizontally and all I have to do is grab the trigger to open fire. While I walk and look, I open a can of C rations and begin eating chopped ham and eggs while I walk. I do this often. There are twelve basic C ration meals—three of them most people have trouble eating. They are chopped ham and eggs, pork slices, and ham and lima beans. The guys who get these three meals usually refuse to eat them, and they give them to me. I have four army socks tied on the back of my gear. Each sock holds nine cans of C rations. The four socks are usually full. I have them in case I get cut off from the other guys for days or even weeks. That way I will not starve. Each C ration meal has nearly two thousand calories. I eat four or five C ration meals a day. I am taking in eight thousand to ten thousand calories each day.

I am carrying twice the weight of most of the guys, and I feel like I need twice the chow. Most of the guys have trouble eating in this heat. I don't. The average infantry soldier came over to Vietnam weighing 165 pounds. After eight or ten months in the field, they weigh 130 pounds. I came over weighing 225 pounds, and after eight or ten months, I'm weighing 255 pounds, and all of it is solid as a rock. My thighs are huge from carrying all this weight, walking all day, and digging a foxhole at night. The guys are just thankful that each time I have been wounded, I have been able to walk out on my own.

We get a new mission order. Bravo Company and another company from our battalion will move out after dark en route to an "abandoned" village that at one time was a sanctuary for enemy troops. Military intelligence believes that a large enemy force is moving into this village each night to rest. This makes me very nervous. The idea of three hundred American soldiers stumping around in the dark going into an enemy sanctuary scares the hell out of me.

Going out with a squad or even a platoon is one thing, but two full companies is crazy.

We gear up at dusk and move out. I am glad that I'm somewhat in the middle and not close to the front. It's hot, and the mosquitoes are out in clouds. We move through the jungle for more than an hour, and then the jungle ends. The only light is from the stars, and it's pretty dark. The word is passed down the files that we have reached our objective. We are told that the village has a berm of dirt five feet high and three-feet thick around the village. There are only two openings in the berm. Bravo Company will enter one and the other company the second.

I'm so scared I can hardly breathe. If the enemy unit is "home," we will be sitting ducks. If the enemy is not there, he may have all kinds of booby traps waiting on us. We spread out and move into the village. I'm holding the machine gun tight with my thumb on the safety and my finger on trigger. Sweat is dripping off me, and it's not all from the heat.

Bravo Company takes its half of the berm. Our platoon and another rifle platoon are ordered to secure our half of the berm. Our other rifle platoon will search our half of the hooches. There are about ten of them.

I'm glad I'm on the berm. I place the machine gun on the berm and face toward the wood line that I cannot see in the dark.

Our search platoon checks all the hooches and find nothing. They then take up positions between us and the hooches. There might be hidden tunnels in those hooches. The ground is rock hard, but we do not dig after dark, so there is no chance of us digging foxholes. The two platoons on the berm have the berm protecting us on one side but not the other three. If we come under a mortar attack, we are in serious trouble.

I'm sweating a mortar attack, a ground attack from the wood line or infiltrators out of hidden tunnels in the hooches.

Then the word is passed. We have hot chow. Have they lost their minds! How did we get that in here? We are in a very stressful situation. We don't need this added stress. We are all carrying C rations if we get hungry. Now we have the added stress of having to figure out how to get this chow and not expose ourselves more than we already are. I'm angry at the stupidity of this action. It's after 2000 hours in the evening (8:00 p.m.).

The word is passed that they will set up the chow line in the open area between us and the hooches. We are also told that they have only brought chow for the two companies. They have an insulated can of sliced roast beef, one of mashed potatoes, one of green beans, and one with peach halves in syrup. They also have two containers holding cold Kool-Aid. The catch is they can only send two cans to each company and one container of Kool-Aid. Then we get the only gem of good news. Bravo Company will get the roast beef and peaches. The other company will get the potatoes and green beans.

We start heading to the chow line in the dark, one man at a time, from the lowest-ranking man first and then up. I send my ammo bearer, Lambrett. He returns, and then I send my assistant gunner, Graves. When he returns, I borrow his rifle and leave them with the machine gun. In the dark, I make my way over to the chow. I get a heavy paper plate. The soldier behind the first can gives me two slices of roast beef and two pieces of bread. The second man gives me four peach halves. The third man fills my canteen cup with cold Kool-Aid. I then make my way back to my gun. I give Graves his rifle back, take my two slices of roast beef, and place them between my two slices of bread. I then eat this thick sandwich. It's really good. I then eat my peaches and drink the syrup off the plate. I then drink my big canteen cup of cold Kool-Aid.

The rest of the night passes with just a few snipers rounds coming in from the wood line. The enemy unit knows that we are here! Daylight comes, and the engineers fly in to blow this abandoned village up. Bravo Company and the other company start company-sized patrols. We patrol all day and find nothing. We return to the perimeter before dark and begin the squad ambushes and night patrols again.

A few days later, Bravo Company gets a new assignment. The enemy have been ambushing and interdicting our truck convoys on Highway 13. These truck convoys have been resupplying us with weapons, ammo, and chow. They are very important to Operation

Junction City. Our battalion is going to patrol down to the highway and set up security along the sides of the highway.

We arrive at the highway at midmorning, and Lieutenant Fletcher and Staff Sergeant Evans "set us in." We will set up in four man teams, one every fifty meters. First Squad with my gun, then Second Squad with the lieutenant, and finally Third Squad with the other gun and Staff Sergeant Evans. Sweatt will have the third radio at this end of the line. Four First Squad men have the first position on the northern end of the line. The second position is Jerry Sweatt with the radio and three other guys. Then it's my gun position. I have my crew, Graves and Lambrett, as well as a First Squad rifleman, Jerrigan. He's a tall brown-haired soldier who tends to be on the quiet side, but he's "seasoned" and knows his job. Second Squad's first position is next. The platoon is covering about three-eighths of a mile on one side of the highway. Another company is on the other side of the road.

There is a fringe of bushes along the highway. Then past the bushes, there is elephant grass with a few bushes. I set us up in pairs. Graves and me, then Lambrett and Jerrigan. I want one man watching out into the field and the other watching back toward the highway. These positions are fifty meters apart, so I don't want an enemy unit to reach the highway unseen and walk up behind us as we all watch the field. I have Graves watching the highway as I watch the field. I tell the other two guys to take a nap. I'll wake them in a while and then have Lambrett watch the field while Jerrigan watches the highway.

We sit in the shade of the bushes and rest. This sure does beat walking all day with all this weight on our backs. I eat a can of C rations and drink some water as I watch the field. *Suddenly*, a long heavy burst of fire sounds out from what sounds like Third Squad's position. It's either an M-60 or M-14 as they sound much the same. Then it's M-16s and enemy rifles popping away. The four of us come to full alert. The gun crew is watching the field and Jerrigan the highway. Our weapons are at the ready as the firing gets heavier. I've decided that it's an M-14 I hear firing away down in Third Squad's area. That means that either McVey or Craft's position is in contact.

I hear someone coming from First Squad's positions. I ready my gun in case it's enemy troops. But it's Sweatt and his radioman. He tells me that Third Squad is in contact and Second Squad along with Lieutenant Fletcher and Staff Sergeant Evans are moving to help them. First Squad and my gun crew's orders are to hold in place and guard this flank. We are to also be ready to reinforce the rest of the platoon if they have bitten off more than they can chew.

The firefight goes on for another couple of minutes, and then I hear artillery rounds landing. The Lieutenant has cannon fire coming in to support us now. The firefight dies out. It's hard for the enemy to take those 105 mm shells dropping on their heads.

Then I hear more movement from Sweatt's position. He joins me with his team and the other First Squad team behind him. He tells me that we are to move up and join the rest of the platoon. He says he will go first with one team and the radio, followed by my gun and then the other team. We will move single file down this fringe of brush until we make contact with the platoon. I sure hope the platoon knows we are coming. I do not want to get hit with "friendly fire."

We reach the platoon's positions, and I find that it was McVey's position that had the contact with the enemy. Mac tells me that a file of enemy soldiers walked into his position as they headed toward the highway. Mac says that he opened up on them with his M-14 and the guys with him with M-16s. The enemy returned fire with AK-47s and carbines. They had a hot firefight going until he started getting reinforcements from the Second Squad and the rest of Third Squad. The enemy then pulled out as Lieutenant Fletcher called in artillery fire on their positions.

I notice that Mac has a lot of empty M-14 magazines lying about. I ask him if he is low on ammo, and he says he is. I've got 1,400 rounds for the M-60. I hate to, but I give Mac 200 rounds to reload his magazines. He begins breaking down the belts and loading up. That leaves me with 1,200 rounds, and I know that the other gun only has 900 rounds. If we run down this enemy platoon, I hope that they do not stand and fight for too long. The 1,200 rounds will not last me more than three minutes in a close, hot firefight.

The Lieutenant then forms up the platoon, and we begin searching the area for the enemy platoon. We find a couple of blood trails and follow them. We have helicopter gunships overhead to support us and artillery rounds hitting the tree line in the distance. I'm pumped. I think if we run down this enemy unit, we will "wax" them. But I also know that they will hurt us as they die.

We follow the blood trails for a while, and then they disappear. The enemy has managed to stop the bleeding wounds on their wounded. We then lose the enemy's trail completely. The helicopters above us are unable to see any enemy movement either. We have lost the enemy platoon. I'm disappointed. We patrol back to the highway and set up in our old positions to secure the highway. Truck convoys are going by heading further north. Well, at least Third Squad has prevented the enemy unit from ambushing the trucks today. Third Squad has also hurt the enemy a little as well. We have no men hurt, so we have had a blessed day.

CHAPTER 17

The Centurion

March 1967

I've turned twenty the month before and have been in Vietnam nearly nine months. We are on Operation Junction City, the largest operation of the Vietnam War. We are working near the Cambodian border and have been fighting four "crack" enemy units. The Ninth, 101st, Eightieth, and the Phu Loi Battalion. It is the entire First Infantry Division, Twenty-Fifth Infantry Division, 173rd Airborne Brigade. And the Eleventh Armored Cavalry Regiment on our side. There has been a lot of combat, and some of our units have been badly hurt, but the enemy has suffered much greater losses.

Bravo Company is preparing to air assault into a company-size landing zone. We will have six helicopters to deliver us. The first lift will be Third Platoon, a few of us from Second Platoon, and Company First Sergeant Bill Perry with his two radiomen. The second lift will be the rest of Second Platoon and part of First Platoon. The third lift will be the remainder of First Platoon and the small mortar platoon. They tell us the LZ is long and narrow so all six helicopters can land at once.

A rifle company is led by a captain. The second-in-command is the senior lieutenant in the company, the executive officer who handles administrative duties, and is usually in the rear area at Di An. The company first sergeant E-8 runs the company. First Sergeant

Perry does just that. He runs the company like a sheepdog herds a flock of sheep. He can chew us out like the best of them, but I can tell that he really cares for us all. The First Sergeant is affectionately called Top by us because he is the "top soldier" in the company.

The choppers come in, and we mount up, seven soldiers per chopper. We rise high in the air, and it is much cooler than it is on the ground. It's not a long trip, and we start descending. I don't know if the LZ will be hot or cold, but my insides twist into knots.

We drop into the LZ, and the choppers hover for an instant, and we all jump from the choppers. Four soldiers out, one side of each chopper and three soldiers from the other side. We hit the ground and face toward the wood line on each side while lying on our stomachs. The choppers start to lift off, and the wood line on one side bursts into heavy automatic weapons fire. Some of the choppers take hits, but all make it out of range with no disabling damage.

We are all putting heavy fire back into the wood line where the enemy is in small camouflaged bunkers. We are pinned down on the LZ. The enemy fire is too heavy for us to move. Most of us pull off our packs and web gear and place them in front of us and fire from behind what little cover they offer. I know there will be no way the helicopters will be able to bring the second lift in to reinforce us.

The enemy bunker line is about forty meters from us, just inside the wood line. There appears to be an enemy machine gun in the center of the enemy unit, and it's putting out a huge volume of green tracer rounds. We are in serious trouble as we all fire as fast as we can. How long will it be before we run low on ammo? We've got to put out this volume of fire to keep the enemy's heads down so they cannot drop their fire and begin hitting us. The enemy fire, as it is, is only about two feet above our heads.

Suddenly, First Sergeant Bill Perry stands up and charges the machine gun bunker. How can he not be hit by either their fire or ours? A young Third Platoon soldier attempts to follow him and give him cover. Top Perry makes it to the enemy bunker as we fire even faster, giving him all the cover fire, we can.

Top Perry jumps on top of the enemy machine gun bunker and tears off part of the bunker roof with his hand and shoots the enemy gun crew to death. The other enemy soldiers begin to pull out without their machine gun to support them. We move into the wood line firing, but the enemy has pulled out.

We check the enemy machine gun bunker and find that the enemy machine gun was a Chicom RKP with large quantities of ammo. The enemy gun crew is NVA with fresh haircuts. If it had not been for Top Perry, they would have kept us pinned down until we either ran out of ammo and were forced to move and would have then taken heavy causalities.

I don't know how First Sergeant Perry had the courage to do what he did. I did not, and neither did any other soldier on the ground that day. Some of us are alive because of Top Perry's actions. Top acts like it's just another day at the office. Maybe for him it is. After all, he was fighting in the Korean War when I was a small child.

CHAPTER 18

Base Camp Charlie

We are near the Cambodian border in late March 1967. I've been in Vietnam on my first tour for nine months. I've turned twenty the month before and have been wounded twice, in September and December of 1966. I'm one of the two machine gunners in Bravo Company's Second Platoon. We are less than a click and a half (less than a mile) from the Cambodian border. The enemy has been regularly shelling us from inside Cambodia. Despite this, our artillery and mortars are not allowed to fire back, because Cambodia is a neutral country. We are still on Operation Junction City.

Our battalion—Second Battalion, Eighteenth Infantry Regiment—is dug in around a large opening in the jungle. Our side of the perimeter is just inside the wood line. Some of Charlie Company's positions are dug in out in the open. I prefer where we are. The enemy has to get close to see us. On the other hand, they can get a lot closer to us before we see them.

We have been at this location a number of days; and every chance I get, I work on our bunker along with Lambrett, who is now my assistant gunner and Mohr, my new ammo bearer. Mohr is a medium-tall guy from the Midwest with black hair and is as nearsighted as me. Graves has left the gun crew and became a radioman. We have three claymore mines placed in front of our bunker. One is as far as the cord will go, which is a hundred feet. The second is about thirty feet closer to the bunker, and the third is only about forty feet out from the bunker. Each mine is placed with a solid tree behind it to stop the back blast. The electrical cords run back to our bunker and are plugged into the detonators. The one on the left is the far one, and the one on the right is the closer one.

I have cut five "fields of fire" through the bushes out from the bunker. They all go about a hundred feet long, and none are higher than about two feet. If we are under ground attack, I can see the enemy's legs. If they are charging in, they cannot see the little passageways I've cut into the brush.

We are making strong contacts here with large enemy units. They are running their patrols from their large base camps inside Cambodia; therefore, we are only running platoon-size day patrols and squad-size night ambushes.

Our chain of command tells us to expect a mass attack any night. Intelligence units tell us that the enemy Ninth Division and the NVA Eightieth Guards Regiment are massing just inside Cambodia and planning to overrun one of our battalions. I'm a twenty-year-old specialist 4, but I think this is ridiculous. We know where the enemy is, their unit numbers, and what they plan to do. But we are not allowed to hit them with giant B-52 bomber "arc light" attacks that can destroy sections of jungle a quarter of a mile long and two hundred meters wide.

The enemy are sure not treating Cambodian as a neutral country. Every time we get seriously on the enemy's case, they run into Cambodia to rest, rearm, merge replacements into their units, and plan where and when to attack us again. This is a terrible way to fight a war.

Today, we have palace guard. First and Third Platoons are out on patrols. Second Platoon, with help from part of the mortar platoon, is guarding the company's perimeter. We are spread out in twos and occasionally having to leave a bunker vacant. The mortar platoon only has one machine gun, but it's on the perimeter along with Second Platoon's two guns. The mortar platoon has their three 81 mm mortars set up behind us and have left enough crew on each to work them if they are needed.

We have worked on our bunker some but have rested a lot. This is the life, lying behind the bunker and watching to the front. We are not walking all day carrying nearly one hundred pounds of ammo and gear. One-man naps while the other watches.

It is getting on into the afternoon. We are expecting our platoons and the platoons from Alpha and Charlie Companies to return to the perimeter soon. Then we'll send out squad-size ambush patrols. We have a couple of two-man observation posts placed out in the jungle to give us early warning in case we are attacked.

Suddenly, heavy gunfire breaks out just to our front! Red tracer rounds are zipping in and hitting around our bunkers. *Red tracers, that's our weapons firing.* I wonder what's happening as I dive into our bunker and grab my machine gun. None of us open fire, because we know that there are Americans out there.

In less than a minute, the firing peters out. We then hear Americans shouting, and we shout back. Then Americans come into sight, walking into our bunker line. It's a platoon from Alpha Company. I see Wirth, a tall thin guy with thick glasses, who I went through infantry training with at Fort Polk. I ask him what happened. He tells me that they were coming in on the perimeter after a hard day on patrol. He said that they had passed one of our observation posts when they walked up the back of a squad of enemy troops that were crawling in on our perimeter. They quickly opened fire, and some of the enemy fired back while others attempted to dart away. It was over quickly. They killed some of the enemy, and some escaped. I see some of the guys carrying enemy web gear and rifles. Wirth shows me a fancy porcelain cup. He tells me that one of the dead enemy soldiers had it in his pack.

I'm relieved. Alpha Company has saved some of our lives. If the enemy had gotten any closer, they would have opened fire and killed or wounded some of us before we could bring our fire to bear on them. I tell the Alpha Company guys how thankful I am for them. They are pumped up. Their adrenaline is still high. Some are loud and shouting, and others are white as sheets and very quiet. They move off to their location on the perimeter. I keep watching to the front as Lieutenant Fletcher, Staff Sergeant Evans, and the squad leaders check the OPs (observation posts). I expect those poor guys are going to get a royal chewing out for not seeing the enemy soldiers crawling in.

Our First and Third Platoons return to the perimeter, and we set in for the night. Bravo Company will be sending out a couple of squad ambushes, but I'm not on them. Then in the distance, we hear the "pop" of mortars leaving their tubes. We all shout, "Incoming!" and roll into our bunkers. The mortar rounds start impacting all around the perimeter. I'm watching to the front with just my helmet and eyes above the lip of the bunker. I'm worried about a mass attack. I'm also worried about the enemy mortars coming in. I can tell that they are enemy 82 mm mortars. It takes five layers of sandbags to stop a 82 mm mortar round. We've got three layers of sandbags on top of our bunker. That will stop a 60 mm mortar round but not an 82. Those were all the sandbags that they gave us when we dug in. When the enemy mortars left their tubes, it sounds like they were located to the north, not northwest in Cambodia. I guess I was right because our three mortars along with Alpha and Charlie Companies' mortars are firing back at the sound of the enemy mortars.

We have a large artillery position about three clicks (two miles) from our location. A battalion of 155 mm artillery is stationed there. There are eighteen of the big guns, the barrels of which are more than six inches in diameter. That's two inches bigger than the smaller 105 mm cannon. The 155 throws a shell a lot farther than the 105 and nearly twice the weight. A shell from a 155 can completely destroy a large house. They call this location Base Camp Charlie for some unknown reason, and they are firing their big guns at the enemy mortars. I would hate to be where the enemy is located. Finally, the exchange of shells end, and it's quiet. Lambrett, Mohr, and I set up our guard watches for the night. I'm taking third watch because that's when I think the enemy will come. The two men sleeping will sleep inside the bunker. It's not as comfortable as sleeping behind the bunker, but we are having too much contact to take any chances.

Sometime during the night, I awake in my sitting position inside the bunker. Mohr is on watch. I hear heavy firing in the distance on the other side of the perimeter. One of the ambush squads from one of the other companies has blown their ambush on an enemy unit. The firing soon peters out, and I go back to sleep. Lambrett wakes me. It's time for my watch. I stand in the bunker and look into the blackness to our front. I take a canteen of water and wash my face and take a drink. I'm awake now. I take the gun and put it against my shoulder and watch out into the dark. I'm so glad that I'm not on LP tonight. I've got this bunker around me and the claymores out to the front.

Another day dawns. and Second Platoon has patrol. We patrol slowly and quietly for half a day, putting out cloverleaf patrols and changing direction often. About noon, we stop and form a circle in the jungle. We all sit and face out. We open cans of C rations and eat while we watch.

We are just finishing eating when we hear heavy fire in the distance. There are American weapons firing but a lot of enemy weapons too. The Lieutenant and Platoon Sergeant listen on the radio and announce that a platoon from one of the other companies is in contact with a large enemy unit. They've got mortars and artillery support coming in to help them, but I can hear them screaming on the radio for help. My blood runs cold. We may lose an entire platoon. We are the closest friendly unit to the platoon in trouble. We form up and start in the direction of the distant fight. We are being very careful. We fear an enemy ambush on our way to help. As we move, we encounter a large thicket of bamboo that we cannot penetrate. We have to go around it. That takes more time. The firing in the distance has not slacked off at all. I can hear the lieutenant's radio pretty well, and it sounds like an American is crying on the radio, begging for help. It almost makes me cry wishing we could get there quicker, but I realize that we will be no help if we are ambushed.

There's more noise and talking on the radio that I can't understand. The lieutenant says that General Hollingsworth has had his helicopter land him at the scene of the fight and taken charge of the action. I can't believe it—a General on the ground in a platoon-size fight. I've seen the General at a distance a couple of times and only thought of him as a very old man in his forties with gray hair in a crew cut. I have heard that this is his third war and that he has more medals than he's able to wear.

We keep pushing and come to a small opening in the jungle where the beleaguered platoon has made their stand. The firing is still heavy, and I see General Hollingsworth *standing up* and firing an M-60 machine gun at the wood line on the other side of the small perimeter. The General has no helmet on, and his gray crew cut really stands out. His jungle fatigues are starched, and his jungle boots are spit shined. He's spraying the hell out of the wood line. The crippled platoon members are also firing, but they are down in the grass. Many of them are wounded, and there's blood everywhere.

We pull up online with our brother soldiers and put our heavy fire out into the opposite wood line. We move across the small clearing and push into the jungle. The enemy has pulled out. We set up security, and dust-off helicopters start coming in and taking out the American wounded. The General seems to be directing the scene. Then his helicopter comes in and takes him away. We then form up with the remains of the other company's platoon and head back to the perimeter slowly and carefully.

We reach the perimeter and sit in our bunkers just as a large firefight breaks out just a few hundred meters from our perimeter. We gear up in case we need to help this unit. Staff Sergeant Evans puts the word out that it's a platoon from Charlie Company and they have made contact with a large enemy unit. We expect to have to go to the rescue, but we don't get the word to saddle up. The firing goes on and on, and it seems to be getting closer. The word is put out that the Charlie Company platoon will enter the perimeter through our lines and for us to be prepared to give them cover fire. I'm glad it's still daylight.

The firing gets closer and closer. It seems as if the enemy will just come into the perimeter with the American platoon. The firing seems to be less than a hundred meters from our bunkers, and we even see an occasional red or green tracer round. Then the firing seems to be slowing down quite a bit, and the Charlie Company point man comes in sight in the jungle to our front. The Americans start coming by our bunkers, some are carrying wounded buddies, and others are helping wounded friends walk. The firing has stopped now just as I see the last American come into sight. He's the platoon sergeant, an old man in his late thirties. He's backing toward us with his rifle pointed back into the jungle, and he's lost his helmet. His face is hard as a rock, and his eyes are cutting back and forth watching the jungle. As he walks backward past our bunker, he seems to take a deep breath. The Charlie Company platoon heads toward their section of the perimeter as dust-off helicopters start coming in to take out the wounded. We watch the jungle expecting a ground attack, but apparently the enemy unit has had all the action they wanted for the time being. Darkness begins to fall very quickly like it does in the tropics, and a heavy fog begins to form. We know if the enemy is prepared for a mass attack, the fog will be his friend. We get very little sleep. We can't see ten feet in the fog, and I'm expecting hordes of the little SOBs to come charging out of the fog at any minute. Dawn finally comes, and the fog starts to disappear. I'm so relieved. Apparently, the enemy was not quite ready to hit us in force.

Staff Sergeant Evans comes by the bunkers and tells us we will be leaving this perimeter today. Another battalion will switch with us. We'll be going to Base Camp Charlie to provide security for the big 155 mm cannon. Helicopters will bring the other battalion in one company at a time, and our battalion will load on the helicopters one company at a time and fly to Base Camp Charlie. I'm relieved in a way and disappointed in another way. I'm glad that I'm going to have a better chance of surviving, but I'm disappointed I won't get a chance to go head to head with the enemy unit that we've been sparring with.

The helicopters pick us up and fly us to our new location. It only takes a couple of minutes. I see Base Camp Charlie from the air. It's a very big open area with those eighteen big guns sitting in it. It's surrounded by dusters. They are twin 40 mm antiaircraft guns on light tank chassis. They are also quad-50-caliber machine guns loaded on flatbed trucks. All these weapons are pointed toward the wood line. There are also huge pits dug by bulldozers where the artillery shells are stored. All this is surrounded by bunkers for the infantry. I'm glad this is the dry season, or this would be a forty-acre mud pit.

We land, and each company and platoon is assigned their bunker areas. Staff Sergeant Evans shows me the bunker for my gun. I notice that one of the 155 mm cannon is only about forty feet behind our bunker and the muzzle is pointed right over the top of our bunker. I know that this is going to be very loud. We settle into our bunker and put out three claymore mines. There are no trees, so we place a full sandbag behind each mine to soften the back blast. It's about one hundred meters to the wood line, and those trees look splintered and broken. Apparently, these big guns have been firing canister rounds into the wood line.

Darkness is approaching, and I'm glad I don't have ambush tonight. I feel for the guys who have a listening post inside that splintered wood line. We hear mortars leaving their tubes and guys shout, "Incoming!" but we are all in our bunkers. The enemy mortar rounds start landing inside our perimeter. Our mortars are firing back, and *then* the big 155 mm opens fire. When the gun behind our bunker fires, it lifts us off the ground even though we are inside the bunker. It also stuns us and leaves our ears ringing. I wait for the incoming fire to stop, but it doesn't. I'm looking out the firing port of our bunker toward the wood line expecting a mass attack. I hear the calls for medics back among the 155 mm guns. These guns have walls of sandbags around them, but they have no roofs. Tonight, I'm glad that I'm not firing the cannon.

This seems to go on forever, and then there is a slight lull in the incoming fire. The lieutenant works the bunker line and tells us that the enemy is attempting to overrun the First Battalion, Twenty-Sixth Infantry Regiment that is dug in about three clicks (two miles) from our location. The big guns we are securing are supporting our sister battalion, and the enemy is attempting to knock these big guns out. Maybe we've fallen from the frying pan into the fire. Another round of heavy incoming fire falls on us. That 155 mm right behind our bunker is beating my brains out. I find out the next day the enemy are firing 60 mm, 82 mm, and 120 mm mortars at us, as well as 107 mm and 122 mm rockets and 75 mm howitzers. They are hitting the First of the Twenty-Sixth with the same weapons and mass ground attacks.

Suddenly, a large piece of hot shrapnel comes flying into our bunker, bounces around the bunker, and goes down Lambrett's collar. He screams, and we tear his shirt open to check him for wounds. All he's got is a two-inch blister on the back of his neck.

Enemy rounds are impacting in one of the artillery ammo dumps about one hundred meters to our right rear. The ammo dump begins to explode. It does not go off in one big blast just a sustained cracking, roaring sound. The ammo dump then begins to walk out of its big hole and across the open ground ever so slowly. It seems to be heading in our direction a few feet at a time.

We are still watching the wood line waiting for the mass attack, but apparently all that effort is against our sister battalion. The incoming fire intensifies, and I don't know how the artillerymen can keep up that steady out going fire, but they do. This goes on all night as the exploding ammo dump makes its way closer to us. We are watching it and the wood line.

Apparently, sometime in the past, this area was hit by our B-52 bombers. There are a few old bomb craters around the perimeter area. They are about twenty-five feet wide and about fifteen-feet deep with four or five feet of dirty water at the bottom. There is one of these bomb craters about sixty feet to our right rear. We watch as the exploding ammo dump reaches this crater and falls in. It is still exploding but not as much, and it doesn't come out of the crater.

Dawn breaks, and the incoming fire ends. Our outgoing fire also stops. The lieutenant checks the bunker line for injuries. I tell him that Lambrett has a very minor injury and to send a medic by. Lambrett says he does not need one, but I tell him that we want him to get a Purple Heart.

The platoon and the company senior medic come by and check his huge blister but says it doesn't rate a Purple Heart because it didn't bleed. I pull my little p-38 can opener and tell Lambrett to let me see his neck, I'll make it bleed. He says no, and we all get a big laugh.

There are helicopters coming to bring in supplies and taking out wounded. Staff Sergeant Evans comes by our bunker and tells us that our sister battalion has eleven men dead and nearly sixty wounded including our Brigade Commander Colonel Grimsley, who was dug in with them. He says that Lieutenant Colonel Al Haig, the battalion CO of the First of the Twenty-Sixth is taking over the Second Brigade. He also tells us that so far, they have found the bodies of 609 enemy soldiers on the scene. The attacking enemy unit was the entire NVA Eightieth Guards Regiment. Well, that is nearly half their men dead, and we don't know how many dead and wounded they were able to drag away to Cambodia. That enemy unit will be out of action for months until they get their wounded back and lots of replacements.

Later, the lieutenant's radioman comes by and tells me to report to the platoon command post which is the lieutenant and platoon sergeant's bunker. I borrow Lambrett's rifle, leaving the gun in the bunker with the gun crew covering our area of responsibility. I walk down and find the lieutenant and Staff Sergeant Evans sitting on their bunker. The staff sergeant asks me if I had to give up my gun who would I like to see get it. I don't hesitate, I tell them Lambrett. They ask me why; and I tell them he likes to shoot, has a lot of guts, and is always thinking tactically. They then tell me that Gonzales has left on a helicopter headed back to Di An. He is rotating home. They tell me to give my gun to Lambrett that I'm the new Second Squad leader. I say, "Yes, sir," turn, and walk back to the gun bunker. I tell Lambrett that he is now the gunner and I am Second Squad leader. I gather my gear and walk the short distance to the Second Squad area and tell Cisero, Sepulveda, and the guys that I'm their new squad leader.

CHAPTER 19

The Squad Leader

During the first week of April 1967, we are still on Operation Junction City after nearly seven weeks. We are seeing some type of action nearly every day. There are steady changes in Bravo Company due to causalities and guys rotating home after their year in Vietnam. Liberato Gonzales has rotated home, and I've been made Second Squad leader. The responsibility is heavy on my shoulders.

This morning, I have my first day patrol. My senior team leader is Phil Cisero. He's an average-sized Italian from Connecticut. He's been with the company since November and carries an M-14. He's a good soldier and a good friend, and I'm glad he's my number two. My junior team leader is Raul Sepulvedo from San Diego. He's been with us since December. He's Hispanic with a light complexion and a good soldier. His only drawback is that his English is poor as he grew up in Mexico.

The machine gun crew that will be going out with me is my old gun. Lambrett is now the gunner, and Mohr is assistant gunner. The ammo bearer is brand-new, and I have not learned his name yet.

We form up with Cisero running point on the right file and then the gun crew. I have a fairly new guy running point in front of me in the left file. He is Bob Keck, a short White soldier from Ohio. He has been here a couple of months and has already been wounded once. He is making into a good soldier and point man.

It is really hot, and I'm sweating even more than usual. I have my compass and map. We will be out all day and will change direction several times. I am praying that I don't get us lost. As always, I pick out a tree some thirty or so feet in front of me and pray that I live to reach that tree. When I reach it, I then pick out another tree and pray more.

We start out and slowly move through thick jungle. My count man tells me when we have moved three hundred meters. I stop the squad, and we all get down. I nod at Cisero, and he takes another soldier and does a small cloverleaf patrol to the right. They return, and I then nod at Sepulvedo at the end of the left file. He takes another soldier, and they cloverleaf to the left. They return, and then we move out again. In two hundred meters, we do it all again. In another two hundred meters, we reach our first checkpoint. I stop and radio the platoon leader that we've reach the checkpoint. We cloverleaf both sides, and then I change direction.

We work this way all day looking for movement and listening for sounds. We change direction four more times. We know that the area is crawling with enemy troops, but we've seen nothing, nor have we heard anything all day.

We are getting close to where the perimeter is, and I pray that I've not gotten us lost. My nerves are tight, and then I see a couple of American soldiers beside a foxhole. Relief floods over me, but I keep my stone face. I radio that we are coming in, and I get an okay. We move in and take our foxholes back. I tell the guys to clean their weapons, one at a time.

I walk over to the platoon command post. Lieutenant Fletcher asks me how it went, and I grin and tell him that it was a piece of cake. Staff Sergeant Evans tells me that we've got hot chow coming in on a helicopter shortly and he needs one man from me to help the soldiers from the other squads unload the chow and then serve it. Staff Sergeant Evans then tells me that Second Squad has ambush tonight and we will have Bicket's machine gun crew with us. He tells me to come back after chow and he and Lieutenant Fletcher will brief me.

I return to the squad area and tell Cisero to send one of his men to the CP for detail. I then tell the guys that we have hot chow coming in shortly. That brightens everyone up, and then I tell them that we have a squad ambush tonight. They then crash and burn. I sit down and clean my M-14. In a few minutes, a helicopter comes in, and the guys unload the containers of hot chow.

The call comes out to send guys up to pick up their chow. I tell Sepulvedo to send one of his men. When that man returns, Cisero sends one of his men. While they do this, the rest of us face out toward the jungle as we sit by our foxholes.

I notice as the guys start returning with their heavy paper plates that we are having fried chicken, mashed potatoes, green beans, and peaches. There is also a full canteen cup of cold lime Kool-Aid.

After all my guys have been to chow, I send Sepulvedo. The highest-ranking man always eats last. Sepulvedo returns, and Cisero heads out to get his chow. He returns and he is upset. I ask him what is wrong, and he tells me that he's dropped his chicken. I ask him where, and he points out the general area. It is my turn to go to chow, and I walk the way Cisero has returned, and I see a beautiful chicken breast and wing attached lying on some leaves. I pick it up and put it in my pocket.

I get to the food line and find out that all the white meat is gone. I get a leg and thigh along with the potatoes, beans, and peaches. I take out my canteen cup and get it filled with Kool-Aid. I return to the squad area, and Cisero asks did I find his chicken. I tell him that I did and I have it in my pocket. He asks if I am going to eat it. I tell him I sure am that it was lying on clean leaves. He asks if he can have the chicken leg if I'm going to eat the breast. I tell him that's what I had planned, and he takes the leg off my plate. We finish eating and dig a small hole and place our paper plates in it and cover them with dirt.

It gets dark, and we form up to move out on ambush. I place the files just like they were on patrol today except that I have Bicket's gun crew instead of Lambrett's. We head out of the perimeter into the darkness. We move slowly and as quietly as we can, stopping often to listen. In about an hour, we locate the small trail that we will be ambushing. I place Cisero with Bicket's gun crew on the trail, and I also set up on the trail about forty feet down from the gun. I have Keck, my radioman, and an M-79 man with me. I place Sepulvedo and the rest of the squad in the jungle to our rear. We all put out claymore mines and wait.

In a couple of hours, a heavy firefight breaks out on the other side of the perimeter. I listen on the radio and learn that a Charlie Company ambush has been blown on an enemy patrol. In a couple of minutes, the firing dies out, and flares are hanging in the air in the far distance. I know that the Charlie Company Squad is now searching the kill zone for any enemy dead. They do not call for a dust-off helicopter to take out any wounded, so apparently, they have had no men hit in the fight.

The rest of the night goes quietly for us, and as it gets gray in the east, we pull in our claymore mines and form up. I radio Lieutenant Fletcher that we are leaving our ambush sight and heading back. We move back very slowly worrying that we may trap an enemy unit between us and the perimeter. We reach the perimeter in time to fill in our foxholes. The battalion is moving to another location.

We patrol as a battalion all day and find nothing. About 1600 hours, we reach the new area that we will work out of. Each platoon puts out a two-man observation post. We then dig foxholes. They will be deep because we keep expecting an enemy mass attack. Some of our sister battalions have been partially overrun on this operation.

It will be a good night. Second Squad does not have ambush tonight, and another squad leader is taking out the three-man listening post. I feel comfortable and relieved.

It's getting close to dark, and I sit on the back lip of my foxhole with my legs dangling into the hole. There's still enough light that I can see a squad in First Platoon gearing up to move out on night ambush. I've got friends there, but I'm glad it's them and not me.

The First Platoon squad moves out into the jungle and all gets noticeably quiet. I sit there hoping to get some quality sleep tonight when a *heavy* burst of fire bellows out from the jungle where the First Platoon squad has gone. They have only been gone about ten minutes. How could they have hit something this heavy this soon? The roar of their weapons and enemy weapons numbs my ears. It sounds like a great monster growling. We have all jumped into our foxholes and are facing out with our weapons ready. I think that the squad has bumped into an enemy unit that is moving in to attempt to overrun our battalion.

The heavy roaring fire goes on for at least two minutes and then slacks off. We wait for the attack against our perimeter, but it does not come. I cannot see the First Platoon area in the dark, but I hear their squad move back into the perimeter. Staff Sergeant Evans moves from foxhole to foxhole in our platoon area filling us in on what has happened. He gets to my foxhole and tells me that the First Platoon ambush squad had only moved about two hundred meters out from the perimeter when they bumped into at least an enemy squad moving toward our perimeter. The First Platoon squad has had no one hit but believe that they have hit at least two or three enemy soldiers. I ask if they swept the area after the fight, and Staff Sergeant Evans says no. They were low on ammo, so they pulled back into the perimeter. They will replace their ammo and move out in another direction to a secondary ambush sight. I do not feel comfortable any-more. The night will be scary, and every little sound will make me jump. I get a little sleep but not much. Morning comes, and we eat cold C rations and get ready for another patrol.

We continue for a couple more weeks of brushes with enemy troops and being hit with mortar attacks. I am getting punch drunk from lack of sleep and all the action. Finally, after fifty-six days of no showers and little sleep, we board helicopters and fly back to our base camp at Di An. They tell us that our unit has had fifty-four days in a row of contact with the enemy.

We arrive and clean our weapons. We then drop the rags that we are wearing and hit the cold-water showers. We then pick clean pants, shirts, and socks from piles and dress clean. It is great being clean and having complete pants on.

The brass tells us to head over to battalion headquarters for a steak cookout. This is great. I leave my rifle, web gear, and helmet on my bunk; pull an Army baseball cap from my duffle bag; and head over to the cookout with my friends.

We arrive and find that the cooks have piles of small steaks and are cooking away on grills. We all fall in line and go through the chow line. I get a steak, fries, and salad. At the end of the chow line are barrels of canned cokes and beer. I get a Coke and go and eat with my friends. I finish my meal quickly and hope for seconds. In a few minutes they call seconds, and I go through the line, and this time, I just get one of the small steaks. I finish it quickly, hit the line again for another steak, and eat it. I do this until I've eaten nine of the wonderful little steaks, and by then they have run out. A lot of the other guys have hit the chow line for seconds or even thirds. The battalion is very understrength due to all the causalities we took on Operation Junction City. Apparently, they had steaks for a full battalion.

They have set up a Filipino band on a flatbed truck, and they are knocking out some pretty good rock and roll music. They have a girl singer who sounds good as well. Three or four hundred of us are crowded around the truck, singing along with the band and having a really good time.

The girl singer comes up to the mic and says that she is going to sing a song that we will all like. It is "Where the Boys Are." Then she says that the song will really fit because she has never seen so many "boys" in her life. A great angry roar goes up from the crowd, and my voice is one of them. The crowd surges toward the flatbed truck, and I see stark fear on the face of the singer and the band. The singer asks over the mic in a frightened voice, "What did I say?" A big Black soldier in front of her shouts, "Lady, there ain't no boys in the crowd." The singer looks confused, and the big Black guy then says, "Ain't nothing but *men* out here, Lady."

The singer then understands and sings the song substituting the word *men* for the word *boys*. The crowd roars with approval. I listen to some more good songs, but my belly is full of steak, and my eyelids are getting heavy. I walk back to my hooch, take my gear off my cot, and crash. I am looking forward to nine hours or more of solid sleep with no breaks.

CHAPTER 20

The Bunker Line

I t's the middle part of April 1967. We are back at base camp at Di An. We have just returned from Operation Junction City. It had been the largest operation in Vietnam history. The First Infantry Division; the Twenty-Fifth Infantry Division; the 173rd Airborne Brigade; the Eleventh Armored Calvary Regiment; some South Vietnam units were against the enemy Ninth Division, which contains three Regiments: 271st, 272nd, and 273rd; 101st NVA Regiment; Eightieth NVA Guards Regiment; the famed enemy Phu Loi Battalion; and assorted smaller enemy units. The operation began in mid-February and went into mid-April up near the Cambodian border in deep jungle.

Our battalion was out for fifty-six days without a shower or change of clothes. The only saving grace was it was all in the dry season, so no monsoon rains. But the heat was unbelievable. We have broken the record for days in contact with enemy units. They tell us that our unit was in contact with the enemy for fifty-four days in a row. During this time, we have had no sleep or maybe two to three hours of sleep out of a twenty-four-hour period. When we came into Di An, my body was so numb that I could not feel it. After a cold shower, clean clothes, hot chow, and two nights of unbroken sleep, I am feeling human again.

While out on Junction City, the last of our sergeants except for SSG Paul Evans rotated home. We got no replacement NCOs.

171

We still had First Lieutenant Fletcher as platoon leader, and with Staff Sergeant Evans as platoon sergeant, we made it through the big operation. They had made me Second Squad leader, and it's a heavy load to bear. Jerry Sweat has First Squad, and Doug McVey has Third Squad. Jim Norberg has the machine gun squad. We are all specialist E-4s in staff sergeants E-6 slots. All the others are draftees, whereas, I joined up.

SSG Paul Evans calls for the squad leaders to a meeting and tells us First Lieutenant Fletcher has been moved to another platoon and we are not getting a new lieutenant. Staff Sergeant Evans will be platoon leader, and Doug McVey is being moved up to platoon sergeant—an E-4 in an E-7 slot; that was crazy. Burner Craft will move up and take Third Squad, another draftee E-4 in an E-6 slot. This is getting very scary. Craft is a very good man from St. Mary, Ohio; but like me, he's only been in the army sixteen months, and, like me, he's only been an E-4 for two months.

Then Staff Sergeant Evans gives us the really bad news. We'll be flying out in the morning on a new operation. They are going to call it Operation Manhattan. We will be up on the Cambodian border just like on Operation Junction City. We'll be going against the same enemy units that we crippled on the last operation. I feel like I'm getting on a first-name basis with members of the 272nd Regiment of the Ninth Enemy Division. We've fought them half a dozen times in the ten months I've been in-country. The enemy will have Cambodia to duck into when we get on their case too hard, and they will fire mortars and artillery at us from the "sanctuary" of Cambodia. What a "fun" war this has become.

Staff Sergeant Evans gives us the orders for the air assault the next morning. He tells me he wants me to take Second Squad into the wood line about three hundred meters after we land if the LZ is not hot. We've never done this before, but Evans says the brass want a squad screen three hundred meters out in the jungle in case a large enemy unit moves against the LZ.

I get my map in plastic with grease pencil overlays and head back to the Second Squad tent. I call a squad meeting, lay the map out on a cot, and give Second Squad a detailed briefing. I have eight men. Phil Cisero is my senior team leader and assistant squad leader, a specialist 4 like me. He has been in-country for six months and in the army for as long as I have. He is a draftee carpenter from New England and a good soldier. I am glad I have him. My junior team leader is Raul Sepulvado, a PFC from San Diego, California. He's a good soldier, but his English is poor. I tell them we will get on line if the LZ is cold and sweep into the jungle for three hundred meters and then set up and wait for Staff Sergeant Evans to tell me on the radio to pull back.

The next morning, we are waiting on the helicopter pads for the choppers. They come in and pick us up. We fly for a long time. It is cool this high up. We approach the landing zone, and I tighten up. I hope it is not hot. We land, jump out, and head for the wood line. The choppers leave, and it is deadly quiet. The LZ is cold. I am relieved. I place the squad on line, and we push into the jungle. We count our steps until we gauge that we have come three hundred meters. We stop and set up. I call back on the radio and advise Evans that we're in position. I set up with my radioman on Sepulvado's side of the line. He is my more inexperienced team leader, and his English is poor. I know that Phil Cisero can handle the other end of the line.

We sit for a couple of hours and neither he nor I see anything. Then Staff Sergeant Evans calls on the radio for us to return to the LZ. I pass the word down the line that we are reversing and heading back to the LZ just like we came. We head out, moving very slowing and keeping a sharp eye out in case the enemy has moved between us and the LZ.

We arrive back at the LZ, and as we come out of the jungle, I see that Cisero's team is not with us. Staff Sergeant Evans storms up to me wanting to know where the rest of my squad is. Evans is right, I have dropped the ball. Someone on the line did not pass the word when we moved out. I take Sepulvado's team and head back into the jungle to find Cisero. We move about 150 meters and bump into Cisero and his team coming out. Phil is looking genuinely concerned, as he should. We drop on a knee, and I tell him what has happened and tell him how sorry I am that I did not make sure that he got the word. We then move back to the LZ and join the rest of the platoon and company. We saddle up and move out on a battalion-size sweep that lasts all day. Late in the afternoon, we move into a large open area, much larger than our foxhole perimeter will be. We put out observation posts of two men each in the edge of the jungle. The battalion digs in for the night. Second Squad digs our three foxholes shoulder deep as dark approaches.

Each company will have a squad ambush out tonight, and each platoon will have a three-man listening post out in the jungle. One of the other platoons has the squad ambush tonight, and our platoon always has a three-man listening post out each night. A squad leader always takes the listening post out, puts them in place, and then returns to the perimeter. So each fourth night, one of the squad leaders has to take out the LP. This is my night. I am not too terrified tonight.

It is one hundred meters to the wood line in front, and they want the LP about fifty feet inside the wood line. I can handle that.

Darkness comes and falls like a hammer. I move down to Third Squad and get a man from Craft. Then I pick up the man from my squad. I move over to First Squad and get Sweatt's man. We then move to the platoon CP and get a radio. I assign the radio to one of the men. I then tell them who will be in charge.

We pass the word up and down the line that LP is going out. We move out from the perimeter in single file with the point man first, then me, then the radioman, and last tail-end Charlie. We reach the wood line and move inside it. We move even more slowly in the brush, trying to keep down the noise. We reach where I think we need to go, and I set the team in. I whisper their last instructions, turn, and move back to the wood line. I pause there for a minute listening and working up my nerve to step out into the open. What if an enemy team has moved up to the edge of the wood line near me? It takes all the courage I can muster to step out and move very slowly back toward the perimeter. My fear now is being shot by a trigger-happy GI on the perimeter.

As I approach the perimeter, I loudly start whispering, "Fedrick coming in." Cisero answers me, and I move into the perimeter and make my way to my foxhole. I have the middle foxhole in my squad area with Cisero on one side and Sepulvado on the other. I have only one man with me while both the other holes have three men each. If the LP has to come in because of enemy contact, the Second Squad man will be with me. This means that the man with me, each of us will have to pull watch two hours on and two hours off.

We have a quiet night, and morning comes. The lieutenant tells the LP to come in on the radio, and I see them walk out of the jungle and come across the one hundred meters of open space. My man comes to me and drops his gear. He sits with me and the other man and joins us in a cold C ration breakfast. I ask him if anything happened last night, and he says that they did not see or hear anything. I start to hope that this operation will be quieter than the last one. Maybe most of the enemy units have fled to Cambodia and we'll have a walk in the sun.

The squad leaders are called to the platoon CP, and Staff Sergeant Evans and McVey give us the word. Bravo Company will head into the jungle on the other side of the perimeter in a box formation. Two rifle platoons in the front, each in column or two files. They will be followed by the other rifle platoon and the mortar platoon. That is always how the company works in the jungle. The mortar platoon is always in one of the rear positions. Today we will follow Third Platoon. First Platoon is on the right followed by the mortar platoon.

I have Second Squad in the left file; Third is in the right file. The First Squad is broken in half and tacked on to the rear of Second and Third Squads. Staff Sergeant Evans is in the file with my squad and McVey toward the back of the right file. It's just like we always work it. That way, it is harder for us to lose our platoon leader and platoon sergeant at the same time. I have Cisero running point, and I'm second. Staff Sergeant Evans is behind me with his radioman next and then Lambrett with the machine gun. But we have all of Third Platoon ahead of us, so I feel pretty good even though we have a new company commander. Captain Dishman has rotated home along with 1SG Bill Perry. It seems that all our experience has gone.

We move about three hundred meters into the thick, triple canopy jungle. The files are twisting around a little, and we are a little closer to the front of Third Platoon than we should be. I can see the

Third Platoon point man, Curt in my file, a tall White soldier. The second man is a smaller Black soldier. Suddenly, the Third Platoon point man throws his rifle to his shoulder, and the entire jungle in front of us explodes. I fall forward, and in a split second as I fall, I see the bunker. It is only about twenty feet in front of the Third Platoon point man. It is low and wide and well camouflaged. Its firing slit is about ten inches high and six feet wide, and I see "them." There are four gooks firing out the firing slot. Three are firing AK-47s, and the other is firing an RPD-56 Chicom machine gun. I see their foreheads and their hair as they fire but not their eyes or lower faces.

I hit the ground, and green enemy tracer rounds are zipping just a couple of feet over us, cutting down limbs and leaves. Terry Frye in Third Platoon rushes the enemy bunker firing his M-14 on automatic. He's hit and goes down beside the point man. The cover man (the second man in the file) appears to have been hit multiple times as well. Terry lies with his back to the enemy bunker and puts a fresh magazine into his M-14. He then rolls over and starts crawling toward the bunker firing his M-14 again on automatic. The enemy mass their fire on him. Terry and his rifle are both hit numerous times. His canteen, cover and all, was shot off his web gear and bounced high in the air. Terry has bought us time. Third and First Platoons are putting out heavy fire into the enemy bunker line. I take Second Squad, and in a low crawl position, we move up to the side of Third Platoon so we can add our fire to theirs. The enemy green tracers are thick coming in. Lambrett crawls up with his assistant gunner and starts laying down heavy fire into the enemy positions. Cisero and I are grinding out bursts with our M-14s. I call up the rest of Cisero's team to add their fire to ours. I tell Sepulvado to have his team watch our flank in case the enemy flanks us and hits us from the side. The noise is unbelievable with all our fire and all the enemy fire. We've got artillery coming in now behind the enemy bunker line, but our closest troops are within twenty feet of the enemy positions, and our artillery has to be at least seventy-five meters to our front, or we will be hit by our own fire. Maybe our shells will keep the enemy from bringing up reinforcements.

Lieutenant Lockery, who leads mortar platoon, crawls up to us and then crawls past us. I wonder where he's going. I then see him crawl into the kill zone, grab the wounded cover man, and drag him back well within Third Platoon's positions. We are all firing heavy cover fire as he does this. I'm amazed by the lieutenant's courage. He then crawls back and grabs Curtain, the point man, and drags him back to another location within Third Platoon's positions. How was this lieutenant able to do this without being hit? At times, the primary enemy machine gun bunker is less than twenty feet from him.

The lieutenant crawls back a third time, grabs Terry Frye, and drags him back to my side. Terry is groaning and thrashing about, but he seems unconscious. He has been shot a number of times. The company medic and Second Platoon medic start working on Terry right away, pushing plasma into him. The lieutenant then crawls back into the kill zone a fourth time and grabs the three rifles and the web gear of the three wounded soldiers and drags them back. I see that Terry's M-14 has multiple bullet holes in the wooden stock. The smell of burning gunpowder is hanging heavy in the air; it is sickening sweet to smell.

I am putting out burst after burst with my big M-14 with the steel butt plate beating my shoulder. The enemy fire has not slackened a bit. I have only lain here a few minutes, and I am covered in limbs and leaves that their fire has cut down. Green enemy tracer rounds are zipping by just a foot or two over our bodies. I look around and see the new company commander. He is sitting upright and looking off into the distance. His radioman, Russell Bridges, is talking on the radio and attempting to hand the handset to the Captain. But the CO seems to be in a daze and is just sitting there looking off into the distance and refuses to take the handset. I do not know how he is not hit by enemy fire.

I am changing magazines and shout at the medic next to me to give Terry something for the pain. The medic looks at me and says that Terry will be gone in a minute. I pound out another magazine at the enemy bunkers and look back as I change magazines again and see that Terry is not moving. The medic looks at me and shakes his head. Damn! Terry and I were always trading western novels, and now he's dead. He was just three days younger than me.

Lambrett is putting out long bursts with the M-60 and shouts at me to get the rest of his ammo brought up. I tell Cisero to tell his two riflemen to crawl back and get all Lambrett's ammo. I then tell Cisero to have his M-79 man to start firing at the bunkers. Cisero says that the brush is too thick. The M-79 shells must travel twenty-nine feet before they arm themselves. I tell Cisero to have him fire anyway, that some of the shells will get through, and we need all the suppressive fire we can get. The M-79 man begins firing, and about every third shell reaches the enemy bunker line and goes off.

Word is passed that Third Platoon will fall back through Second Platoon and we will give them cover. At the same time, First Platoon will fall back through mortar platoon. We put out heavy fire, and Third Platoon crawls back through us carrying their wounded troops. I see that Terry is dead now, as well as Curt, the point man. The cover man is gravely wounded but still alive. After Third Platoon is past us, we are told to start crawling backward while still putting out heavy fire. We do this an inch at a time while they back up the impact point of our artillery shells.

We get about seventy-five meters from the enemy bunker line, and now our artillery shells are falling on their bunker line. This lessens the enemy fire, and we are finally able to rise to a crouched position and duck walk backward, still firing back at the enemy location as the artillery shells tear up the jungle. We get back a couple hundred meters from the bunker line, and now we have our shells coming down between us and the enemy in case any are attempting to follow us. We now move in a crouched position backward while still firing. We break out of the jungle and head to our foxholes that have been manned by a skeleton crew while we have been in the fight. I drop in my hole and drain an entire canteen of water. I ask the two men in the hole with me if they are all right, and they say they are. I then shout to my team leaders on each side of me and ask if they and their men are all right. They say they are. I've been just in time. Staff Sergeant Evans shouts for a casualty report. I shout back that Second Squad is okay. I then tell Cisero and Sepulvado to do an ammo check. I do it for myself and the two men in the hole with me. I've only got two loaded magazines left. Just 40 rounds, I've fired 360 rounds. I get a total of what Second Squad has fired, and I almost double it. This fight is far from over. Lambrett calls out that he's fired 850 rounds in the machine gun, and I realize that he had only a 50-round belt left when we got back to the foxholes.

We've got jets bombing the enemy positions in the jungle now with bombs and napalm. I hope we French fry some of them. By midafternoon, it's gotten quiet, and helicopters take out our dead and wounded. One of the other companies has hit the same bunker line at another location, and they also have casualties. Then choppers start bringing in ammo and water for us. I detail two men up to the platoon CP to help carry it back from the chopper pad to our location. Each squad has two men on the detail while the rest of us cover the wood line from our foxholes.

We get our ammo, and I fill all twenty of my magazines. I then place two hundred rounds of loose ammo in an empty claymore bag that I will carry on my shoulder. I told all my guys to carry a double load of ammo. If we do not get hit with a ground attack tonight, then we will go up against that bunker line tomorrow. We ran extremely low on ammo today, and that cannot happen again.

The call comes out for squad leaders to meet at the platoon CP. Craft, Norberg, Sweatt, and I head up there moving in a crouched position and carrying our rifles. We sit around the two foxholes that make up the CP. The four squad leaders along with McVey, Staff Sergeant Evans, their RTOs, and the platoon medic meet at the CP. Evans tells us that the company is going to put Terry Frye in for a posthumous Silver Star and the mortar platoon leader, Lieutenant Lockery, is being recommended for the Distinguished Service Cross. I tell Staff Sergeant Evans that that is not enough. I tell him Terry bought us those few seconds that it took us to get a heavy base of fire out and get the enemy's heads down. Evans says he will pass my feelings up the chain of command. He then gets down to the plan. We will go in the next day in a different location. The other companies will be doing the same. Second Platoon will be up front with First and Second Squads leading the files. Second Squad will be on the left, and First Squad will be on the right.

I say, "Sarge, let me run something past you." He tells me to go ahead. I tell him that I want Lambrett and his assistant gunner as third and fourth in our file. He reminds me that he's usually third and his radioman fourth. I agree that's fine on a patrol, but we know we are going to hit that bunker line within three hundred meters, and I want that M-60 up there where he can put out a heavy base of fire right away. I tell him it's not like we are looking for the gooks, because we know right where they will be, that's if they don't hit us with a ground attack tonight. He thinks for a minute and tells me that we'll try it my way. I tell him thanks that it might save us getting some men hit.

Evans looks over at Craft and tells him that he will take out the listening post tonight. Craft already knew that and just nods. Sweatt and I tell Craft that we will have our man ready. We head back to our squad areas, and I tell my man to get ready for LP. He does not look happy, but I wouldn't be either. I stand in my foxhole and ask the guys in the holes on both sides of me if they can hear me, and they say that they can. I tell them we are going in first tomorrow in the left file of the left column, that we will hit that bunker line in a different place where we hope that it is not as strong. I tell them that artillery will pound the enemy all night and in the morning, we will hit them with air strikes and then follow in a walking barrage of artillery fire. I'm trying to sound positive and upbeat, but I don't feel it, and I don't think that the guys are buying it. They look as afraid as I feel.

Usually, I alternate my two fire teams, one in front one day and the other the next day. I am not going to work it that way tomorrow. I need Cisero up front with his M-14 and experience. I tell them that Lambrett will be third man in the file with that M-60. A couple of them nod. Then I drop the big one on them. I have been struggling with it since we got back to the perimeter. I keep asking myself, *What would Staff Sergeant Ben Garza do?* But I know what he would do and what he always did in bad situations. I cannot let him down, now or ever. I tell the squad that the next morning I'll be running point going into that bunker line, Cisero will be second, Lambrett third, his "assistant Gunner," Mohr fourth, then Staff Sergeant Evans, his radioman, and then the rest of the squad. I tell them what position I want each man in. I then look at Sepulvado and tell him that if Cisero and I both go down that he will have the squad and to watch our left flank in case the gooks hit us in a flank attack. I close the briefing with more bright info. I tell the guys to be alert tonight, that I think the gooks will hit us with a ground attack before morning.

The briefing is over, but I look over at Cisero and say, "Phil, I need you up front tomorrow." He nods like he is flattered and understands, but he is not too happy about the honor. That is how I would feel. This is no game; it is deadly serious.

It gets dark; and Craft comes by with his man, picks my man up, and heads up the line to get Sweatt's man. I am glad I'm not taking out the LP tonight. I am also glad that I'm not on LP or that my squad doesn't have ambush. I firmly believe that we will get a ground attack before daylight. I pray to God for my life and barring that, that He take my immortal soul.

Craft comes back by my foxhole after taking out the LP. He stops and kneels by my hole for a moment. I tell him to hang tough, that it may rain tonight. He says, "It's not going to rain. It's the dry season." I reply, "I didn't mean rainwater." He snorts. "You're just full of happy thoughts, aren't you?" I chuckle, and he heads on down to his squad area.

It's fully dark, but the sky is clear, and the stars are beautiful. It's like that in the southern hemisphere. I tell the soldier in the hole with me to catch some sleep. He doesn't say a word and just rolls up into his poncho liner. I sit in the foxhole and look at the blurred black tree line in the distance. Our artillery from far away is pounding the enemy base camp behind me. Then I hear the little hollow thumps in the distance. Incoming mortars. I get deeper in the hole with just my helmet, and my eyes above the lip of the hole. The enemy mortar rounds start impacting in and around our perimeter. I expect the enemy to come boiling out of the wood line at any second.

In a while, the enemy mortars stop. It sounds like our artillery shells are trying to search out their mortar positions. I know that they have already moved those mortar tubes and will soon drop shells on us again. No one is asleep now. An hour or so goes by, and some of the guys are dozing off again. That hollow thump again, guys shouting, "Incoming!" I am one of them. The shells start hitting around us again as I wait for the ground attack. In a while, the enemy mortars stop. It is quiet again. Apparently, our ambushes or LPs have not made contact. Why haven't they hit us on the ground? Are they sucking us into coming against them in their base camp or are there not enough of them to hit a full battalion with a ground attack?

Morning finally comes as it breaks gray in the east. No ground attack, I am surprised. I do not think I've slept any at all during the night. Maybe that is what the enemy was trying for. I am terrified this morning because I'm running point going against that bunker line. I may have given myself a death sentence. It was what I had to do. I could not put one of my men in that position. Ben Garza would not have put one of his men in that position. I can do no less. I pray.

The LPs and ambushes come in from the jungle. The word comes down for us to get in our foxholes with our helmets on and our heads down. Artillery is going to be called in at the edge of the wood line where we will be entering the jungle. We follow orders, and the shells come in sounding like freight trains. The shells tear up the wood line for a while, and then they back the shells up about fifty meters into the wood line. We line up and get ready to move. I hope no one can see me shaking. I would not want anyone to think that I have nerves or fear. I have eaten nothing and drank very little water. If you are badly wounded, you stand a better chance of living if your stomach is empty.

We start out with me up front followed by Cisero, Lambrett with the machine gun, his assistant gunner, Mohr, Staff Sergeant Evans, and his radioman. First Squad is to my right with a tall Black soldier named Ellsworth Johnson from Arkansas by way of Chicago running point. Jerry Sweatt is second, then Charles Bicket with the other machine gun. Two files of Third Platoon are on the other side of Sweatt's squad.

I move into the jungle with Johnson even with me and twenty feet to my right. The artillery impacts are then moved back to one hundred meters from the wood line. There is still dust and gunpowder hanging in the air from the artillery shells exploding. There is also the smell of fresh cut wood from the shell-splintered trees and fresh dirt turned up by the shell impacts. Those three smells, gunpowder, fresh split wood, and fresh turned dirt will bother me the rest of my life.

One good thing about this shelling, it should set off any booby traps that the enemy has set for us. No sooner than I think that, I see my first trip wire. I move up and check it. The booby trap is tied to a tree, and the wire stretched about fifteen feet to another tree. Then I see barefoot tracks and knee prints in the freshly torn-up earth. Damn, the gooks are between us and where the shells are impacting. How can they do that and survive?

I pass the word back—"booby trap." I then take C ration toilet paper out and drape it over the wire. I then step over it and continue on. I am looking for enemy soldiers and trip wires. I am soaked in sweat, and it hasn't gotten hot yet. I am sure it's fear.

I see Johnson find a booby trap and mark it the same way that I did. We keep moving very slowly, and I see another one and mark it the same way. The artillery is moved back another fifty meters as we progress. Johnson and I each find a couple more booby traps and mark them the same way. All the trip wires have been from ankle to knee high. I am focused on that now as the sweat pours off my body. Then Johnson saves my life. I hear him whistle. I look over at him, and he's pointing up with his chin. I look up and ahead, and I see it. There's a trip wire two feet in front of my face. I have been looking at the ground. This trap would have killed me by taking off part of my head. I look back at Johnson and nod. I then mark the high wire with toilet paper. I pass the word back that we have got a high wire. I move on slow as a turtle. I'm still seeing fresh footprints and knee prints in the freshly torn earth. I don't know how the gooks can survive working that close to the exploding shells.

I glance back at Cisero and Lambrett. Their eyes are darting from side to side and their weapons posed looking for a target. They are as soaked in sweat as I am.

We have come about three hundred meters, and it has taken three hours or more. The tension can be cut with a knife. The shells are landing about one hundred meters in front of us. I believe that the shells must be hitting inside the enemy base camp. I do not know if I saw something, I heard something, I felt something, or my nerve just broke. I fall forward firing my M-14 on automatic. Cisero is falling and firing on my left, and Lambrett is doing the same on my right. The jungle in front of us explodes with enemy fire, and green tracer rounds are zipping a couple of feet over our heads. Johnson, Sweatt, and Bicket are firing to my right; and the Third Platoon is firing to the right of them. This bunker line seems as strong as the one we hit yesterday.

We lay there and fire. My M-14 is beating my heavily bruised right shoulder and my right cheekbone. I pull the rest of Cisero's team up on line with us, and we are putting out a heavy base of fire. Sepulvado and the rest of the squad are covering our left flank. Staff Sergeant Evans is on the radio attempting to get the artillery dropped closer to us. I think it is futile. The enemy bunkers are within thirty feet of us. If the shells are brought in that close, they will kill us.

We shot it out with the bunkers for an hour or more when suddenly there's much heavier firing from Third Platoon's side and shouts. We are now getting enemy fire from our front and from our right. The enemy fire directed at Third Platoon is also reaching us. Green tracers are zipping over our bodies only a foot or so above us. I am lying flat on my stomach and firing to the front. The big brown buttons on my shirt are the size of nickels. I feel that this places me too high off the ground. I reach down and unbutton my shirt. This gets me a sixteenth of an inch lower. The heavier firing goes on for perhaps a minute, and then it slacks back to the previous level. I look behind me at Staff Sergeant Evans. He is listening on the radio. I ask him what has happened. He tells me that the enemy has hit Third Platoon's right flank with a strong probe. Third Platoon has stopped the enemy cold, but they have casualties including one KIA. I flinch. I have lots of friends in Third Platoon. Some of whom I went through AIT with at Fort Polk.

I pass the word back to the rest of the squad regarding what has happened to Third Platoon and tell them to watch that flank. The gooks may try the same move with us. I am covered with leaves and branches that the enemy fire has cut down. It's like a rerun of yester-day. Smoke is pouring off the barrel of my M-14. Cisero has the same problem with his M-14 and Lambrett with the M-60.

We exchange fire for a couple more hours, and despite the large amount of ammo we have carried in, we're running low. I pass the word to Staff Sergeant Evans, and he tells me he has just gotten the word to pull back. Just like yesterday, we crawl backward firing to keep the enemy's heads down. We need to get one hundred meters back from the bunker line so we can call our shells down right on their bunkers. That will get them in the bottom of their bunkers and protect us from their fire.

Finally, we get there after crawling backward and firing for nearly one hundred meters. The big shells are dropping right on them now. We rise to a crouch and walk backward still firing. We move faster toward the wood line still firing back toward the enemy. Third Platoon is doing the same.

We break out of the jungle and head toward our foxholes only one hundred meters away across the open area. I see four Third Platoon men carrying someone in a poncho. A second poncho is covering the body. He looks like a big man, and his boots are big. I ask one of my friends in Third Platoon, "Is that Marty?" He shakes his head yes and then says, "He caught one just above his right eye." Damn, Jose "Marty" Martinez was a big Puerto Rican whom every-one in the company loved. He had five weeks left in-country, and I have seven weeks left. This is not good. I wonder if I'm going to make it out of this.

I ask the Third Platoon guys what happened; and they tell me that Marty was down with Dave Beck, a dark-haired burly soldier from Pennsylvania. Beck is armed with one of the new XM-148 "over and under weapons." The enemy begins their "probe," and there is a heavy exchange of fire. Marty is hit above the right eye with an AK round and is killed instantly. Beck shoots and kills that enemy soldier at close range. A second enemy soldier rushes in to retrieve his buddy's body. Beck's M-16 jams, as usual, so he feeds a canister round into his M-79 tube and shoots the second enemy soldier with it. Third Platoon then beats the enemy probe back.

We drop into our holes, and I tell the Second Squad to clean their weapons, one man at a time. I then get an ammo count. We've shot more than we did yesterday. It could be because we were carrying more ammo. I'd carried 600 rounds out and brought 60 back. Lambrett has fired nearly 1400 rounds with the machine gun.

I give my ammo count to McVey so he can call for more ammo to be brought to us by helicopter. While I'm at the CP, Staff Sergeant Evans calls for a squad leaders' meeting. I sit on the ground, completely wasted. Sweatt, Norberg, and Craft arrive and crash beside me. Evans tells us we have done well that day. I do not know about that, but we are alive. Evans then tells us that some promotions have come through. He, Evans, has been promoted to sergeant first class E-7. That is really fast. Evans has only been in the army just over seven years, and it takes seven years and a waiver for a man to make E-7 in that short of time. He then tells us that McVey and Jerry Sweatt have been promoted to sergeant E-5. That is great—McVey will still be an E-5 in an E-7 slot, and Sweat will be an E-5 in an E-6 slot, but at least they will be sergeants.

Evans then looks at Craft and says, "Craft, you, Norberg, and Fedrick will make sergeant E-5 at the end of next month." That is four weeks away, and I have seven weeks left in-country. I do not expect to live to make sergeant. Evans then reminds Norberg that it is his night to take out the LP. He then gives us the order of March for the next day. He wants Second and Third Squads up and First Squad behind us. I am surprised. It is Second Squad's turn to follow the other two. Evans was looking right at me when he gave that order. I start to say something, but I see that Evans has not made a mistake. He has said what he wants.

We break up and head back to our squads. I brief Second Squad, and when I tell them we are up front again tomorrow, there are angry comments. I tell them that is the order that I got. I sure as hell did not volunteer us to be on point another day. I tell them that Second Squad's order of March will be the same the next day, me on point and Cisero second, then Lambrett's gun. Cisero turns white and looks at me. He was expecting Sepulvado up front tomorrow. I just look at him with my "hard face," and he looks away. I remind the guys that the gooks may hit us with a ground attack tonight and to straighten the safety pins in their hand grenades. It is almost dark, and Norberg comes by to pick up a man from each of the rifle squads. The Swede's square jaw is set, and he looks twice his age, which is twenty. The word is passed that the LP is going out and they leave out past my foxhole. I tell the guys that the Swede will be coming back soon and not to shoot him.

In about thirty minutes, I see some moving in front of me and get my rifle ready just in case. I then hear the whisper, "Fedrick, Norberg coming in." I reply, "Come on in, Jim." He comes by my foxhole and whispers, "Damn." I whisper back, "Ain't this fun?" He heads off to his position without answering.

I have a different soldier in the hole with me tonight. Someone else needs to be in the two-man hole so the man from last night can get a little more sleep. I hear those hollow thumps in the distance and shout, "Incoming!" The enemy mortars start impacting in and around our perimeter just like last night. Our artillery that had been pounding the enemy base camp is now switched to attempt to hit the enemy mortar tubes. I know that the enemy has fired about ten rounds from each tube and grabbed them and are running to a new position. Our artillery fire might get one of them or at least keep the gooks off balance.

I wait for the ground attack that doesn't come. In a while, it gets quieter, just our artillery hitting the enemy base camp in the distance. The man with me is sleeping while sitting in the bottom of the hole. I'm glad it's the dry season. Rain would make this night even more miserable. I hear those hollow thumps again and shout, "Incoming!" It is a rerun of the last time and again with no ground attack. The rest of the night goes like that with me not sleeping and praying quietly to myself.

Morning comes, and SFC Evans calls on the radio for the LP to come in. We pass the word up and down the line that the LP is coming in. My man from LP comes to my hole. He looks like a whipped dog. I ask him if they heard or saw anything the night before, and he shakes his head no as he opens a can of C rations. I'm not eating again this morning, because I fully expect to be at least wounded today, and if my stomach is empty, I've got a much better chance of living. I tell the guys to bend the safety pins on their grenades before they put them back on their web gear. We don't need a grenade going off on someone's web gear and killing him and wounding the rest of us.

Suddenly, I hear cheers from the other side of the perimeter. I look and see four M-48 Army tanks breaking out of the wood line and heading toward our perimeter. I cheer too. This may save my life. The tanks enter our perimeter and stop. The tank platoon leader gets out of one of the tanks and starts talking with our leaders. I sit on the edge of my foxhole and breathe the breath of "the saved."

In about thirty minutes, the squad leaders are called back to the platoon CP. Sergeant First Class Evans gives us the new briefing. Bravo Company will head into the jungle behind two of the tanks. Second Platoon will follow the tank on the right, and First Platoon will follow the one on the left. Each of our files will go in while walking in the tracks of a tank tread. I will be in the right, and Craft and Third Squad will be in the track of the left tread of "our" tank. That will put our two files a little too close together, but we will not worry about stepping on a mine by walking in the tank tracks. We are told that we will keep at least sixty feet back from the tanks because they will, without a doubt, be setting off booby traps. Another company will follow the other two tanks a few hundred meters down from us.

Our artillery tears up the wood line again and then moves back into the jungle. We line up behind our tank and start toward the wood line. I'm only very scared and not terrified now that we have the tanks going in first.

The tank reaches the wood line, puts his track against a fair-sized tree, and just runs over the tree. We enter the tree line about fifty feet behind our tank just as the tank trips a booby trap. The shrapnel bouncing off the tank sounds like BBs bouncing off a car door. This is great! I'm feeling better by the minute. I glance back at the guys, and Cisero is grinning. Craft nods at me from the other file.

We keep in the tread tracks and moving forward. We are moving much faster than the days before. The tank trips another booby trap. The tank to our left in front of First Platoon is also tripping traps.

We are getting close to the enemy bunker line and start taking small-arms fire. The tanks begin firing their machine guns and their cannon. That is what I'm talking about. Those big tank cannons will destroy a bunker in a flash. We crouch down and keep moving forward. The tanks' main cannons are firing as fast as they can reload. I see a bunker with a muzzle flashing from its firing port. I fire back. Cisero and Lambrett are firing as well. The tank cannon takes out the bunker as we move forward.

The tank in front of us is in the bunker line. It drives on top of a bunker, does the "twist," and crushes the bunker. I scream with glee and shout to the guys to grenade the bunkers even if they are crushed, in case there are still live gooks in them.

Suddenly, a gook darts from a bunker just to our right. He is running back into the base camp, and I'm firing at him. Just as my tracer rounds reach him, the tank hits him with a canister round from its cannon and then runs over him with one of its treads. As I push by the dead gook, he looks like hamburger. It's a turkey shoot now. The gooks are abandoning their bunkers and running for their lives. We are all shooting and shouting. The tanks are putting out an unbelievable rate of machine gun and cannon fire. I hear screams for medics coming from the First Platoon area. Damn, First Platoon is taking casualties.

It's over in a few minutes. The gooks either are dead or have escaped. We are throwing grenades in all the bunkers, but it's over. We have the base camp. I hear that First Platoon has a KIA. Damn, this base camp has been expensive. I find out later that a good soldier named Ray has been killed by small-arms fire. We secure the enemy base camp, and they fly in engineers. The engineers work the rest of the day blowing the enemy bunkers and supplies. I am calming down from my adrenaline high. I am just real beat. Then I recall that I have not slept the last two nights and haven't eaten today.

The day is nearly gone, and we're heading back to our perimeter. Sergeant McVey walks up to me and says, "Fedrick, we've got hot chow coming in tonight." McVey really knows how to perk me up! We've got hot chow coming in. Sweatt is taking the LP out tonight. My squad does *not* have ambush tonight. I'm making Sergeant in four weeks and going home in seven weeks. Life is good!

CHAPTER 21

Third Platoon Overrun

1967

Bravo Company continues operations as usual. The mortar platoon hits a booby trap while out on patrol. Lopez is killed. He had finished his one-year tour and had extended for another six months in order to stay with his squad. He also wanted to make sergeant E-5 as a squad leader. The mortar platoon will miss him. He was a very brave man but pushed his luck.

Bravo Company's Third Platoon has a night ambush patrol going out. SFC E-7 Oliver is in charge of the patrol. He is a very competent NCO and well-liked by the men in Third Platoon. He has been in the Army for eighteenth years and is thirty-seven years old. The same age as my dad. Some of the soldiers going out with him are Seadorf, Grisson, and Chrisco, the medic.

They move in the dark to their ambush location and begin setting up. They place claymore mines out, and accidentally one of the mines is set off. No Third Platoon soldiers are injured in the accident, but this causes the ambush to have to switch their ambush location as this one has been compromised.

They move to a secondary location and set up. What they don't realize is that the enemy has been alerted by the explosion and has followed them to their secondary ambush location.

The night progresses until suddenly an enemy force in strength attacks the Third Platoon position while putting out a heavy volume of fire. The Third Platoon troops fight back, but they are heavily outnumbered and soon are overrun. Sergeant Oliver and a second soldier are killed outright while Seadorf and three other soldiers are so badly wounded that they cannot fight or run. The other members of the patrol fight their way through the enemy ranks and escape out into the jungle.

Seadorf and the other three badly wounded soldiers play dead as they lay with Sergeant Oliver and the other dead soldier. The enemy starts stripping the American bodies of their weapons, billfolds, watches, and rings. When they begin stripping one soldier, he fights them, and they shoot him a half-dozen times and kill him. Seadorf and the other two wounded soldiers continue to play dead, and the enemy soldiers strip them and then fade away into the jungle.

A relief force responds to the scene and finds the dead and wounded Americans. They also locate the soldiers who escaped into the jungle. They get the wounded and dead dusted off and return to the perimeter with the other soldiers.

The next day, Vern Bramlett, a particularly good Third Platoon soldier and a good friend of Seadorf, travels to the Army hospital where Seadorf and the other two wounded soldiers are located. Bramlett talks at length with his friend Seadorf and gets the full story of the ambush gone wrong. Bramlett then returns to the base camp at Di An. A few days later, Seadorf dies in the hospital.

A few weeks later, Alpha Company has an ambush set up in the same area where Bravo's Third Platoon was overrun. They have been in their ambush position on a trail for a while when an enemy squad walks into their ambush kill zone. The Alpha Company unit opens up with a heavy volume of fire on the enemy squad. In a minute or so, the firing stops, and the Alpha Company soldiers sweep the kill zone. They recover three enemy bodies along with an AK-47, an SKS carbine, and an M-16 rifle. A check of the serial number on the M-16 the next day reveals that the M-16 belonged to one of the Bravo Company's Third Platoon soldiers who had been killed earlier when Third Platoon was overrun. Alpha Company got some payback for the guys in Bravo Company's Third Platoon. All combat is a tragedy. The death of a close friend in combat is similar to losing a member of your family. It's something a soldier will always remember, and it will always hurt.

CHAPTER 22

That Deep Slapping Sound

Late May 1967

I have less than a month left in-country on my first tour. I've just been promoted to sergeant E-5 and am still Second Squad leader in Second Platoon Bravo Company. That's still a staff sergeant E-6 slot, but the army has grown so big so fast that there is no one to fill the slots. Myself and the other squad leaders have worked a couple of months in E-6 slots as E-4s. McVey, the platoon sergeant, was also an E-4 working in an E-7 slot.

It is early morning, and Second Platoon is about to depart on a platoon-size day patrol. The terrain we will be patrolling is an area that is mostly brush and elephant grass. The platoon is trying a new formation on platoon patrols. One squad will run about one hundred meters in front of the other two squads and the two machine gun crews. It is Second Squad's turn to pull this point squad detail. They are doing this so if there's an ambush, the enemy will just ambush one squad and not the entire platoon.

I do not like the idea of being out on a limb without a machine gun. I ask the platoon leader if I can take a machine gun crew with me, and he says no. The directives from on high say that we will run the patrol like he has said. I say, "Yes, sir," and start getting the squad ready for the patrol.

My squad is woefully understrength. There are only six of us instead of ten. The other five men are all PFCs. What makes it worse is that both of my team leaders are out of pocket. One is on R&R, and the other is in the hospital with very serious wounds, and I doubt that he will ever return to us.

My most experienced soldier is Bob Keck, a short dark-haired guy from Ohio. He has been with us about four months and has already been wounded once. He is making into a fine soldier and point man. Today he will be my second-in-command.

I am going to run the squad in two files of three men each. Keck will run point on the left with me second. The third man will carry the radio. He is King, a tall, thin Black soldier from Illinois. He has been with us a little over two months and is a quiet, competent soldier and is good on the radio.

Haviland will run point on the right file. He is medium tall with brown hair and a red face. He's only been with us six weeks, but I like the way he's working out. The second and third soldiers in the right file are both brand-new. It's their first patrol. The second man is very big, even larger than I am. The third man is shorter and stocky, and his voice is very loud. That concerns me.

I am carrying the big M-14, and the big man in the right file is carrying one of the new test weapons. It's an M-16 with a large tube under the barrel that fires an M-79 shell. The army calls it an XM-148. We call it an "over and under." The Army says that it will give the soldier the M-16 for self-protection, but his primary job is to fire the M-79. I have concerns about this. Our men with the old break-down single-shot M-79 carried at least forty high-explosive (HE) rounds. The SOP with these new weapons is only twenty HE rounds. The soldier does have the M-16 with at least sixteen magazines, but that is not his primary job. Unless we are in very thick vegetation, he is supposed to be firing the M-79. I have also heard that in some of the other platoons the squad leaders have told their grenadiers to just carry a half-dozen rounds for the M-79. I cannot believe that. In Second Platoon, the grenadiers carry at least twenty M-79 rounds.

I have my compass and map, and King is doing double duty as count man as well as radioman. I tell Haviland to stay even with Keck. I tell the big man to cover Haviland and look to the flank often. He is brand-new and gives me that "deer in the headlights" look. Damn, he doesn't know what I'm talking about. I tell the shorter, stocky man at the end of the right file to keep a sharp eye to our rear in case any enemy get behind us. I get another of those blank looks. Six men instead of ten and no machine gun. Also, half the guys are green as grass. This scares me.

We start off slow and easy. King tells me when we have gone one hundred meters, and I tell him to inform the platoon leader so he can start the platoon moving behind us. We keep moving until the platoon leader advises that he is stopping the platoon to cloverleaf small patrols to his right and left. I stop the squad, and we all face out. The shorter man in the right file says something to the big man in front of him. You could hear his voice for a quarter mile. I quickly move over to him, and in an extremely low voice, I chew him out. I tell him that this is not Fort Polk or back home, that his loud voice will get us all killed.

The platoon leader advises that it's time to move. We move a while, and then the platoon leader advises that it is time to change direction. I check my compass and map and do this. We stop a number of times for the platoon to cloverleaf. We also change direction a couple of times.

The shorter man says something again to the big man. Again, it could be heard for a quarter of a mile. I lunge at the shorter man and shove my nose against his. I snarl at him that if he does that again, I will hurt him. I tell him to not say another word on the patrol unless he sees enemy soldiers. He hangs his head and nods. I think that he believes me.

It is the middle of the day, and the platoon leader tells us on the radio that it's time to break for chow. I look around and see a big log. I tell Haviland and his guys to set up behind the log for chow. I tell Haviland to watch to our rear and each of the new men to watch the flanks. I tell the shorter man to keep his mouth shut. He nods.

I set Keck, King, and myself up in the elephant grass about forty feet to the right front of Haviland's position. I set up in the middle with King on my left and Keck on my right. I advise King to watch the front and the left side and Keck to watch the front and the right side. I will watch the front. I hope that our rear is covered.

There is a bush by where I set up. The trunk is about as thick as my arm. I check around it for trip wires or booby traps and find nothing. I keep all my gear on and my rifle in my lap with its strap still around my shoulder. I put my back against the bush and sit down. I break out a can of C rations and open it with my tiny P-38 can opener. I then eat while I watch to the front. We do not realize it, but there is a well-used trail about twenty-five feet to our front in the elephant grass that goes from our left to our right. We can't see it.

Sitting with my back against the bush, I can just see over the elephant grass. King is ten feet to my left and Keck ten feet to my right. They have taken off all their gear, and King has also taken off that twenty-five-pound radio. I have kept all my gear on because I have my back braced with the bush. It is quiet and hot. The little shade from the bush and the elephant grass helps a little. I'm expecting the platoon leader to call us any time and tell us to saddle up.

I hear Keck whisper to King. He asks if King has any Kool-Aid in any of his canteens. King says he does, and Keck asks if he can have a drink. King whispers that he can. Keck stands up to move the few feet to King's location. Keck is so short that only his head and shoulders are above the grass. I open my mouth to tell Keck to keep his head down. I never get the words out. *Suddenly*, a heavy volume of AK-47 fire falls on us like a heavy hailstorm. I hear that loud deep slapping sound. If you ever hear that sound, you will never forget it. It's the sound of military-grade high-velocity rifle rounds striking the human body. I hear Keck and King both give out large, deep grunts as I roll over on my stomach. Enemy rounds kick dirt, leaves, and twigs into my face as they hit just inches in front of my face in a line from my right to my left. If the enemy soldier had held his weapon's muzzle just an inch or so higher, I would have been hit numerous times. Thank God for my eyeglasses. They have kept the dirt and twigs out of my eyes. I shove the big M-14 against my shoulder and fire three long bursts out into the grass toward the sound of the AK-47s.

Keck falls against my right side and says that he is hit hard. I leave my empty M-14 hanging from my shoulder, grab Keck by his pants belt with my right hand and his hair with my left hand, and start crab running toward the big log that Haviland is looking over with his rifle to his shoulder. I shout for him to fire cover to the left front, and he begins firing as fast as he can pull the trigger on his M-16 toward the sound of the AK-47s.

I reach the log within seconds and fall over the log with Keck still in my hands. Keck has blood pouring out of both his thighs like faucets on high volume. I shove a fresh magazine into my rifle and shout to Haviland that I am going after King and to give me cover on the way back. I jump over the log and crab run toward King's location, firing quick bursts with the M-14. I reach King, and he's trying to crawl toward the log. His pants are soaked with blood. I let my empty rifle hang from my shoulder; and, like I did with Keck, I grab King by his pants belt with my right hand and his hair with left and start crab running toward the log as Haviland fires an entire magazine toward the enemy positions. King and I fall over the log, and I shove another magazine into my rifle.

I look over at the two new men to my left. They are both huddled against the log and doing nothing. I shout at them to put out fire to our left front. The short man fires one shot with his rifle and then gets back down. The big man fires one M-79 round, and he also gets back down. I rip off a magazine in a long burst, shove in another, and do it again. While I change magazines, I see that Haviland has cut Keck's pants away with his knife. Keck has two holes about the size of dimes on the outside of his right thigh. The two rounds have exited on the inside of his right thigh, leaving two holes about the size of nickels. Then apparently, the same two rounds have entered the inside of his left thigh, leaving holes about the size of quarters. They have then exited the outside of his left thigh, leaving holes as big as the palm of my hand. These two exit holes overlap, and bone shards are sticking out. Blood is pouring out.

The army has an SOP that you never put a tourniquet on a wounded soldier. This keeps a soldier from losing a limb if the tourniquet remains in place too long. Haviland doesn't hesitate; he cuts strips of cloth from Keck's ruined pants and places tourniquets on first his left leg and then his right. The blood flow stops. He has saved Keck's life. He then turns to King, who is not bleeding nearly as bad as Keck was. He cuts Kings pants open and places tourniquets on his legs. King, however, does not appear to have double hits on his legs, and it appears that he has no arteries or bones damaged. I am always amazed that the exit wounds on Black soldiers are as pink and red as they are on White soldiers. I realize we are no different except for the color of our skin.

While Haviland is working on Keck and King, I'm firing long bursts to the left front, and when I change magazines, I shout at the two new men to fire. Each time they each fire one shot and then get back down. Haviland has stopped the bleeding on Keck and King, and I tell him that I've got to get the radio and for him to cover me on the way back. I go over the log firing bursts until I reach the radio. I don't hear enemy weapons firing now. Have they pulled out, or are they flanking us? I grab the radio by a strap and head back with Haviland firing away. I fall over the log again and quickly reload my rifle. I tell Haviland to keep firing. I pick up the handset and hear people talking on the channel. I say, "Break, break," and they quit talking. I shout into the radio, "Two-two to two-six" (my call sign and the platoon leader's call sign respectively). The platoon leader answers, and I tell him we have received heavy automatic weapons fire from our left front and that I have two "echo mikes" (enlisted men) that are "whiskey India alpha" (wounded in action). I advise that we need assistance and medics. He okays my request and advises that the platoon is moving toward me.

It seems that the enemy fire has ceased. I hope that they have pulled out and are not just flanking us. I tell the two new men to watch our left flank and if they see anyone but Americans to fire at them. Keck and King seem to be resting quietly. I am sure that Keck is in shock, and King may be as well. I tell them that the platoon and medics are on the way. King nods his head. Keck just stares at me and breathes through his mouth.

Haviland and I have our weapons at the ready and are attempting to watch in all directions. I have no confidence in the two new men. The platoon breaks from the brush to our rear and move into our position. The medic kneels beside Keck and cuts off his tourniquets; the huge blood flow has stopped. The medic then adds pressure bandages. He then does the same for King. Dust-off helicopters are en route to medivac the wounded men.

The platoon moves forward and secures the area that the enemy fire came from. The platoon leader asks me what happened, and I tell him. He asks how many enemy soldiers were involved, and I tell him that we did not see them, that they saw us. We had just fired at the sound of their weapons. I tell the platoon leader that I did not see them but I think that there were only two or three, four or five at the most or they would have overrun us when Keck and King went down. We will never know. The platoon leader is taking no chances. He's got artillery rounds coming into our front and left. I do not blame him. Those shells are cheap compared to the lives of soldiers, but I think the enemy has pulled out.

The dust-off helicopter comes in and takes out Keck and King. King will return to the platoon in a few weeks, but Keck will be shipped to an Army hospital in Japan and then hospitals in the States where he will remain for over a year. Keck will write me for years and tell me that the VA had taught him to walk again. His second Purple Heart was a noticeably big one.

The platoon leader forms the platoon up to continue our patrol. The war must go on. I have only three men left, so he puts Craft's Third Squad out on point. I am relieved. I have less than four weeks left on this tour, and I wonder if I will live to get home.

I set the "squad" up in the right file to take Craft's Third Squad's place. Haviland will run point with me second. Then it's Lambrett's machine gun crew with my two green troops coming next. The new platoon sergeant and his radioman will bring up the rear. I place the loud soldier in front of the platoon sergeant and tell the platoon sergeant how loud the shorter man talks. He says he will keep him quiet.

The platoon leader and his radioman are third and fourth in the left file with Sweatt running second behind his point man. The other machine gun crew follows the radioman. Then the rest of First Squad follows the gun crew.

We move for a while, and the platoon leader stops the column and calls for cloverleaf patrols to the right and left. I take the shorter loud soldier and do the right cloverleaf myself. My thinking is that I can keep the shorter soldier quiet. We move about thirty meters to the right of the column, make a small circle, and return to the column. I see that First Squad's two men have also returned. The platoon leader gives us the word to continue the patrol. We move a while, and it's time to cloverleaf again. This time I send Haviland and the big soldier. They return, and we continue our mission.

This goes on all afternoon. I am feeling completely wasted. I have used a lot of energy in that firefight. I am also very concerned about Keck and King. I feel that it is my fault for not being more alert. I don't think this would have happened to Ben Garza.

Finally, in late afternoon, we arrive back at the perimeter. The one bright spot is that I see that my team leader, Raul Sepulvedo, has returned from R&R. I fill him in on what has happened as best as I can. He's a good soldier, but his English is very poor, and my Spanish is worse than terrible. We have five men in the squad now, and Raul has been here six months and is seasoned.

We take up positions for the night. Second Squad has two fox-holes to man in the center of the platoon. We also have to supply a man for the listening post. I place Raul and the big soldier in one foxhole and Haviland and myself in the other. Sweatt will be taking out the listening post tonight. I take the shorter, loud soldier down to Sweatt's position and tell Sweatt he will be Second Squad's man on LP. I then tell Sweatt how loud the man is. The shorter soldier hangs his head. Sweatt says that his man Mike Yaw will be in charge of the LP. We call Mike over, and I tell him how loud the new soldier is and for him to keep him quiet. Mike says he will do it. I hope that embarrassment will keep the shorter man quiet. Sweatt walks down to Third Squad's area and gets a man from Craft. He's a low-key country boy from Kentucky and very dependable. He will carry the radio.

On my way back to my position, I stop by the platoon command post. I tell the platoon sergeant that I'm working with a five-man squad. I ask him when we will get replacements. He tells me that we'll be getting "fresh meat" any day now and I'll just have to make do until we do.

I move back to Second Squad's position and check on Raul and the big man. I tell them that we will be getting new people in a few days and in the meantime we will just have to "hang tough." They don't seem to be very happy about it. I move back to my foxhole with Haviland. I fill him in, and then we set up guard shifts. It will be two hours on and two off and then do it again. If nothing happens, we will each get four hours' sleep in two-hour increments. I wonder what it will be like when I get back to the world and am able to sleep for eight hours' solid in a bed instead of a few hours' broken sleep on the ground.

In a couple of days, we do get a couple more new men. I try to break them in as best I can, but my only really experienced man is Sepulvedo. Haviland has done really well in the firefight that Keck and King were wounded in, but he still has less than two months in-country.

The next couple of weeks, we are providing security for Rhome Plows. These are large bulldozers, and they are being used to clear brush away from a road. We are putting out a lot of observation posts (OPs) and making short squad-sized patrols.

The dozers are occasionally tripping booby traps out in the brush. A couple of the drivers receive minor shrapnel wounds. We are getting sniper fire every day but only a couple of quick brushes with enemy troops where they exchange fire with us and then run. We have gotten a new platoon leader who thinks he knows it all, and we've had a new platoon sergeant for a couple of weeks. The sergeant is an old guy, well into his thirties, with about twelve years in the Army. He is only an E-5, but he's trying hard and has a lot of experience but none in combat. I am starting to think I might survive this tour of duty.

Finally, it is just a handful of days until I'm due to go stateside. It's time for me to give Second Squad to someone else. In a way, it is kind of hard. I meet with the new platoon leader and suggest Sepulvedo as the new squad leader. The lieutenant turns down my suggestion. He says that Raul's English is not good enough for him to be a squad leader. I don't agree, but it's not my call. The lieutenant says that his radioman, Watson, will take my squad. Watson is a short stocky blond soldier and is a good man. If not Raul, then I think Watson will be a good squad leader.

I walk back to the squad foxholes, pull Raul over to the side, and tell him the platoon leader is going to put Watson over Second Squad. Raul is not happy about it, and I tell him that Watson did not want the job but the lieutenant's word is law. I tell Raul that he will still be senior team leader and support Watson all he can for the squad's sake. Raul shakes his head.

I grab my gear and rifle and prepare to take the next chopper back to Di An. I shake all the guys' hands and tell them that Watson will be the new squad leader. I walk toward the platoon CP, and Watson catches me. He seems upset and tells me that he did not want this job and he will do everything Sepulvedo tells him. I strongly tell him that he cannot do that. He's in charge, and Raul is just his second-in-command. He has to be strong and give the orders. I shake his hand and walk toward the landing helicopter.

I arrive in the rear at Di An to process out. Over the next few days, a number of my buddies arrive in the rear to go home. There's Burner Craft and Jerry Sweatt. Both are squad leaders like me. McVey and Norberg have already left. The platoon has all new squad leaders. Charles Bickett and Leo Franovich also show up. We are all glad to be alive.

Lieutenant Robert Leary, the company executive officer, sits me down for a serious talk. He wants me to extend my tour for another six months like he has done. I am very tempted because I miss the platoon already, but I cannot do that to my family. I tell him that, and he says he understands. I will regret that decision the rest of my life.

It's the day before I'm due to go to Saigon to get on the 707-plane going home. Craft and I walk down to the beer tent in the evening. We walk in and see Nelson Taylor and Bobby Beathea sitting at a table. We walk up and speak. They are the two troops who left the platoon four months before for jobs in the rear security platoon. Bobby makes mention of Craft and I being sergeants now, and he wonders what they would have done had he stayed in the platoon. I tell him that if he and Taylor had stayed, they would have these stripes now instead of Craft and me. I remind him that they were grooming Taylor and him to take Second and Third Squads, but they left for those good rear jobs, so it fell to Craft and me. Taylor tells him to be quiet that he, Taylor, could not have taken four more months of fear in the field. Bobby settles down, and they all have a beer, and I have a Coke. Taylor and Beathea are both going home in the next few days, so they are very happy about that.

The next day, we are trucked to Camp Alpha in Saigon to catch that big plane back to the "world." I also run into a number of guys at Camp Alpha that I had infantry training with at Fort Polk. We are glad to see each other. Some of the guys look at the ribbons on my chest and make mention of the fact that I have received two Purple Hearts on this tour. Some of them have one, and some have none. They are impressed. I tell them it is because of my clumsiness. We talk about the several guys that we went through training with that have been killed in the last year. We are sad about that but glad that we are alive and going back to the "world."

They come out with a manifest for the next plane. Craft, Sweatt, and I are going to be on the same plane. Craft is near the head of the list. Jerry Sweatt and I are in the middle. I ask Craft to save Jerry and me seats with him. We all toss our bags in a pile to be placed in the belly of the plane. We then line up to board. Jerry and I are together and Craft up close to the front. We start into the plane, and as Jerry and I enter, we see Craft up toward the middle left. We get to him, and I tell him to move over. He says no, that he saved the seats, so he gets the aisle seat. I laugh and say that is fine. I then ask Jerry if he wants the window or middle seat. He says window, so I take the middle one. We settle in, and the plane takes off. Everyone cheers. It is good to be going home sitting between two guys whom I have just spent a year with, in combat.

We arrive at Fort Ord in California and process out. I have orders to Fort Benning; the other two are going to other forts. The three of us share a cab to the airport. We are all going to be on different planes going to different cities. In the terminal, we all shake hands and then head down different concourses. I will never see either one of them again. We have had a full year together, and I will remember it all, day by day, for the rest of my life.

CHAPTER 23

Fort Benning

July 1967

I'm driving from Memphis to Fort Benning, Georgia. I have completed my first tour in Vietnam and have had leave in Memphis. I'm twenty years old now and am a sergeant E-5. I was wounded twice while in Vietnam, in September and December 1966. I still have a lot of numbness in my right thigh from a rifle bullet in September as well as a terrible scar.

I arrive at the in-processing center at main post at Fort Benning. They check my records and notice that I have a physical profile on my right leg. This means that I might have trouble performing full field duty. I don't tell them that I have just fought for the last eight months on that leg. They decide to send me to Brigade Headquarters Company of the 197th Infantry Brigade located on Kelly Hill. They tell me that being in Headquarters Company, I will have very little, if any, field duty. That is fine with me. I don't want to spend long periods of time in the woods. I am very allergic to poison ivy and will get it if I'm in the woods. I'm so glad that they didn't have that in Vietnam. If they had, they would have had to make me a gunner on a helicopter or give me some rear job where I would not have been exposed.

I travel to Kelly Hill and report to the company. They decide to place me in Brigade S-4 (supply) where I will supervise menial tasks. It sounds fine to me. I'm assigned a room in the barracks with another NCO and settle in. Then it begins. It's Sergeant Fedrick take four men and cut the grass. Sergeant Fedrick take four men and rake leaves. Sergeant Fedrick pick four men and after evening chow have them clean the Brigade Headquarters Building. Sergeant Fedrick check out a jeep and run errands for the company first sergeant. It's all very *boring*.

Each night, the company has a charge of quarters, a sergeant E-5 who is in charge of the company at night. He has a private for a "runner," and if anything, big happens, he calls the Company First Sergeant E-8 at home. I pull this detail nearly once a week even despite the fact that there are many sergeant E-5s in the company, but I understand. Most of the other E-5s have assigned jobs. I'm the floater with no real job just handling details. It's really not a bad deal, just terribly *boring*.

In the fall, I'm called into the orderly room, and the first sergeant tells me that they have a new NCO Academy starting up at Fort Benning. It's the third army NCO Academy. A senior NCO Academy of sergeant E-5s and staff sergeant E-6s to teach them how to become sergeant first class E-7s and a junior NCO Academy for private first class E-3s and specialist 4 E-4s to teach them how to be sergeant E-5. Our company has to supply a sergeant E-5 for the first class in the academy. They can do without me easier than any other sergeant E-5 in the company, so I've been picked.

I gather my gear and drive to where the academy is located and report in. I'm assigned a bunk in a barracks and start meeting the other students. They are all sergeant E-5, specialist 5s, staff sergeant E6s, or specialist 6s. Most have been in the army much longer than me, and most have families. There are truck drivers, artillerymen, supply men, cooks, helicopter crewmen, infantrymen like me, and even a dental assistant. They tell us that over the next six weeks, each of us will spend a week in each of three different leadership positions. Also, there will be a written test each week. If we fail the test, we'll be bounced from the academy.

My first leadership role will be as a squad leader. No problem, I have been a squad leader. That week passes smoothly. We get up early and have classes all day on many different army subjects. We then study during the evenings and help each other with quizzes. The only bad part is I do not have evenings off. I have been hanging out in the day room after evening chow back in the company. I watch the evening news on TV and then programs that I have not seen in the last year and a half due to my six months of training and then my year in Vietnam.

The barracks behind us belong to the junior NCO Academy. The barracks back up to each other where we all tend to sit on our back porches, polish our boots, clean our weapons, and talk. One day, I notice a much older PFC on the other back porch. He is a Black stocky soldier and looks familiar. I walk forward. He looks at me. He walks toward me, and then I realize it is Hearn. He was a corporal in one of the other platoons in Bravo Company when I was in Vietnam. He is also a Korean War veteran and sports a star on his Combat Infantry Badge, meaning that he's been in two different wars. He has to be at least thirty-five years old, and I remember that in Vietnam he had been saying that he was getting out of the army. Hearn may have his faults, but when I was four years old, he was fighting the Chinese army in the snow in Korea. I have great respect for that.

I shout, "Hearn," and he shouts, "Fedrick." We grab each other and hug. We come apart, and I tell him that I thought he was getting out of the army. He tells me that he did, but those civilians expect you to work on their jobs, so he came back in. We both laugh, and then he begins telling the young soldiers on his porch about the day that I was shot in the leg over a year ago. Most of them are not combat veterans, and they listen closely to Hearn's inflated story. I notice some of my classmates are listening as well. It's a little embarrassing. We talk a while about battles, we were in. We then wish each other good luck and go inside our respective barracks.

The third week of the academy, I am placed in a platoon sergeant position. I have watched platoon sergeants for nearly two years now and am able to go through the motions. I make it that week without too many errors. This isn't a bad school. Just shine your boots, keep your uniform sharp, and study for the test.

The fourth week begins, and I wonder what my final leadership role will be. I hope it's not company commander or first sergeant. In midweek, some of my fellow classmates approach me and others. They have stolen the answers for the test on Friday. It's always a multiple-choice test, and they have the "key." It is a choice. A third of the class elect to use the key and cheat on the test. The other two-thirds of the class, including me, elect to take the test clean and not cheat.

We take the test Friday afternoon, and soon after, we are called to formation. The instructors call out a list of names and have them fall into another formation. It is about a third of our number. The commander of the academy then announces that these men have cheated on the test and will be expelled. He calls for the Sergeant Majors of all the men involved and have them come to the academy and take their disgraced men away. The Academy Commander then tells us that this is a black mark on the first class of the academy, but he is proud of us. He tells us that we are honest men and that we have character.

The fifth week of the school goes by fast with no bumps. The start of the sixth week begins, and I find out my third leadership position. I will be the company executive officer. I have watched what the executive officer has been doing at the academy. Mostly, I move ahead of the company as they go from class to class and make sure where the company is supposed to be. It is not a bad job. The company commander only chews me out once during the entire week.

The week comes to an end, and we graduate. We have a small ceremony, get our certificates, and then return to our units. Then it is back to the same *boring* grind.

The end of January 1968 comes, and I have another lackluster day. I eat the evening meal and then go to the day room to watch the evening news. The news comes on with a map of South Vietnam covered with sites that are having heavy fighting. The North Vietnamese Army and Viet Cong units have attacked all over the country. They are calling it the Tet Offensive. It's the heaviest fight the Army, and Marines have experienced since the Korean War. It is force against force, and no one is backing up. I am stunned as I watch. Our soldiers are not looking for the enemy. The enemy is in their face. I sit by the TV and wait for the ten o'clock news. I watch scenes from Vietnam as the fighting grows heavier.

I lay awake in my bunk all night. I know what I must do. I can do nothing else and still call myself a soldier and a man. The next morning, we hold formation and then go to chow. After chow, I go to the orderly room and ask the clerk for a form 1049. The First Sergeant asks me what I'm doing, and I tell him I'm putting in a 1049 request to return to Vietnam. He asks why. I tell him that there's heavy fighting there and I cannot stand not being involved. He asks if I am sure, and I tell him that I lay awake all night thinking it over and I can do nothing else. He says for me to fill it out and he will send it up to Brigade. I fill it out, and the First Sergeant puts it in the mail pouch and has the clerk take it across the street to Brigade headquarters.

A couple of weeks go by as I watch the heavy fighting on TV. I feel very frustrated that I am not a part of it. The Soldiers and Marines in Vietnam are not having to look for the enemy. The enemy is right in front of them.

I check on my 1049 request and find that there is no record of my 1049 being submitted. I angrily fill out a second 1049 and submit it. I wait a couple of weeks as I watch the fighting in Vietnam slow down. I check on my second 1049 and find there is no record of it either. I am really angry now. It seems that I have missed the Tet Offensive. I submit a third 1049, wait a couple of weeks, and check on it. There is no record of my third 1049. My mind is set now. I think that someone is trying to look out for me. I do not want to be looked after. I am a grown man, just turned twenty-one years old, combat hardened with three stripes on my sleeve. I make up my mind that I am either going to Vietnam or Leavenworth Federal Prison.

My buddy in the company is SPC5 Bill Shutes. He's a Vietnam veteran but was in the "rear with the gear" during his tour, but he can type. I ask Bill if he will type a letter for me with seven carbon copies. He says sure and asks who I'm sending eight letters to. I tell him the president, vice president, two senators, and two congressmen from Tennessee, as well as the secretary of defense and the secretary of the army. He lets his breath out and sits down. He asks if I'm serious, and I tell him I am. He tells me he will type it for me if I swear I'll never tell anyone that he typed it. I tell him if anyone asks, I will tell them that I did.

We sit down, and Bill types me a long generic letter as I dictate, explaining about my three "lost" 1049 requests and my desire to return to Vietnam where my combat experience can be used. He finishes, and I already have the eight envelopes addressed. I sign each letter and place them in the envelopes, and we walk together to a mailbox, and I drop them in. I have done it now. I may go to jail. Time will tell.

It is April 4, 1968, and I have charge of quarters tonight. I make sure that my runner and I are the first in the chow line for the evening meal. We then report to the orderly room, and I take charge of the company. The company first sergeant, the clerks, and all the officer's leave. I sit behind the desk and wait for the phone to ring or some other problem to arise.

My phone rings, and I answer it the standard way, "Headquarters Company, a Hundred and Ninety-Seventh Light Infantry Brigade, Sergeant Fedrick, Charge of Quarters speaking, Sir." I find that it is my friend SPC5 Bill Shutes. He says he is in the day room watching the evening news, and the news is that Dr. Martin Luther King has been shot and killed in Memphis, Tennessee. I'm shocked. I tell Bill that he better not be joking about this that if he is serious, I'm going to call the Company First Sergeant at home. Bill swears he is telling the truth. I hang up the phone and call First Sergeant Price's home number. He answers the phone and tells me that he has seen the news and is putting his uniform back on and will be back at the company shortly.

First Sergeant Price arrives, followed closely by the platoon sergeants, the company commanding officer, and the other officers. They start organizing the company to be deployed. The news is that there are major riots in every large city in the nation and some of those cities are on fire. First Sergeant Price knows that I'm from Memphis and finds a young Black private that is too. He tells us that if we are deployed to Memphis, we will guide the company. That makes me a little uneasy. I know Highland Heights, Binghampton, and Downtown. I know almost nothing about North Memphis, South Memphis, East Memphis, Parkway Village, Orange Mound, or Frayser.

We began packing vehicles on into the night with tents, supplies, and weapons. The news continues to be bad. Cities are burning, and some people are dying. We all load up and convoy to the airfield. This is getting serious by the minute. We arrive at the airport, and the number of army vehicles is staggering. There are hundreds of vehicles and thousands of men. The entire Brigade is here.

We then get the update. The brigade will fly into Andrews Air Force Base near Washington, DC, and then convoy into Baltimore. I am relieved. I will not be a guide. I have never been to Baltimore.

Some of the guys are getting naps in the vehicles and beside the vehicles. I stay beside the first sergeant assisting him, running errands and working details. Finally, in the wee small hours of the morning, the big Air Force cargo planes begin to land, dozens of them. We begin to load men and vehicles. We then take off, and I get a little sleep sitting in a jeep car seat. We land at Andrews Air Force Base in the morning and unload. We then form up the convoy and head toward Baltimore. The convoy is miles long. We drive through a part of Baltimore that is still burning with many people standing on the sidewalks. They are doing nothing and saying nothing. I suppose that we are doing a "show of force." It seems pretty effective.

We arrive at Druid Hill Park in the middle of the city. The park is really big, and I guess it's usually beautiful, but now it's full of soldiers putting up large tents and parking army vehicles all over the grass. It is organized chaos. Some mess tents go up first, and the cooks are already cooking the evening meal. I like that. After all, an army moves on its stomach. We have our brigade operations tents up, and they are directing activities for the entire Brigade. The line companies are about to start jeep patrols with heavily armed teams in each jeep and at least two jeeps together at all times. We have the full four-thousand-man Brigade in the park.

First Sergeant Price tells me that I will be in charge of the ammo for the company and to issue one twenty-round magazine for the

M-14 to each man in the company. I get right on it keeping a record of each of nearly two hundred men whom I give a magazine to. I keep *two* loaded magazines for myself. The first sergeant then tells me that I will be in charge of the company's guards. They will guard the company area and keep civilians out and soldiers in. There is always some soldier who wants to go to a bar. I get my guards together. I have one sergeant E-5 who is junior to me and two specialist 5s. I also have twelve private first classes and specialist 4s. I divide them into three shifts with the sergeant or one of the specialist 5s and four men on each shift. They will work four hours on and eight hours off, and those on duty will walk guard mount around the company area. The ones off duty will be ready to respond to any crisis.

It is the middle of the night, and I'm getting a little sleep on a fold out cot in one of the tents. One of my specialist 5s wakes me and tells me that there has been an incident. I get up and go with him. I find that one of the company soldiers has attempted to leave the company area. He was stopped by one of my guards and told he could not pass. The guard said that the man appeared to be half drunk and said that he was going to town to party. He tried to force his way past the guard, and the guard struck him in the head with his weapon. This knocked the soldier out and placed a large cut on his head. I make sure that a medic is on the way and send for the First Sergeant. The medic arrives and bandages the soldier's head as he awakens. The First Sergeant arrives and sends for the military police. They arrive, take the injured soldier into custody, and take a statement from the guard. The military police leave with the injured soldier, and the First Sergeant tells the guard that he did his duty. The First Sergeant and I return to our tents to get a little more sleep before day light.

A few days later, the First Sergeant comes to me and tells me to find a young private with no important job that he has a detail for me. He tells me that the city is going to send a repairman out to fix the many broken or shot out streetlights and he needs protection. The First Sergeant is going to send me and one man to ride with him tonight to guard him. It sounds like a nice break in the routine. I find a young private who has just been doing work details and tell him to get his rifle and make sure he has his ammo.

The city work truck arrives, and we meet the repairman. He is a tall brown-haired White guy in his thirties. He tells me he's sorry, but he refused to go out without protection. I tell him that I welcome the change in routine. I tell the private to get in the middle of the seat and I will be by the door. We place the butts of our rifles on the floor with the barrels sticking up in front of us. I make sure that both rifles have the magazines locked in place but no round in the chamber. We only have to work the bolt to have the rifles hot. I don't want an accidental discharge going through the roof of this city truck. I don't want to be demoted to corporal.

It is still daylight as we move around the city. The repairman stops often to repair lights. When he stops, the private and I stand on each side of the truck with our rifles at port arms. I don't think this is too threatening, but it shows people that we are armed. We run into no trouble. No one shouts at us or throws anything at us. I'm thinking that this riot is just about over.

It is getting on toward dusk dark, and we are driving slowly down a residential street. The houses are older two story frame houses but appear to be neat. As we approach one house on the right, we see a double window upstairs with four or five adult White men hanging out the windows with rifles and shotguns in one hand and quart bottles of beer in the other. They are watching the street. I tell the repairman to stop in front of the house; and he, the private, and I roll out of the truck on the left side away from the house. I tell the repairman to call for the police on his radio. I tell the private to get down behind the bed of the truck and cover the house. I tell him to put a round in the chamber of his rifle but make sure that the safety is on. I load a round into my chamber and lean over the hood of the truck with my rifle pointed at the fools in the window. They jump back inside and close the window.

In a few minutes, eight police cars come sliding up beside us. An old silver-haired police lieutenant in his late forties comes up to me and asks what I've got. I tell him, and he sends a couple of his men to the rear of the house. He then tells me to come with him as he heads toward the front door of the house. I tell the private to stay with the truck and the repairman and guard them.

We reach the front door, and the old police lieutenant draws a nickel-plated revolver and just opens the door and walks into the living room followed by some of his men and me. The lieutenant shouts that it's the police, but no one appears. The lieutenant has his men search the downstairs, and they find nothing. I say they all still must be upstairs. The lieutenant says that we will go up there and see. He tells me to go first up the stairs with that big M-14. I'm surprised. I wish this M-14 was fully automatic, but it's not; it's semi only. I start up the stairs with the rifle at the ready. The old lieutenant is right behind me with his pistol ready. A couple of other policemen follow the lieutenant.

We arrive at the upstairs landing, the lieutenant calls out, a door opens, and the four White guys come out with their hands up. The lieutenant asks them what they were doing, and one of them says "nothing." The lieutenant says that he is lying, that the Army Sergeant here said, "You were hanging out the windows with rifles and beer." The other policemen find their weapons and unload them. They also find their beer and pour it out. The lieutenant is chewing the guys out big-time. One of the guys tries to say that they believed that the riot was over. The lieutenant calls him a liar and tells the men that if the police get another call to this location, they are going to lock up everyone in the house and take their guns. The men all hang their heads. The police and I walk outside, and the lieutenant thanks me, and they all leave. The private, repairman, and I get back into the truck and continue on with our duties.

We stop at another location to repair lights, and an army jeep pulls up with a Captain in the passenger's seat. He has no camouflage cover on his helmet, so I assume that he and his people are National Guard. He grins and asks what's going on. I come to attention, salute, and say, "Sergeant Fedrick, Hundred and Ninety-Seventh Infantry Brigade out of Fort Benning, Georgia, Sir." The Captain seems surprised and tries to return my salute first with his left hand and then his right. I get the idea that he has never saluted before. I explain about our detail, and he says okay. They start to leave, and I come to attention and salute, and the Captain does a better job returning it this time.

A few days later, the riot seems to be over. The brigade packs the vehicles; and we drive to Andrews Air Force Base, load on planes, and return to Fort Benning. When we arrive back in the company area, it takes us days to unpack. It only took us hours to pack it all, but then that was an emergency. The riot was not very exciting, just hard work. It is really boring to be back in the same boring routine again. I am wondering what became of the letters that I wrote. Well, at least they are paying me. I wonder how people stand the peace time army.

A few weeks go by, and I am ordered to report to the Company Commander. I walk into his office, come to attention, salute, and say, "Sergeant Fedrick reporting as ordered, Sir." The Captain looks puzzled and tells me that he has received orders that I am to put on my dress uniform with all my ribbons, awards, and badges and report to main post. I am to see the post Command Sergeant Major, Walter Cannon. He is the senior enlisted man on post and is in charge of some thirty-five thousand soldiers. I know who he is. Before I departed Vietnam, he was the Command Sergeant Major of the First Infantry Division. He had replaced Sergeant Major William Woolridge who departed Vietnam to become the First Sergeant Major of the Army.

I tell the Captain that I know what it is about. I tell him about my three missing 1049s and the eight letters that I wrote. The captain turns pale and sits back in his chair. His mouth is hanging open. I ask him if he thinks I am going to prison. He says he doesn't know but that I better get to main post as quickly as I can. I salute, turn, and head for my room to put on my dress uniform. I am really afraid that I'm going to be locked up. Well, I had promised myself that I was either going to Vietnam or jail.

I drive to main post but keep within the speed limit. I don't need to get a ticket from the military police. I park and walk into the infantry center. It is huge, but I've been there before while running errands. I find the post Command Sergeant Major's office and walk in.

The outer office is really large with a dozen clerks looking very busy. The front desk is manned by a large old Master Sergeant with blond hair. He looks like a bulldog. I walk up to him and tell him who I am and that I have orders to see Sergeant Major Cannon. He looks me up and down with distaste and says to me, "Young Buck Sergeant, do you know your chain of command?" I tell him I do. He says, apparently, I do not. He then has a clerk check to see if the Sergeant Major is ready for me. My stomach is in knots. The clerk says the Sergeant Major is ready for me. I walk into the Sergeant Major's office, and I see him. He is a much older man in his late forties, average sized with a gray-brown crew cut. He is in his shirt-sleeves and tie. His uniform coat is hanging on a hanger from a hat rack. I have never seen so many ribbons on a uniform coat in my life. I see ribbons from WWII, Korea, and Vietnam. I am in awe.

The old man smiles at me and says, "Son, come over here and talk to old Walter." He sounds country as a butter bean. I think he is just leading me on before he drops the hammer and calls in the military police. He has me sit down, and he sits in front of me. He says, "Son, why did you write all those old letters when you could have just come and talked to old Walter?" I try to tell him about my "lost" 1049s and my desire to just return to Vietnam and put my experience to use. He says, "Then you just want to go back to the Eighteenth Infantry and the First Division?" I tell him that is correct.

He then gets on the phone and calls the Sergeant Major of the Army, William Woolridge at the Pentagon. I am stunned. He gets Sergeant Major Woolridge on the other end of the line and says, "Bill, this is old Walter down here at Fort Benning. I've got that young Buck Sergeant that wrote all those letters sitting here with me. Bill, all he wants is to go back to his unit in the First Infantry Division. Some idiot lost all three of his 1049 requests." He listens on the phone for a minute and then asks me if I can clear post today. I tell him I can try. He then asks me how much home leave I need. I ask for ten days. He then says to the phone, "Yeah, Bill, you are going to teletype his orders right now. Bill, you'all come see us you hear." Sergeant Major Cannon then turns to me and tells me to see that old Master Sergeant out front that my orders should be coming in now. I shake his hand and thank him. He laughs and says, "Next time, son, just come see your Sergeant Major. We run the whole Army you know." I stop at the old Master Sergeant's desk, and he hands me my orders without saying a word, and I leave.

I have to clear numerous places on post to show that I owe no bills. Somehow, I manage to do it and still return to my company's orderly room before the end of the duty day. I advise the First Sergeant that I have cleared post and am on my way to Vietnam after a few days in Memphis. I clear out my room and place all my belongings in my 1965 Chevrolet. I call home before I start the nine-hour drive to Memphis. I tell my family that I am going back to Vietnam after a few days of leave. I lie and tell them that I will be in operations when I return to Vietnam and will be somewhat to the rear. That seems to ease their fears. I sure hope I don't get killed. They would never forgive me.

In a few days, I fly to Fort Dix, New Jersey, and report in to the "repo depot." It usually takes a day or two for them to get you on a plane for Vietnam. I make my first formation and am surprised to see Staff Sergeant Bass from my first tour holding the formation. He reads off a list of names going out that morning and advises that the next formation will be after noon chow. He dismisses the formation, and I walk up to him and say, "Staff Sergeant Bass." He turns to me and growls, "What do you want, young Buck Sergeant?" Then he recognizes me, grabs, and hugs me while shouting my name. We then talk, and I tell him I'm heading over for a second tour. He then loads me in his car and takes me to a firing range where SFC John Hall is in charge. He was our Platoon Sergeant in Vietnam. The range is closed, and then Staff Sergeant Bass takes me by Sergeant First Class Hall's quarters, but no one is there. I tell Staff Sergeant Bass to tell Sergeant First Class Hall that I am so sorry I missed him. Staff Sergeant Bass then takes me to lunch at the NCO Club. We then return for the afternoon formation, and my name is not called. Another formation is held after evening chow, and Staff Sergeant Bass does not hold this formation. Another NCO does and calls my name. I go back to the barracks, get my duffle bag, and report to the bus that will carry me to the plane.

I board the plane, and unlike the first time, I went over about a third of the soldiers on board have stripes and Vietnam Service and Campaign ribbons on their uniforms. They, like me, are going over for their second tour. Well, at least this time I know what to expect.

CHAPTER 24

The Drunks

Summer 1968

I'm at Di An on my second tour. I'm a sergeant E-5, and I am twenty-one years old, one of the oldest guys in the unit. I am in Third Platoon, and we are working day patrols out of Di An. It is evening time, and we are in our hooch. Some of the guys have already gone to sleep on their cots. A couple of guys are talking. I am sitting on my cot reading a Louis L'Amour western novel. There's laughter and noise outside, but we have got a troop of the First of the Fourth Calvary parked near us with their tanks and armored personnel carriers. The cavalry is always loud, but it sure is good to have them in the area. They have saved my bacon a couple of times on my first tour.

Suddenly, the north door of our hooch flies open, and five soldiers I have never seen before storm in. Four are White, and one is Black. They are all very drunk. The soldier in the middle is very tall and thin, and his hair is very blond. I see he has specialist 5 rank on his shirt. That is the same pay grade as my sergeant E-5, but he is not an NCO, just a senior specialist. He is shouting, "Who in here called the First of the Fourth SOBs?" I shout back at him that no one in here has said a word. He has got the wrong hooch. He shouts back that I am a lying SOB. I shout at him, "That is Sergeant SOB," to him. They have apparently had someone shout at them from another hooch and, in their drunken state, have mistaken which hooch the shout came from.

There is a short stocky White soldier standing to the right of the tall soldier. He is so drunk I can't understand his roaring slurred speech. The Black soldier is a real "moose." He is bigger than I am, and he is trying to curse us but is so drunk he's having trouble saying his words. The other two White soldiers are also shouting curses and threats at us. I am standing ten feet from the five of them shouting for them to get out of our hooch. My guys are starting to get up off their cots; some awaken from sleep. I am very concerned. We have these guys outnumbered, more than two to one. That tells me that these guys are armed. Even drunk I don't believe that they would be this aggressive if they weren't packing. My rifle is lying on my cot by my knee. According to SOP when in base camp, we take the magazine out of our weapons. My magazine is lying on the cot beside my weapon. I know that it would take too long to seat my magazine and load a round into the chamber. This is really getting scary.

The tall specialist 5 shouts, "How long have you been in-country, big man?" I shout back at him, "Which time?" He stops in mid-shout and waves his hand. His four men quiet down. The tall specialist 5 looks at me and asks me if this is my second tour. I tell him that it is. He asks what unit I was with on my first tour. I tell him I was in this unit, B-2-18. He gives me a questioning look and asks me if I was up on Highway 13 in the summer and fall of 1966. I tell him that I sure was. A huge grin spreads over his face, and he shouts, "Homeboy." He then runs over and hugs me, saying he was up there, too, with the First of Fourth Cavalry. His four friends are also trying to hug me. I shout to my guys to break the beer out of our cooler, that we have "kinfolk" visiting. A party breaks out with the cavalry guys trying to hug all my guys. I make sure each one of the cavalry guys has a cold beer in their hands as the tall specialist 5 and I talk about the big battles back in 1966.

The drunks all get a second one of our beers. They are having a good time now. The specialist 5 shows me that he's carrying a .25-caliber automatic in a shoulder holster under his shirt. The short stocky soldier and one of the other White soldiers raise their shirts, exposing

.45-caliber pistols in their waistbands. The big Black soldier and the other White guy show us switchblade knives that they are carrying. I was right; these guys were "loaded for bear and drunk as lords."

The specialist 5 tells his people that they have to get back to their APC (armored personnel carrier) that they are moving out early in the morning. They stagger out the door with us slapping them on the back and telling them to come again. They lean on each other and begin singing as they stagger toward their area.

After they are gone, I look at my guys and tell them that was a close call. It could have been a tragedy. If it had gone bad, they would have "popped" two or three of us before we got our rifles going. We would have then "waxed" all five of them. Then we would have had seven of eight dead Americans from each other's hands over nothing. Drunk armed nineteen-year-old men are very dangerous. I tell the guys that we need to get some sleep, that we have another patrol early in the morning.

We then hear that an ambush patrol from Second Platoon is in heavy contact somewhere "out there." We gear up, ready to go to their aid. We then get the word to stand down. The fight seems to be over. We get the word that the Second Platoon has two wounded and they are dusting off by helicopter. We also hear that they have a body count of enemy soldiers.

The next morning, we get the word as to what happened with Second Platoon. They had an ambush set up on a small dirt road near a village. The machine gun position on one end of the ambush consisted of Mahosky on the machine gun. He's a tall raw-boned blond with thick eyeglasses from Pennsylvania. He has the reputation as a very good gunner. Freeman, a short stocky, friendly Black soldier, is his assistant gunner. Morrison is the M-79 man. He's a stocky brown-haired soldier from Oregon. Landweir is an average-sized light-haired soldier from New York. The man in charge of the position is a medium-tall sergeant E-5 with dark hair.

They are close to the road and have set out two claymore mines down from them and angled out facing the road. These mines are also close to the road. Then they see an enemy squad walking down the road in single file coming toward them. The sergeant grabs the detonators for the two claymores and readies them to fire, one in each hand. Mahosky tells everyone to hold their fire until the enemy gets very close. He whispers to the others that you do not get a body count unless the enemy is very close.

They observe that there are nine enemy soldiers with eight carrying AK-47s or SKS carbines. The ninth soldier has an RPG (shoulder-fired rocket launcher). The other guys say that the closer the enemy gets, the bigger Mahosky's smile becomes. When the enemy point man is almost on top of them, Mahosky opens fire with the M-60 machine gun. His tracer rounds strike the point man in the torso, exit out his back, and hits the second man in the file. The other guys open fire, and the sergeant sets off both claymores. The claymores are a little too close to the road to get a good spread, but their pellets shred the legs on two of the enemy soldiers.

The enemy has tough professionals and fires right back; even their wounded are firing. The RPG man fires his rocket, and it explodes near the machine gun position. Landweir takes a hit in the chest and goes down. Morrison is hit in the hand but spins around and keeps firing the M-79.

Then Mahosky *stands up* and steps out onto the road, all without taking his finger off the trigger of the machine gun. A steady stream of tracer rounds is coming from the muzzle of the gun. Morrison then grabs the more badly wounded Landweir's rifle and lunges out onto the road with Mahosky. They are both firing and walking toward the enemy soldiers; many of whom are down on the road.

The three hundred round belt of ammo in the gun runs out, but it's over all in a little over half a minute. Seven enemy soldiers lie dead on the road, and two have escaped. The Second Platoon recovers half a dozen enemy rifles and an RPG. They then call in a dust-off helicopter for Morrison and Landweir. Both of whom will return to the platoon when their wounds heal. The Second Platoon then moves to a secondary ambush location and set up for the rest of the night. The rest of the night is quiet.

CHAPTER 25

The Plantation

Summer 1968

I am back in Vietnam on my second tour. I am a sergeant E-5 and am now twenty-one years old. I have managed to get back with Bravo Company, Second Eighteenth, First Infantry Division. They have placed me in Third Platoon, instead of Second Platoon, but at least I'm back with the company. It is good to be back. Those months I spent at Fort Benning, Georgia, between my tours were the most boring of my life.

There are twice as many soldiers in Vietnam now as there were on my first tour. There are over half a million soldiers in-country. We are working very differently from my first tour. The First Cavalry Division, the Twenty-Fifth Infantry/Division, the Eleventh Armored Cavalry Regiment are working up north around the Cambodian border. The First Division's First and Third Brigades are with them. They are breaking up the large enemy units as they enter South Vietnam from Cambodia.

Down near Saigon, the First Division's Second Brigade (us) along with the 199th Infantry Brigade and the Australians and New Zealanders are guarding the approaches to the capital. Each battalion now has a Delta Company as well as Alpha, Bravo, and Charlie Companies. Each battalion in the Second Brigade (First-Eighteenth, Second-Eighteenth, and Second-Sixteenth) has an area of responsibility. The Second-Eighteenth works companies out of Di An, the Thu Duc Water Plant, VC Island, and a fourth perimeter along a tiny road in the middle of nowhere. Each company works each area for about six weeks, and then the companies all switch. This keeps the companies from becoming stale.

The six weeks Bravo Company is at a given location, we work one rifle platoon on daytime squad patrols and two rifle platoons work squad night ambushes. This leaves the day platoon and the mortar platoon to secure the perimeter during the night. This makes things a lot better than my first tour. We get a hot meal nearly every day and more sleep. The drawback is we are usually in the mud even in the dry season. We have a lot of swamp and also rice paddies in our area.

We are working out of Di An and have night ambush. We head out after dark. The Lieutenant is with us and a machine gun crew. The Lieutenant is working the compass and map. We walk a long time and finally arrive at our ambush location. It appears to be some kind of plantation with small trees about eight feet high planted in rows. They are not fruit trees, and I think that they are tea bushes, but I do not know. There is a twenty-foot-wide road running east and west in the plantation and a small road about ten feet wide running north and south that crosses the wider road.

We set up northwest of the intersection. The Lieutenant's position is facing the small road, and the machine gun is facing the wide road. I've got the position facing the rear into the rows of trees. I have three other men in my position. Doug "Duke" Scallions, an average-sized soldier with curly brown hair and an olive complexion, is from Georgia and is one of the best soldiers in the platoon. The second soldier is a small quick-moving soldier with blond hair named Tom. The third soldier is the Third Platoon's Kit Carson Scout. This is a new program that has happened since my first tour. A Kit Carson Scout is a former VC (Viet Cong) or NVA (North Vietnamese Army) soldier that has "rallied" to our side. They have been put through a training program, and then one each has been placed in American rifle platoons. I don't trust the guy, but the Third Platoon guys swear by "Chin." His story is that he was a schoolteacher and was "drafted" into the elite VC Phu Loi Battalion. He served with them for two years and then surrendered to American forces. He is a very big Vietnamese. He is five feet eight and about 135 pounds. He is also an old guy of thirty-five.

The moon is out even as a storm threatens in the west. We can see a good way out into the trees with the moonlight. We've only been in position about thirty minutes when I see something move in the little trees about a one hundred meters from our position. I whisper to the other guys, Tom on my right and Duke on my left, to look; and they see them too. A file of men is spread out and walking in the trees from our left to our right. I whisper to Duke to crawl back to the Lieutenant and tell him what we have and bring the machine gun back with him. He crawls off; and Tom, Chin, and I keep our rifles trained on the people in the distance. In a minute, Duke crawls back and tells me that the Lieutenant says just to monitor the situation. *Monitor the situation!* I grab Duke and growl at him to go back and bring me a machine gun. He rises to a crouch and starts toward the machine gun position, and the enemy see him move. They open fire on us. Tom, Chin, and I and then Duke return fire. I'm knocking out bursts with the big M-14 beating against my right shoulder. I notice that the other three guys are firing fully automatic with their M-16s. On my first tour, we didn't fire the M-16 on automatic. It jammed way too fast if we did. I have noticed that the M-16s the guys carry now look a lot different from the ones we had on my first tour.

The enemy muzzle flashes are winking at us in long bursts. Rounds are hitting around us as the Lieutenant, his radioman, and the machine gun crew fall in among us. They all open up on automatic. The machine gunner is firing long bursts, but I notice his tracer rounds are floating about three feet above the enemy positions. I crawl over to him, grab his collar, and shout into his ear that he needs to lower his fire and hit the ground around the enemy muzzle flashes. He changes his grip on the gun and puts out a long burst that kicks up dirt around the enemy positions. I shout that he is on target and to keep it up.

I start back putting out fire with the M-14. All our tracers are hitting around the enemy positions. How are they surviving?

Suddenly, we realize that we are getting no return fire. We see nothing moving and slack off on our fire. Have we killed all the enemy? We have not seen them run away. We have flares hanging in the air, so we can see pretty well.

The Lieutenant tells me to take a team and search the kill zone. My guts tighten up. I tell Tom, Duke, and Chin that we will move two at a time covering one another. Tom and I and then Duke and Chin. We will move about twenty feet at a time while the other two cover us. Tom and I move out about twenty feet and drop with our weapons ready. Duke and Chin move up on line with us and drop. We lay there a few seconds, and then I tell Duke and Chin to move. They do and drop. Tom and I move up even with them and drop. Tom and I then move. We are not receiving incoming fire, and I hope that the enemy is not just waiting for us to get closer.

We reach the area where the enemy was located, and I see what has happened. There is a small footpath running east and west, and beside it is what I guess is a small irrigation ditch. The ditch is about two feet wide and two feet deep—just big enough for small enemy soldiers to take cover in. There are a lot of expended rifle shells lying around. I also see a pair of tan pants in the ditch. I pick them up and see that they are soaked in blood and have bullet holes in the front. We have hit one of them! I hand the NVA uniform pants to Tom and tell him that we have hit at least one of them. We then move back to the Lieutenant's position two by two, just like we've moved up.

We reach the Lieutenant, and I report what we found. A ditch and NVA uniform pants with blood on them and bullet holes in them. I ask Tom what he did with the pants, and he says he threw them down. No big thing, the Lieutenant calls it in on the radio, and we get ready to move. The Lieutenant says we will move across the small road two at a time and set up on the northeast corner of the intersection much like we had set up on the other side of the road. We wait until the flares die out and then move across the road two at a time.

Suddenly, the rain comes in great cold sheets. I shake with the cold and just keep looking out into the black night and the cold rain. I cannot see five feet. If the enemy tries to find us, they are going to have to be very close for us to see each other. The rain falls all night and slows up just before dawn. I cannot wait for daylight and us moving back to base camp. Before morning, we hear heavy firing in the distance. Another squad has ambushed an enemy squad at close range.

The day finally breaks gray and cold. The Lieutenant comes over and tells us that they are bringing in a scout dog team to track the enemy squad from last night. I am amazed—it rained hard all night. They will not be able to find any scent. I tell the Lieutenant this, and he says there is nothing he can do. The order comes from battalion level.

We move out and secure the intersection. In about an hour, a helicopter lands, and a soldier and a large black dog exit. We form up with him and move into the ambush site looking for booby traps and mines. We locate the enemy pants now washed clean. The K-9 soldier works the dog all-round the ditch and the pants but says the dog cannot find a scent. I tell him we have gotten about five inches of rain since the ambush. He is amazed and asks why they sent for him and his dog. I tell him it is a mystery to me that the order came from battalion. He laughs and shakes his head.

We form up and start to walk back to base camp with the dog and his handler. The dog is big and has a German Shepherd head but is black as sin. I ask the handler what kind of dog he is, and the handler tells me he's half German Shepherd and half Lab.

As we move toward the perimeter, we come across the scene of the other "blown" ambush. We had heard the gunfire from the ambush before daylight. Our Company Commander is there along with a squad from another platoon. There is also a squad of ARVN soldiers (South Vietnamese Army) with our guys. Were they set up together?

There is a trail through the elephant grass where they had the ambush set up. On and in the grass beside the trail are the results of the ambush. There are eight dead enemy soldiers scattered about. Three of them are lying close together with one lying over the top of another. One is missing an arm. Another is lying a way up from those three, and half his head is gone. Another body is further up, and apparently, he was wounded and tried to crawl away before he bled out. He has at least twenty feet of his intestines stretched along the trail behind him. All eight enemy soldiers are riddled with bullets, grenade fragments, and pellets from claymore mines. The other soldiers have placed the enemy's rifles and web gear in a pile. Their equipment is as bullet riddled as their bodies.

Our Company Commander and the ARVN Lieutenant are standing on the pile of three dead enemy soldiers. They are smiling, and our troops and ARVN soldiers are taking photos of them as the officers take up poses with their weapons. It reminds me of big-game hunters posing with dead lions—except these enemy soldiers were much more dangerous than lions.

I hear a strange noise and look around. I see one of the new guys on his knees in the grass throwing up. I walk over and help the new guy to his feet. He says, "Sergeant, this is terrible. I've never seen a dead person before. I've never even been to a funeral." I tell him, "Troop, this is not terrible. This is wonderful. None of these eight enemy soldiers will ever kill you or any other American. This is a good day for us and a very bad day for them. This makes your chances of getting home alive much better." We then form up and head back toward the perimeter.

We arrive back at base camp and clean our weapons, and I check our ammo resupply needs. I find that I have fired ten magazines or two hundred rounds. That left me ten magazines or two hundred rounds. I have fired up all my magazines that were loaded with duplex ammo. Most of the other riflemen have fired six to eight magazines. The M-79 man has fired ten shells. The machine gunner has fired four hundred rounds. I turn my ammo request over to the company First Sergeant. I know I will not get duplex ammo on the resupply, so I walk to the battalion ammo supply point. Duplex ammo is hard to come by and is mostly used by chopper gunners. But I really like having thirty-six projectiles coming out of a twenty-round magazine instead of twenty projectiles. There's a Staff Sergeant E-6 in charge of the ammo distribution point. The story is that he has been in the Army about twelve years, so he was too young for the Korean War. This is his first tour in Vietnam, and he was assigned to one of the other companies in the battalion. He spent a couple of months in the field and received his Combat Infantry Badge, but he could not deal with the fear and danger of combat. The brass took pity on him and found him this good rear job at the ammo distribution point.

I approach the Staff Sergeant and ask him if he has any 7.62 duplex ammo. He asks me what I need it for, that only a few days before he had given me two hundred rounds of duplex ammo. I tell him that I know that, but I have shot those up. He tells me that I should use regular ball ammo on the range. I look at him like he has lost his mind and tell him that I haven't been to a range since I was at Fort Benning. I inform him that I fired all that duplex the night before in a firefight with enemy soldiers. He looks embarrassed and tells me to get a two-hundred-round can of duplex but no more than that. He says he is low on duplex ammo. I tell him thanks, pick up a can, and head back to my tent. I load my empty magazines with the duplex and set these magazines up so they will be the first I fire. I then crash and try in get some sleep in the heat of the day. We have another ambush tonight.

CHAPTER 26

The Swamp

Summer 1968

I am a twenty-one-year-old sergeant E-5 on my second tour of duty with Bravo Company, Second Battalion, Eighteenth Infantry Regiment, First Infantry Division, the "Big Red One." On returning, I have been placed in Third Platoon, instead of Second Platoon; but at least I'm back in the company.

We are working day patrols out of our main base camp at Di An. The Lieutenant has taken half the platoon, and the platoon sergeant has taken the other half on patrols in two different areas. I'm the senior NCO with the Lieutenant's patrol. We are working the swamp attempting to locate enemy base camps. We have been told that there are elements of the NVA Fifth Infantry Division in this area. These enemy soldiers came down the Ho Chi Min Trail with two uniforms, one pair of boots, and their weapons. When these uniforms wear out, they wear what they can; sometimes uniforms made in enemy base camps in Cambodia and sometimes black pajamas. They also wear sandals or go barefoot after their boots are gone. Most of the supplies coming down the trail are weapons and ammo, so they wear what they can.

We are working in muddy swamp filled with clumps of bushes and small trees. The mud is ankle deep with each step we take. We are working in two files. The Lieutenant has the one on the left. He is second in the file. His point man is SPC4 Hardy, a six-foot, 180-pound Black soldier with a medium complexion. He is a very good soldier and likes to run point carrying an M-79. I have not seen this before, but if Hardy likes being up front with just a single-shot M-79, then more power to him. We have recommended that Hardy be promoted to sergeant E-5.

I've noticed since I've been back that they have taken the XM-148s out of the field. This was an M-16 with an M-79 attached under the barrel of the M-16. This replaced the M-79 just before I left the first time. This was supposed to give the M-79-man close personal protection with the M-16. The XM-148 man was supposed to carry a full load of M-16 ammo and half a load of M-79 ammo. I noticed before I left that in most of the squads, the XM-148 men were only carrying five or six rounds for the M-79 and almost never firing that weapon. The squad leaders let this slide. A major failing in leadership on their part. You need M-79 rounds going out in a firefight. Apparently, some one noticed this and put the M-79 back into service and took up the XM-148.

I'm running point in the right file with my M-14 with the machine gunner behind me. We are coming up on two large clumps of bushes, one to our left front and one to our front.

Suddenly, Hardy says look! I look to the left and see a Vietnamese man's head sticking out of the large clump of bushes to our left front. The Lieutenant shouts, "Fire!" I jump to the right to get Hardy out of my line of fire as the gook ducks back into the brush. Hardy fires a HE (high explosive) round, and I fire a twenty-round burst into the clump of brush. I am trying to shove a fresh magazine into my rifle, and Hardy is reloading his M-79 *when* I see them! Six gooks darting from the clump of brush to our left front to the clump of brush in front of us. Two are wearing NVA tan shirts and the others black pajamas. All six are carrying rifles. They duck into the brush just as I seat my magazine and fire a twenty-round burst into the thicket, and Hardy fires a HE round. The Lieutenant is firing, and the machine gunner has moved up and is spraying the brush with fire. I throw a hand grenade into the first clump of bushes just in case some gooks did not run with the six that I saw.

Without a word being said, we break into two groups—the right file with me and the left file with the Lieutenant. We lay down a heavy base of fire, and then the two groups advance on line, one group at a time firing while the other group puts out even more covering fire. I am proud of these guys. Everyone here except the Lieutenant and me is a draftee, and they are all doing a professional job.

The enemy is returning our fire with AK-47s, and it's pretty heavy. I wonder if a second squad of enemy soldiers were in the second clump of brush when we jumped the first group. I think not. If there were that many enemy troops, they would have stood and fought until they had wounded one or two of us and then made their escape when we were slowed down.

Everyone is firing on automatic, and most of the fire are twenty-round bursts. Those tracer rounds make it easy to see where your rounds are hitting so you know where you are firing. I'm knocking out twenty-round bursts with the M-14 using my great weight to hold the barrel down as I fire from the waist. I have only every fifth round as a tracer, but I can still see where my rounds are hitting.

We are getting glimpses of the enemy soldiers through the brush. They are about forty to fifty meters ahead of us in the brush and mud and are putting a lot of AK fire back at us. I am surprised that we have not killed any of the enemy or had any of our men hit yet with the amount of fire being exchanged.

I pass by a tree on my right about six inches thick. It's about a foot to my right when AK rounds slap into the tree. A gook has me in his sights! He just put too much finger on his trigger, and that threw his rounds to his left and saved my life. I dive forward toward the ground, putting my rifle out to break my fall. I sink my M-14 and my arms nearly to my elbows in the soft mud. I jerk my rifle out of the mud and lumber to my feet. My rifle has two inches of mud covering it. I hit my rifle against a tree knocking some of the mud from it. I then fire my rifle, and there is one shot and then nothing. I work the bolt and fire. Again, just one shot. The mud has downgraded my rifle to a bolt action rifle. Well, at least I still have a weapon. I keep firing single shots as fast as I can work the bolt as we leapfrog after the enemy.

We come to a creek. It is about twenty feet across and four-feet deep. I see a spot of blood on the near side bank. We have hit at least one of the enemy! We see that the enemy soldiers have not climbed out on the far bank, because there are no marks in the mud. They have gone to the left or right in the stream. I shout to the Lieutenant that I will take my half of the troops and go to the right and he can take the other half and go left. He says no. We only have one radio and one machine gun and there are only sixteen of us, we don't need to have an eight-man squad caught without a radio or one without a machine gun. He is right. I just had my blood up. He says for everyone to catch their breath, and then we will all go left.

Everyone faces out and start drinking water while they watch. I take this chance to do an ammo check. I check with each of the guys and find that some have fired four or five magazines and others have fired eleven or twelve.

The ones who have only fired a few magazines, I take some of their loaded magazines and give them to the guys who are low on ammo. I check with Specialist 4 Hardy and find that he only has eight shells left for his M-79. Damn, he has fired at least thirty-two of the little shells! I check with the other M-79 man, and he has twenty-five shells left. I take my helmet off and tell him to drop eight of his shells into my helmet, and I will take them to Hardy. Hardy really lights up when I bring him the shells. He was worried about running out of ammo. I then check the machine gunner and find that he only has four hundred rounds left for the gun. I tell him if we make contact again with the enemy to fire short bursts.

I check my own ammo and find that I have ten loaded magazines and ten empty ones for the M-14. If my rifle had not gone into bolt action mode, I might have only six or seven loaded magazines left. I also take my rifle and wash it as much as I can in the creek. I hope I have automatic mode back. If we find the enemy again, I will find out.

We saddle up and patrol along the creek to the left watching both sides of the bank for signs that someone has crawled out. We see nothing. We patrol along the creek for about an hour without seeing or hearing anything. The creek keeps getting smaller, and I have decided that we've gone the wrong way. Then we exit the swamp and move into some elephant grass, and the creek completely peters out. We have chosen the wrong way.

We patrol back to base camp and drop our gear, and everyone starts cleaning their weapons. I get an ammo count and turn my ammo request into the First Sergeant. I then clean the M-14. I am making a big decision. I love the M-14, but the rifle and twenty magazines weigh forty pounds. It's all I can carry, and I want more ammo with me. The reasons I went to the M-14 on my first tour was that it didn't jam and you can fire it on automatic.

The army has made a lot of improvements on the M-16 in the last year and a half. I have noticed since I've returned to the company that everyone fires their M-16 on automatic and they do not jam.

The M-16 weighs seven pounds, and each loaded magazine weighs a half a pound. Therefore, the rifle and twenty magazines would weigh seventeen pounds. I am thinking of thirty-one magazines which would weigh twenty-three pounds with my rifle. If my rifle and ammo weigh only twenty-three pounds, then I can carry two hundred rounds or twelve pounds for the machine gun. Even with the ammo for the gun, I will be carrying five pounds less weight than I've been carrying with the M-14. We need the extra ammo for the gun, and I need 620 rounds for my rifle instead of the 400 I've been carrying with the M-14.

I take my M-14 and my twenty magazines down to the supply room and tell the Supply Sergeant I want to turn them in and draw an M-16 and thirty-one magazines. He takes the M-14 and gives me a brand-new M-16 and thirty-one magazines. I wonder why we only have twenty-round magazines for the M-16. Thirty-round magazines exist, but they do not issue them to us. The enemy's AK-47 has a thirty-round magazine, and we have to go up against them with a twenty-round magazine. I believe that someone at the Pentagon or in Washington is saving money by us firing less ammo at the cost of some of our lives.

I'm about to return to my hooch when I'm approached by a Sergeant E-5 from Second Platoon. He says he needs to talk to me. I tell him to go ahead. He tells me that he does not get along with the guys in Second Platoon and his two best friends in the company are in Third Platoon. He asks me if I would switch platoons with him if he can swing the deal. I think a minute. I've gotten comfortable with the guys in Third Platoon, but this guy really wants to switch platoons, and I was in Second Platoon on my first tour. I've also heard that there are some great guys and fine soldiers in Second Platoon. I tell him that I will switch with him. He says that he already has it arranged, that I just need to move my gear to the Second Platoon hooch.

I pick up my gear and move it to Second Platoon area and start meeting the guys. They seem friendly. The platoon leader is a tiny lieutenant with brown hair. The Platoon Sergeant is a Sergeant First Class E-7 with over nineteen years in the Army. He entered the army in the fall of 1948, three years after the end of WWII. He spent the Korean War, 1950–1953, stationed with the army in Germany, so he had eight months left till retirement when he got orders to Vietnam. He has a couple of months left to go now. He seems squared away and an okay guy. We have no Staff Sergeant E-6s in Second Platoon, and I'm the Senior Sergeant E-5.

Two of the other Sergeant E-5s are Jim Morris and Ted Townsend. Morris is an average-sized guy from Oregon. He has flaming red hair and is the best NCO in the platoon. He is an instant NCO, having been sent to the twelve-week NCO Academy after he finished infantry training. The Army has come up with this program because the army has grown so fast that there are no NCOs in the platoons in Vietnam and by the time a private soldier has worked his way up to Sergeant in Vietnam it's time for him to rotate home. Just like it was for me and my friends on my first tour.

Ted Townsend is an average-sized blond soldier from Indiana. He is older than anyone in the platoon except the Platoon Sergeant. He is twenty-four and was drafted later than most guys. He is a good soldier and a fine squad leader. I find out that Morris and Townsend both are like me. They both carry machine gun ammo.

Some Sergeants refuse to do this because they are Sergeants. I think this is stupid. That two hundred rounds of machine gun ammo I carry might save MY life.

The machine gunners are Chet Mahosky from Pennsylvania and Ken Bissenden from Utah. Chet is tall, is blond, and wears very thick glasses. He has the reputation of being one of the very few men who likes combat. It is said that he is always smiling during a firefight. Ken is nearly as tall as me but weighs 135 pounds. He is very strong for being so thin and handles the twenty-three-pound M-60 like a toy. He is said to be steady as a stone when the chips are down.

We have two brand-new guys in the platoon. Rocky is an Italian with a huge smile and a very outgoing personality. Richard "Big Jake" Jacobs is a big teenager from Missouri. He has Black hair and light eyes and is built like a bull elk. He is also the most self-assured young man that I've seen. It is looking like I have made a good move.

Di An has really changed since my first tour. When I was here before, they had a large beer tent where guys in the rear could go and drink a beer or Coke and listen to a jukebox. They have now built the Bamboo Inn. It's a huge building with a stage for bands about fifty cheap tables, each with six or eight chairs at each one. There is also a long L-shaped bar.

The word is that there will be a Philippine band there tonight with singers. I have no duty tonight, so I'm thinking about going down and listening to the music. I eat evening chow and walk over to the inn. My rifle is lying on my cot in the hooch. We are not allowed to carry our rifles to the Bamboo Inn. But I am carrying a survival knife in a sheath on my pants belt under my shirt.

I walk into the inn, and the band is knocking out rock and roll tunes. They sound pretty good. The place is packed. There are soldiers here from the Second-Eighteenth, First-Eighteenth, Second-Sixteenth, and the artillery. There must be three hundred guys here. I guess all the soldiers from these units who are not out on operations or on guard duty are here.

I find a place at the bar and order a Coke. The bartender places the Coke down, and I give him five cents in Military Payment Certificates. I turn and place my back against the bar and listen to the music. This place is *loud*. All the tables are full as is the bar. About 25 percent of the soldiers here appear to be Black, and another 25 percent are Hispanic. The other 50 percent are White guys. Everyone is having a great time. I do notice that the majority of the tables seem to be segregated but not all.

The band takes a break and leaves the stage. The noise is less now. But everyone is still loud. In the middle of the tables, I see a very drunk brown-haired White soldier stand up and tell the guys at his table that he has to go to the latrine. He stumbles toward the latrine going by a table where six Black guys sit. Apparently, he steps on one of the Black soldier's foot. The Black soldier jumps up cursing the drunk for stepping on his foot. The drunk smiles and says, "Damn, boy, I'm sorry." The Black guy knocks the drunk down with his fist, and in a blink of an eye, all three hundred guys in the club are swinging fists and chairs. A few guys break for the doors, but most stay and fight it out. I have never seen a fight this big. I stand with my back against the bar and drink my Coke with my left hand as I watch hundreds of guys slug, kick, and stomp each other. Chairs and tables are flying everywhere. A big Black soldier from Bravo's First Platoon jumps up on the stage, picks up the microphone, and begins to sing off-key.

Then I start seeing the flash of knives in the lights. This is getting serious. I reach down, take my knife out, and hold it behind my right leg with my right hand with the cutting edge up. I am not fighting, but I do not intend to let anyone hurt me.

Suddenly, a large Black guy and a large White guy fall against the bar next to me. They are slugging it out. They then fight over to the jukebox, and I hear the White guy's nose break. This stuns the White guy, and then the Black guy hits him with two big right hands to the left eye. The White guy drops with his entire left eyebrow laid open. Then I realize that the Black guy is from Bravo's Third Platoon. A White guy from Third Platoon runs up and grabs the Black guy and shouts, "Buddy, let's get out of here. The military police are coming." They turn arm in arm and run out the door. The fight starts breaking up, and I see White guys helping injured Black guys to get away and Black guys helping injured White guys to escape. I'm sure that the fight was a racial thing, but now platoon buddies are helping each other back to the barracks. Just like they would do in a firefight in the field. Human nature is a strange thing.

I put my knife away and just stand and drink my coke. The place is in complete shambles. I hear jeeps pulling up outside, and eight military police storm in with a huge Black Staff Sergeant E-6 in the lead. He walks up to me and asks me what happened, and I tell him the biggest fight I've ever seen. He then asks if I was involved. I get an uneasy feeling that I should have left with every one else. If the MPs search me, will they take exception with the knife on my belt? Then one of the bartenders tells the big MP that I did nothing but stand at the bar. The MP then asks me what I saw. I tell him that I couldn't get out the door through the brawl, so I just stood with my back against the bar, took my glasses off, and put them in my pocket in case someone jumped me. Therefore, I was unable to see anything but a lot of movement and colors. That is not true, of course, but I do not want to give a statement. They accept my story, and I ask them if I can go, and they tell me to leave. I'm out the door and head toward my hooch.

I enter the hooch and find guys laughing and talking about the fight. Some have marks on their faces, but none seems to be seriously hurt. The different races in the hooch are laughing with each other about the fight. Vietnam is one crazy place, and not all the danger is from enemy soldiers.

The next day, we find out that nine soldiers of different races are in the hospital with serious knife wounds. We also learn that the drunk soldier who stepped on the Black soldier's foot is dead. He was stomped to death. We also learn that he was a Lieutenant at the end of his year in Vietnam. He had taken the rank off his collar so he could go in the club and drink with his men. Now after living through a year in combat, he is killed in a bar brawl. It is a sad thing.

Second Platoon has an ambush going out a few days later. The platoon travels after dark slowly going toward our ambush location. The platoon notices movement in a far tree line. It's a large unit, either a reinforced platoon or an understrength company. They spot Second Platoon and place a very heavy fire on Second Platoon's position. The platoon is pinned down. Ken Bissenden comes up on one knee with his M-60 and places an unbroken stream of fire on the opposing force. He holds his trigger down and swings his fire left and right into the force in the wood line. That force falls back into the woods and the firing stops. A quick check finds that only one American is hit.

Rocky is down, and he is dead. He has been killed on his first ambush patrol. It is heartbreaking. No one else is hurt. Bissenden has saved the platoon many more causalities by his brave act.

The next day, the platoon returns to base camp and hear a rumor that the opposing force that killed Rocky the night before was a lost ARVN unit (South Vietnamese Army). We continue patrols for several more days with no contact with enemy forces. Then the Platoon Sergeant approaches me and tells me we need to talk. I wonder what I have done wrong. He tells me that the Lieutenant is gone. He has rotated home, and for the time, there is no Lieutenant to replace him. He tells me for the time being he will be the platoon leader and I will be the Platoon Sergeant. Like a good soldier, I say, "Yes, Sergeant," but I am not a happy camper. I came back to Vietnam to run a ten-man squad and have fun, not to have to worry about four squads with all the personnel problems and administrative duties that come with the job of Platoon Sergeant for forty men. I have no choice. I'm the senior E-5 in the platoon, so I'm in the hot seat. I obtain a couple of ballpoint pens and a small notebook. I will need them. I will just pray for either a Lieutenant or another NCO who is senior to me. I now know how McVey felt on my first tour when he was placed in a Platoon Sergeant position and he was only a Specialist 4 in an E-7 slot. I am an E-5 in an E-7 slot, and that is scary enough. This also means that on split ambushes or patrols, I will have half the platoon, and the old Sergeant First Class E-7 will have the other half. On my first tour, I was a squad leader for the last few months and took out many squad patrols and ambushes. But that was with a ten-man squad. Now I will be taking out some twenty guys or half a platoon twice as far out for twice as long. Well, I shouldn't gripe. I volunteered to come back, and I am the senior Sergeant. Well, you should be careful what you wish for.

A few weeks go by, and Bravo Company is working out of Di An Base Camp. Second (us) and third platoons are working squad ambushes at night. First platoon is working squad patrols during the day.

A cold hard rain has fallen all night, and the squad that I have set up an ambush with are all soaked and chilled. We leave our ambush location and work our way back to Di An. The rest of second platoon comes in, and so does third platoon. We all move to our hooch and clean and oil down our weapons. I then strip off my wet shirt and pants, crash on my canvas cot, cover up with my poncho liner, and fall into a deep sleep.

I have been in a deep sleep for a couple of hours and awaken by someone shaking me and shouting, "Sergeant! Sergeant!" I sit up on my cot and see it is the company commander's runner. He is extremely excited and tells me that first platoon is in a hot firefight and taking causalities. I am wanted at the command post. I jerk on my pants and shower shoes. I tell the runner to go to the next hooch and wake the rest of second platoon. I wake some of the guys in my hooch and tell them, "saddle up first platoon is in trouble and need our help." I then trot down to the command post.

I enter the command post and see the company commander, executive officer, company first sergeant, third platoon lieutenant, third platoon sergeant, and the old sergeant first class E-7 that is my acting platoon leader. All huddled around a radio.

I say, "I've got second platoon saddling up. We will be ready to go in five minutes."

The company commander says, "Hold on for a few minutes. This may be over."

I then learn that the first platoon squad has made contact with an enemy patrol, and the first platoon squad has three men wounded, and a "dust off" helicopter is en route to take the wounded to the hospital. The entire enemy patrol has been killed, and their weapons have been recovered.

The company commander tells us all to return to our hooch and tell our men to go back to sleep. I walk back to my hooch and walk in. All the men have their gear on and are ready to go. I tell them that it is over. First platoon has three men wounded and have wiped out an enemy patrol. They all hit me with questions, and I tell them that is all I know and for them to go back to sleep. I then walk over to the other second platoon hooch next door. All these men are geared up as well. I tell them the same thing, and that is all I know, and they need to go back to sleep that we have ambushes tonight.

I return to my hooch, crash on my cot, and pull my poncho liner over me and attempt to go back to sleep. It takes me a while because I have become overly excited about the prospect of going to help first platoon. I finally fall into a deep sleep. We are all awakened about four hours later. It is time to eat and then gear up to go out on ambush again.

We have eaten and are about to depart the company area to head out into the jungle to our ambush location about three miles away. Then the first platoon squad that was in the firefight enters the perimeter. We then get the "scoop" on what happened.

The first platoon squad had been on patrol all morning in the rain when they came to a small group of rice paddies. On the edge of these paddies was a shelter. Apparently, it had been built to shelter rice workers from the rain. I had been by this location before while on patrol. The shelter was about twelve feet by twenty-four feet with a tin roof. The six beams that held the roof up were all about a foot square, and there were seven more of these large square beams connecting the six support beams at the tops and then the inverted V-shaped tin roof. The crossbeams are only about seven feet from the ground.

The first platoon squad elected to set up around and under the shelter and eat their noon C-rations. What the first platoon squad did not realize was that an enemy patrol had taken shelter at the same location apparently to escape from the rain. The enemy soldiers were all lying up on the crossbeams and possibly had even slept there during the rain the night before. The squad pulled in and around the shelter and all faced out for security and began eating their C-rations.

If the enemy soldiers had kept their "cool," they may have survived, but their nerves broke. They tossed grenades down at the Americans only five or six feet from them and then dropped to the ground firing their rifles. The first platoon soldiers reacted, quickly returning fire at close range. The tall lanky blond machine gunner had a one hundred round belt linked in his "gun." He rushed the enemy soldiers, firing a hundred round burst. In the eleven seconds it took the gunner to go through the hundred round belt in his gun, it was over, and the enemy soldiers were all dead. The machine gunner had a bullet wound in the calf of his right leg. The platoon medic, a Japanese American, had taken a bullet just above his left nipple, but the bullet had exited out his left armpit and did no serious damage.

A third soldier had a back full of grenade fragments. None of the soldiers were badly wounded and were all in the hospital in good shape. Fortunately, the enemy soldiers are not so lucky. They are all riddled with bullets and their AK-47s have been taken by first platoon.

It is like we always said. If you live to go on home from Vietnam, then barring cancer or car wrecks, you have got another fifty years to live. Fortunately, most of us will make it home. That is not the case with the North Vietnamese soldiers. The vast majority of them will die in South Vietnam. The NVA soldiers even have a saying. They refer to themselves as "born in the north to die in the south."

CHAPTER 27

The Sinkhole

It is early fall 1968. I'm a sergeant E-5 on my second tour. Half of Second Platoon is working a daytime sweep near the Saigon River. It is hot and muggy, with us sinking ankle deep in mud as we patrol. We have been at it for over half a day searching for enemy base camps in the swamp. We have found nothing, no sign of the enemy. The mosquitoes are thick, the heat is heavy, and the mud pulls at our boots.

Lieutenant Price is the new platoon leader and seems to already have a handle on things. He's got light hair, wears eyeglasses, and is from Ohio. The platoon sergeant is Staff Sergeant Jones, an old soldier and Korean War veteran. This is his second tour in Vietnam. In his first tour, he was with Recon Platoon, Second, Eighteenth. He was here when I was here last time, and we know some of the same people. He's an old, seasoned, experienced Black soldier from the Carolinas with nearly twenty years in the army. He must be nearly thirty-eight years old.

The First Squad Leader is Jim Morris from Oregon. He is an average-sized man with red hair and the best soldier in the platoon. He is a graduate of the instant NCO Academy, a twelve-week NCO school that the army sends sharp troops to after they complete infantry training. The army has gotten so big so fast that there are no NCOs to lead squads. Morris is the best young NCO that I have seen. He is nearly my age but much sharper than I am.

The Second Squad leader is Sergeant Collins from Illinois. He has come up through the ranks and is very confident.

The Third Squad Leader is Ted Townsend, a carpenter from Indiana. A very personable blond-haired man and is one of the two or three men in the platoon who is older than my twenty-one years. I am the weapons squad leader and senior squad leader only because I've been a Sergeant longer than Jim Morris.

Richard Jacobs is a young teenage soldier from near Kansas City, Missouri. He is sharp, very self-confident, and impresses the other NCOs and me. We call him Big Jake because he's six feet one and 215 pounds and because of his self-assurance. His hair is dark, and his eyes are light, and he seems ready for any challenge.

We patrol along the banks of the Saigon River looking for sampans, tracks, and enemy soldiers. Suddenly, there is a shout from among the Napa Palm trees near the bank. I head over to see what the problem is and see Big Jake in the mud up to his armpits. He shouts that he is still sinking. We grab the rope we use to cross rivers and tie it under Jake's armpits and attempt to pull him from the mud. Ten of us are on the rope, and we cannot budge him. We are making too much noise, so I send a couple of two-man outposts out about one hundred feet from our location. I don't want the enemy to walk up on us while we are attempting to help Jake.

We throw the end of the rope through the fork of a small tree, and all of us pull on it. Jake doesn't move. I am getting concerned that the mud is going to suck him down and kill him. I tell two guys with machetes to cut down two saplings about as big around as my arm and about twelve feet long. We then place one under each of Jake's armpits. We tie the rope off to another tree, hoping that between these two efforts that he will not sink any further. We have all walked close to Jake, and the only soft mud seems to be just the small area that he is trapped in.

We call in to company headquarters and tell them the problem we have. I am hoping that they will get us a helicopter to pull Jake out. We put out a third two-man outpost because it looks like we'll be here a while.

Jake is keeping it together, but I know how helpless he must feel. I kneel beside him and tell him not to worry, that we are all staying right here even if it takes all night and into tomorrow before we get him out. After an hour or so, we hear the sound of motors. We look at the river and see a navy riverboat coming up toward us. We pop colored smoke so they will see us and not mistake us for enemy troops. They pull over to the edge of the bank, and a sailor shouts to us that he heard we needed help. We tell him the problem, and he says for us to throw out the end of the rope and that they can pull our man out.

We leave the rope across the fork in the tree and throw the end to the sailor, and he ties it on the boat. The boat starts to move away very slowly. I hear Jake grunt and see him twist. The rope is pulled taunt, and Jake comes up a couple of inches out of the mud. He shouts that it hurts, and I say we've got to get you out. The boat puts on power, and Jake pops out of the mud with a scream. He then starts shouting, "My back, my back." His back is hurt, and he cannot stand. We medevac him out of there by helicopter and then continue patrol and still make it back to the perimeter by dark.

The next day, Lieutenant Price and I travel to the Ninety-Third Evac Hospital to visit Jake. He is on a cot and is doing better.

We talk with him a while and find he is in a good mood. His back pain is much less, and I lose the nagging fear that his back might be permanently damaged.

Lieutenant Price asks Jake if he would mind writing Lieutenant Price's little sister who is in high school. Jake says that he would be glad to write her. Lieutenant Price then writes down the address and her name. It is in St. Mary's, Ohio. My mind clicks, and I think, St. Mary's, Ohio. I ask the Lieutenant if that is a very big town. He tells me that it is not. I then ask him if he knew a Burner Craft. He is shocked and tells me that was his best buddy in high school. I then tell the Lieutenant that Craft was engaged to a girl named Carolyn Rice. He looks even more shocked. He tells me yes and that Craft married her. He asks me how I know Craft, and I tell him that Craft was in Third Squad of this platoon when I was here before and that we made Sergeant E-5 on the same set of orders. We also rode the same plane back to the States and sat beside each other.

We are amazed at how small a world it is. I tell him what a great guy Craft is and a good squad leader. I also mention that Craft had told me that when he got back to the world, he would never talk about Vietnam and if anyone asked him about it, he would tell them to go and see for themselves. Lieutenant Price tells me that is exactly what happened when he asked Craft about the war when Craft got home. Truth is sometimes stranger than fiction.

The next week, we are running squad ambushes. We leave the perimeter just before dark and move in the wrong direction from where we are planning on setting up our ambush. We hope that this will throw the enemy off if they are watching. After full dark, we change directions and head toward our ambush location. We move through thick brush and elephant grass.

We arrive at our location. It seems to have been a small dam at one time. But there is no water on either side just very thick brush. There is a very well-worn trail going across the dam. This trail had to have been made by either enemy soldiers or civilians. There is no village or rice paddies close, so we are betting on enemy soldiers.

We set up three positions on the dam. There's thick brush on both sides of the dam and then heavy thickets in the low places on both sides. We have the machine gun on the end where we are guessing we might have the most activity. The regular gunner is out of pocket, so Freeman is carrying the gun. He is a supernice, short, stocky Black soldier. I set in with the gun.

The rain has stopped, the moon has come out, and it is bright. It is my turn on watch, and I sit behind the gun and watch the trail. The moon is so bright that I can see most of the trail all the way to the end of the dam. As I watch, I see movement at the end of the dam. I freeze in place and only move my right thumb as I flick the safety off the gun. I see them now—two dark figures walking slowly on the trail toward me. I want to wake the other guys with me, but I am afraid to move thinking that the two enemy soldiers would see the movement.

I sit and wait as they walk closer and closer. They are about twenty-five meters from me. I have picked out a large bush beside the trail about fifteen meters from me, so when the enemy reaches that bush, I will kill them. I am not moving, and no other American is moving or making a sound. I do not know if the enemy saw my outline or they just felt something, but suddenly both dive off the dam into the brush on their right side. I pull the trigger on the gun and spray red tracer rounds at the enemy soldiers and where they have ducked into the brush. I hold the trigger down until I have fired a three-hundred-round burst, spraying the brush in the area where the two enemy soldiers disappeared. Burns, an M-79 man, runs up to me from the middle position, and I shout for him to cover the area with his little explosive shells. He starts popping out the little shells, one every five or six seconds. Other guys are firing as well, but I am afraid we have lost the two enemy soldiers.

I give the machine gun back to the gunner, and we saddle up and move down the trail to where the enemy jumped into the brush. The brush is unbelievably thick. I doubt if an American with all his gear could move through it. We have flares hanging in the air, but we can see nothing. I doubt if either of the enemies are hit, but if there is a wounded enemy soldier lying out there, then we are sitting ducks on this dam in all this light. We move off the dam and patrol to our secondary ambush location and set in. I hope that the two gooks I shot at were not the point element of a larger unit and that unit has followed us to our new ambush site. I worry about that the rest of the night and get no sleep. I don't know if any of the other guys sleep either. We are all on edge, but morning comes with no more activity, and we patrol back to the perimeter.

CHAPTER 28

The Well

It is fall in Vietnam 1968. I am back with B-2-18 for a second tour. I made Sergeant E-5 in May 1967 at the end of my first tour. I have now been a Sergeant for over a year, and I am twenty-one years old. I am one of the older men in the platoon. Things have really changed since my first tour. There is nearly twice the number of Americans in-country than there were when I was here before.

The enemy has changed as well. On my first tour, two-thirds of the enemy units we fought were Viet Cong, and about a third were North Vietnamese regular army units. Now even Viet Cong units are made up of mostly NVA replacements, and there are two more full NVA army divisions in the III Corps Area. The enemy is much better armed and trained. All enemy troops now have either AK-47 assault rifles or SKS carbines. They are not carrying the WWII American surplus weapons that many Viet Cong carried when I was here before. Most of the Viet Cong were killed in the February 1968 Tet Offensive. Their replacements are well-trained, well-armed troops from Hanoi. Even small units now seem eager to meet us on the battlefield.

Our tactics have changed as well. Instead of working in a battalion-size operation in different areas each month, each battalion has its own area. All battalions now have an additional line company, Delta Company. The battalion works out of four perimeters with a rifle company in each. The areas are Di An, the Thu Duc Water Plant,

247

VC Island, and a reinforced perimeter set on a tiny Black top road in the middle of the other three. Each company spends about six weeks in each, and then we "switch." This gives new ideas in each area every six weeks. We work day sweeps and night ambushes from these locations. Each of the three rifle platoons spend about two weeks on day sweeps and four weeks on night ambushes. We usually work it by splitting the platoon in half with the Lieutenant taking one unit and the platoon sergeant taking the other. That way, we usually have two weeks of day sweeps and four weeks of night ambushes working out of each company area. Sometimes we even split into squad sweeps and ambushes. This is a little scary, only having eight or nine guys out at a time, but it gives us better coverage.

There is a lot more comfort for us. We get hot chow very often now, and in a couple of the locations, we have a cold shower. We also have heavy reinforced bunkers in all these locations for the small amount of time that we are not out on sweep or ambush. The mortar platoon is usually in the perimeter all the time, manning their three 81 mm mortars and pulling bunker guard on the perimeter. Mortar platoon has become a pretty good job. Except for a few snipers, they are usually only under fire when the enemy mortars our company areas and our mortars are firing back.

We are working out of the Thu Duc Water Plant now. We are one of the two platoons working night ambushes. I am going out with the Platoon Sergeant's half of the platoon. A truck will take us to the factory area of Thu Duc just before dark. The truck has a driver and a couple of mortar platoon guys riding shotgun.

I am impressed by the machine gunner we'll have in this ambush. He's Ken "The Zipper" Bissenden from Utah. He is called The Zipper because he's six feet one and only weighs 135 pounds. He is only as wide as a zipper. He seems to know the gun and handles the twenty-three-pound weapon and lots of heavy ammo with ease.

There are a lot of good troops in the platoon, but besides the Lieutenant and Platoon Sergeant, I am the only one in the platoon who's not a draftee. The army has really changed.

The truck takes us to an out of the way location on the road with no houses visible. We dismount and head into the brush and conceal ourselves. The truck will return to the perimeter another way so the people we have driven by will not see the truck return empty. I don't know if we are fooling anyone, but we hope so.

We let it get dark and head out toward our ambush location. There are sixteen of us: The Zipper armed with an M-60 machine gun, two troops with M-79 grenade launcher, and thirteen of us with M-16s. Even I am carrying an M-16 instead of an M-14. Since my first tour, many, many improvements have been made on the M-16, and now there is a cleaning rod with every weapon. The M-16 seldom jams now. The rifle should have been like this on my first tour when my mother had to send me a .22-caliber cleaning rod. I am carrying thirty-one magazines for my rifle or 620 rounds. The M-16 and thirty-one magazines weigh twenty-three rounds. The M-14 with twenty magazines weighs forty pounds. I would still prefer the stopping power of the big 7.62 round as opposed to the 5.56, but now the M-16 works, and I feel like I need the 620 rounds. The NVA soldiers like to stay a while now and "shoot it out."

It starts to rain on us as we move. That is good; it will help cover our noise and movement. We work our way into heavy brush between the factories and the Napa Palm tree line where the swamp starts. The factories are mostly up on the road, and they work a night shift. The enemy soldiers live in base camps out in the swamp. The NVA like to come out of the Napa Palm Line after dark and move into the factories where they hit the chow line in the cafeteria and abuse the female factory workers. It's our job to stop that.

We reach our ambush location and break into four teams. Three teams, including the machine gun, orientate toward the Napa Palm Line. I orientate my team toward the factories. I will watch our back door and guard against any enemy that might come out of the factories and confront us.

We sit in the rain for about an hour, and then it stops. It is real quiet, and none of us have tried to go to sleep yet. We will have two men up and two sleeping in my position. I tell Ames, a small White soldier, that he and I will take first watch. I tell the other two men to get some sleep.

Suddenly, our other three positions open fire toward the Napa Palm Line. The Zipper is pounding out long bursts with the gun. They are getting heavy fire in return including RPG rockets. The four of us are flat on our bellies facing to the rear and flanks. Suddenly, four NVA soldiers dart from the bushes on our right about fifty feet out, heading toward another clump of bushes to our rear. We open fire on them, and two seem to stumble, and then all four disappear in the bushes. We shove fresh magazines into our rifles and spray the area where they have ducked. Are they trying to surround us?

Green tracer rounds reach out toward us from the area of the factories! They have a machine gun crew up by the factory covering for them as they move out of the swamp. Some of the rounds are impacting near us, and some of the green tracer rounds are bouncing off the ground and going high in the air. I am terrified and fire toward the source of the green tracers.

Ames shouts to me, "Sergeant, I've found a hole." I look ten feet to my left and see Ames drop feet first into a hole. I think Ames has found an old abandoned foxhole, and I dive headfirst into it. I fall and fall. I have my feet and elbows stretched out tearing into the walls of the hole trying to slow my fall. Then I crash into Ames at the bottom. I am still upside down, and in the narrow area, I'm afraid I'll not get my head up. I twist and turn and tear and finally get my head up. I pull the flashlight with the red lens off my web gear and turn it on. Ames and I find our rifles and put our helmets back on. We are both barely able to stand in the close quarters. I ask Ames if he's okay, and he says he is. I play the red light up above us and see we are about twenty feet from the opening. We are in a dry well. I'm glad it didn't have ten feet of water in the bottom.

I tell Ames to climb up on my shoulders and see if he can grab anything higher up. He climbs up, and I point the light up. Ames says that there's nothing to grab, and it's still ten feet to the surface. I tell him to get down. There's still heavy firing coming from above. There's nothing we can do until the fight is over. I just hope our guys are still there when the fight is over.

The firing tapers off. Are our guys still in charge of the ground above us, or are the enemy in control? We listen for voices and then hear some. Is it English or Vietnamese? It gets louder, and it's English! I take the red lens off my flashlight and start waving my light up through the opening. Ames and I start shouting in English so they will know we're Americans. We don't need a hand grenade down here with us.

Some guys look down into the well, and I turn the light on Ames and me. I want the guys to see us. I hear a tall, lanky Alabama country boy named Merrell say, "Golly, Sergeant, what are you and Ames doing down in that hole?" I shout back that we fell in. I'm so embarrassed.

The guys get the rope we use to cross rivers and drop it down to us. I tie it around Ames, and they pull him up. They then lower the rope down to me, and I tie it around my back side and tell them to pull. I walk my feet up one side and brace my back against the other side and try to help the guys. I'm nearly twice as heavy as Ames, so I know they are having a hard time pulling me up. I finally get to the top and crawl out onto the grass. What a relief!

There's artillery flares hanging in the air. We gear up and sweep the area but are unable to find any enemy bodies or gear. None of our men are wounded, and that's a blessing. The flares go out, and then we move to another location in case the enemy either mortars our old location or tries to hit it with a ground attack. The rest of the night passes without incident. When daylight comes, we sweep the area again but are still unable to find anything. We then move up to the highway. In a few minutes, the truck comes and picks us up, and we head back to the water plant.

CHAPTER 29

Friendly Fire

It is early October 1968. I'm a twenty-one-year-old Sergeant E-5 on my second tour in Vietnam with B-2-18. Second Platoon is working ambushes out of our main base camp at Di An. The rear area at Di An has really changed since my first tour. We no longer have squad tents but barracks that hold two squads. The barracks are very simple with a tin roof, concrete floor, and plank sides put in at an angle so the breeze could still come in and the rain would stay out. It's simple, but it sure beats the old squad tents with dirt floors.

We have left the perimeter just after dark en route to our ambush location. We are trying a new formation when we move. The platoon is still in two files or a column. They have now decided that a three-man team should be about fifty feet in front of the platoon, an NCO and two men. The two men are to work side by side and about ten feet apart. The NCO will be between the two men and about ten feet behind them giving the directions. This means that if we hit an ambush, it's the three men up front that take the heat and not the entire platoon.

This all makes perfect sense, except tonight, I'm the Sergeant up front. I've got George Margus to my left front and Howard Morrison to my right front. George is carrying an M-16 and Howard an M-79 loaded with a canister round. This makes the M-79 a giant single-barrel shotgun.

It's a clear night with a good moon out. We are running point for Lieutenant Price's half of the platoon. The Platoon Sergeant is taking the other half of the platoon to another ambush site.

We are moving through heavy brush that ranges from four to eight feet in height. I think that this was once a farm field and has been left to go back to the jungle.

I've got my compass open as it hangs on a cord around my neck. I'm attempting to stay on the correct heading that Lieutenant Price has given me. He's fifty feet behind me, but I can hardly see him or the unit even with the bright moon out. We are moving very slowly. George and Howard stop about every fifty feet and drop to one knee. I then move up and tell them which direction to go each time.

I see George walk by a break in the brush on our left. When I get to the break in the bushes, I look out and see a clear field about seventy-five feet away. The moon is bright, and I see six men lying on the ground in line facing us. As I see them, the man on the end on my left comes up on one knee and brings a rifle to his shoulder pointed at us.

I bring my rifle to my shoulder and begin to fire as fast as I can. All my rounds are tracers, and I work those twenty rounds up and down the line of six men. The entire platoon is blazing away now, but none of them can see the six men, and I can. I slap a second magazine into my rifle and work the six men over a second time with twenty rounds of tracers.

Just as I finish my second magazine, one of the men in the field starts screaming, "We are Vietnamese. We are Vietnamese." We stop firing, and one of the guys back in the platoon shouts back, "So are the Viet Cong, you dumb SOB."

I realize that it's an ARVN unit from the South Vietnamese Army that I've fired up. One of three things has happened. Either we are in the wrong place, they are in the wrong place, or someone in Operations has set a night ambush at the same location for both units. I know we are in the right place, so it's either the ARVN's mistake or Operations' mistake.

Lieutenant Price pulls up with me, and I point the six ARVN out to him in the field and tell him that one of them was about to open fire on us. He calls it in on the radio and then tells me to cover our flank with Margus and Morrison and he takes the rest of the unit in to check the ARVN. We have a medic with us who goes right to work on the ARVN. I see now that there were more than six of them. I only saw their one position.

The Lieutenant calls in a medevac helicopter to take our injured allies to a field hospital. The helicopter leaves, and the Lieutenant returns to my location. He tells me that two of the ARVN are dead and four wounded. He then directs me to continue our mission. I direct Margus and Morrison to continue on.

In about another thirty minutes, we reach our ambush location and set up along a trail. I set in with Margus and Morrison. I tell them that I have first watch. They both lie down on the ground and are instantly asleep. I watch the trail and analyze how I'm feeling over killing two ARVN and wounding four others. I find that I feel nothing. I am so glad that they were not Americans. If they had been Americans, I know that it would bother me the rest of my life. I know that they were about to fire us up and I just beat them to it. It was their lives or some of ours.

We ambush the trail all night with no activity. When day breaks, we saddle up and make our way back to our perimeter. I tell the guys to clean their weapons and then get some sleep. I then head up to the company headquarters. Our old Company First Sergeant is there and pours me a cup of coffee. He's been in the Army for twenty-seven years and must be pushing fifty. He asks if I'm the one that shot the ARVN the night before, and I tell him that I was. He tells me that it wasn't my fault and to not let it bother me. I tell him that I know it wasn't my fault and, no, it doesn't bother me. I say, "Hell, they were probably undercover Viet Cong, anyway." He shakes his head and refills my paper coffee cup. I tell him thanks for the coffee but I've got to go check the guys' weapons and get some sleep. I head toward the barracks thinking about my cot.

CHAPTER 30

The Green Tracer

It's very early fall 1968. Second Platoon has just gotten a new Lieutenant, and I'm so glad to give up this acting-Platoon-Sergeant job. Our old SFC E-7 has moved down from acting Platoon Leader back to his old job as Platoon Sergeant. I've moved back down to senior squad leader/machine gun squad leader/assistant Platoon Sergeant.

Back to a "fun" job. Being third-in-command of the platoon is much better than second-in-command. That means that two people have to go down in order for me to have to lead the platoon.

Our new platoon leader is LT Jim Price from Ohio. He's a medium-tall young man with light hair and eyeglasses. He's younger than me by three months, which still makes me the third oldest man in the platoon after Ted Townsend and the Platoon Sergeant. We all hope that the Lieutenant will work out well.

We are on a platoon-size day patrol, and so far everything is going well with Lieutenant Price. We hear the Captain call Lieutenant Price on the radio and tell him to bring the platoon back to the perimeter. Lieutenant Price okays the command and then continues on with the patrol. The old Platoon Sergeant and I look at each other with questioning looks. We then talk. We wonder where the Lieutenant is taking us. The Platoon Sergeant calls him on the radio and tells him to hold up. The Lieutenant stops the patrol and the Platoon Sergeant, and I move forward and pull the Lieutenant away from

255

the other troops so as not to embarrass him. We then ask him where we are going, he says that he is just learning the area. We remind the Lieutenant that the captain told him to bring the platoon back to the perimeter. I add that they might have an artillery barrage or B-52 air strike laid on for the area where we had been going. Realization comes to the Lieutenant's face, and he says that we'll be returning to the perimeter. That's when I know that we have a good lieutenant. He can take polite recommendations.

A few days later, Second Platoon has a night ambush. We move in the dark to our ambush location. It's a trail and dirt road intersection out in some tall elephant grass. We arrive to find that an old concrete house with most of the walls down overlooks the intersection. We set up in the house. Some of the walls are still partially up and part of the roof. It has a solid concrete floor. This is good. The partial walls will give us some protection from enemy fire, and the partial roof will divert some of the rain.

We lay there in the dark for more than an hour, and then First Platoon calls us on the radio. They are nearly a mile from us but have spotted an enemy platoon headed in our direction. They report that the enemy were too far away from them to take them under fire but they saw them with their starlight scope. They also report that there are twenty-six enemy soldiers in the file, some with heavy weapons.

We all go on alert hoping the enemy will come down the trail to the road where our ambush is located. We are very apprehensive. First Platoon says that there are twenty-six of the enemy and there's only eighteen of us, just half the platoon. The other half of the platoon has an ambush set up at another location. We only have one machine gun with us. This could get very hairy unless we catch the enemy platoon cold in the kill zone.

We wait with no one moving and all barely breathing. *Then* heavy fire falls on us from the side of the house that I'm not on. Green enemy tracer rounds from an RPD-56 Chicom machine gun are hitting all around us. I start quickly crawling across the concrete floor to the side the action is on. I see it floating in. A green tracer round coming right at me. It hits the concrete just a few feet from me. It bounces off the floor and hits me in the right knee. It flips me onto my back, and I finish my crawl on my back. I reach a partial wall and pull up my pants leg. I've just got a deep three-inch gash on the right side of my knee. An inch over and my war would have been over. The medic shouts, asking if I need him. I shout back for him to hold his position, that it's a minor wound.

I then begin adding my rifle fire to the other soldiers. I'm ripping out twenty-round bursts with my rifle braced on a partial window frame. The twenty-red tracer rounds look good going out into the elephant grass in a line under the muzzle flashes of the enemy weapons. Our machine gun and the other riflemen are also putting out a barrage of red tracers. Our two M-79 men are popping the little explosive shells into the grass. This goes on for maybe two minutes with neither side gaining fire superiority. Then our mortars begin dropping shells from back at the perimeter. The enemy unit pulls out then. They can't stand up under those big mortar shells. We've got flares hanging in the air. We then sweep the entire area but find nothing, no bodies or weapons.

The medic then checks my knee and concurs with me that it's just a deep gash. He puts a field dressing on it, and we change location to a secondary ambush site. I'm concerned. We are low on ammo. I hope that we don't have another fight until we can resupply with ammo. I count my magazines and find that I have fifteen loaded magazines and sixteen empty ones. I've fired 320 rounds and have 300 left. I realize that I've just earned my third Purple Heart. I tell the medic to just keep a bandage and medication on my leg and fill out the paperwork for my Purple Heart. I miss no time from the field.

The rest of the night passes without incident. We then patrol back to the perimeter after daylight. We clean weapons and resupply with ammo. I'm carrying thirty-one magazines or 620 rounds for my M-16. Most of the guys are carrying sixteen magazines or 320 rounds. This is only fifteen pounds with the rifle. I suggest to the men that they all add another seven-magazine bandoleer to their gear. This would add 140 rounds and only three and a half pounds of weight. This would give them 460 rounds, instead of 320. I also suggest to the M-79 men that they carry fifty HE rounds, instead of forty. This would only add four pounds of weight to their gear. On the machine guns, they've been carrying nine hundred rounds per gun. I don't leave the perimeter with less than 1,100 rounds per gun. I would prefer 1,300 rounds per gun if we have the men to carry it. We might be able to swing it with SGT Jim Morris, SGT Ted Townsend, and me carrying ammo for the gun. Some Sergeant E-5s refuse to carry machine gun ammo. Morris, Townsend, and I don't see it that way. That extra twelve pounds of ammo may save our lives. We need this amount of ammo in order to gain fire superiority over the enemy's AK-47.

A few weeks later, we are working day patrols in the same area. I'm with Lieutenant Price's half of the platoon. We are in an area of brush and elephant grass with occasional strips of trees. We start taking sniper fire from one of the tree lines. We return fire, and I'm beside Lieutenant Price and behind Big Jake Jacob's machine gun. Grenades are exploding along with the gunfire. I feel a sharp pain in my left arm and elbow area. I know what has happened. I'm an old hand at this now; I'm wounded again. I turn to Lieutenant Price, who is on the radio. I tell him that this is number four. He looks confused and asks me what I'm talking about. I tell him I'm hit. He seems put out with me being wounded again. He calls for a dust-off helicopter to take me out. The firing has stopped. The medic puts a field bandage on my left arm, and when the chopper comes in, I crawl on, and we head to the Ninety-Third Evac Hospital at Long Binh.

We land, and they take me into the operating room and check my arm. They take an X-ray and tell me that there is a large piece of steel in my elbow joint. They find that I've just eaten and they are unable to put me to sleep. They give me a shot to numb my arm and then lay my arm on a stiff board and tie it down. I can see a large hole in my elbow. I watch as a doctor cuts a half circle on one side of the hole. He then cuts a second half circle on the other side. He then takes a large instrument that looks like giant tweezers and plucks the piece of torn flesh out of my arm. I look away and feel like I might faint. I'm glad I'm lying down. The doctors work for a while, and I can hear their instruments grinding on the bones in my elbow. It's really eerie.

The doctor finally stops and tells me that they could get the large piece of steel out of my elbow but it might leave my elbow frozen. I tell them that I would like them to leave it that I do not want a stiff arm. They bandage me up and roll me to a ward.

They settle me onto a cot, and I get comfortable. I notice that they have a TV in the ward. I then realize that it's November 5. It's election day, and I have voted absentee for Nixon. I'm just twenty-one, and it's the first time that I've been able to vote. The other wounded and I watch the election returns. This is before satellites and the election returns are being read to us by two soldiers sitting at a desk in Saigon. Nixon wins easily and I'm glad. He is the best of the three candidates I had to choose from: Nixon, Humphrey, or Wallace.

There's a Tanker lying on the bunk next to me. He's a Staff Sergeant E-6 in his midtwenties, a much older guy. I learn that he was traveling in the hatch of his tank with his upper body above the hatch. The enemy hit his tank with an RPG shoulder-fired rocket. The three men in his crew were killed instantly, and he was blown from the tank but not before he was burned from his waist down. His body from his waist line down is red as a lobster except some areas on his feet that was covered by the partial leather on his jungle boots. The Staff Sergeant from the waist up has not a mark on him. The burns must be giving him terrible pain. He lays there and screams constantly even though the nurses are shooting the morphine to him. I walk over to the nurses' station and speak quietly to the charge nurse. I tell her I hate to say anything, but I wonder if I could move my bunk, because there is no way I can sleep with the Tanker screaming beside me. She tells me not to worry that the Staff Sergeant is going to be flown to an Army hospital in Japan in the next hour or so.

I'm in the hospital for a couple of days and watch TV with the guys. It's canned TV. They have segments of *Bonanza*, *Gunsmoke*, and other popular TV shows; and they play them on the American channel. They then tell me that my arm is not infected, and they send me back to the company on "light duty." I get back to the company, roll my shirt sleeves down, and tell them that I'm back on full duty. No one questions me, and I go out on an ambush that night. A week later, I will have the platoon medic take the stitches out of my arm.

CHAPTER 31

The Ambush

November 1968

Jim Morris and I have just been promoted to Staff Sergeant E-6. I'm amazed that I've made E-6 in thirty-two months in the army. Morris, an instant NCO, has made E-6 in twenty months, but he is really a good NCO and a sharp combat leader. I've made it because there was no one else in the entire battalion with enough "time in grade" as a Sergeant E-5 to be promoted to Staff Sergeant E-6.

I've also received my third and fourth Purple Hearts. In October, we had blown an ambush on a platoon of enemy soldiers. They had an RPD-56 Chicom machine gun. A green tracer round from this weapon hit me in the leg. It was not a bad wound, but an inch or so over and it would have blown out my knee. In early November, we were on day patrol and took sniper fire from a wood line. We moved on them, and I caught grenade fragments in the left arm and elbow. I would carry a large fragment in my elbow the rest of my life. I've been blessed to have received four Purple Hearts and still able to function. Apparently, God has something for me to do.

We are working out of the Thu Duc Water Plant and are pulling ambushes. Army Intelligence has received information that a seasoned combat platoon from the Fifth NVA army division has been slipping into the Coca Cola Bottling Plant at Thu Duc at night. They come from their base camp in the swamp and are going into the Coke Plant to hit the chow line in the cafeteria and abuse the female plant workers. They are well-trained and combat-hardened troops from Hanoi.

The brass has made the decision that our entire platoon will move in and set up an ambush between the Coke Plant and the Napa Palm tree line where the swamp begins. Two trucks take us out in midafternoon and drop us off a long way from the Coke Plant. We act like we are on day patrol for a while and then conceal ourselves so we can move into our ambush position within thirty minutes after it gets dark.

It's dark and begins to rain. That's great; rain will help us stay concealed as we move. The darkness and rain will cover our movement and the sounds we make.

We reach our location in the elephant grass and low bushes. We set up in a number of positions making a rough circle. We don't need the NVA to penetrate our positions. We have three positions facing the Napa Palm Line, Lieutenant Price, and both machine guns. Richard Jacobs has the gun on the right along a faint old wagon road coming from the swamp up toward the factory. Kney is Jake's assistant gunner, SGT Ted Townsend is in charge of the position, and Toney is the M-79 man. They also have a fifth soldier. Lieutenant Price's position is in the middle. The Lieutenant's radioman is Vanderburg. The M-79 man is Morrison, and the medic is Doc Apachlata, and they also have a rifleman. Burns is the machine gunner on the left with Quintana as his assistant gunner. Litaglow is the M-79 man, and Sergeant Collins is in charge. They also have a rifleman. The rest of the platoon is in positions on each flank and the rear.

It's still raining lightly, but the sky is not completely overcast. Our only starlight night scope is in the front. Our guys with the starlight spot 15 NVA soldiers exit the Napa Line walking in single file. They are about two hundred meters from our platoon, but with the starlight, we are able to tell that two of the enemy soldiers are carrying RPG shoulder-fired rockets. One is in the middle of the file, and the other toward the rear. This is a single-shot weapon that takes about twenty seconds to reload, but its shell is twice as powerful as an American hand grenade. The range on an RPG is about a quarter of a mile. It's a fearsome weapon. The remaining thirteen enemy soldiers appear to be armed with AK-47s and SKS carbines. At least they don't appear to have a machine gun.

Our platoon wonders if the enemy platoon will go left to the village or stay on the faint road coming toward us and the Coke Plant. They don't turn left and keep coming toward our platoon. The rain changes from a light rain into a downpour. It's falling in buckets.

The rear and flank positions are ready with hand flares. We did not have these on my first tour. They are a small cylinder, about two feet long that is fired by taking the cap off and placing it on the other end of the tube. It is then fired by hitting that end on the ground. The flare is then fired high in the air, and a little parachute comes out, and the burning flare floats to the ground, putting out a decent amount of light. It's a good stop gap until we can get artillery flares coming in.

Jake and SGT Ted Townsend are being cool in their position. The enemy platoon is walking right into them, and they are holding their fire until the last minute. Jake's a teenager but mature as can be with a lion's courage. He carries the twenty-three-pound machine gun with three hundred rounds of ammo. That's eighteen pounds of ammo. Most gunners only carry the gun and one hundred rounds of ammo. Nearly every man in the platoon who is not a point man, an M-79 man, or carrying a radio carries two hundred rounds for the machine guns. We need more machine gun ammo than we did on my first tour. It seems that over half the enemy soldiers are armed with AK-47s. This weapon has a thirty-round magazine. Our M-16s only have a twenty-round magazine. We need something to over-come the enemy's fire superiority, and a heavy and long base of fire from the M-60 will do that.

SGT Ted Townsend is an old man of twenty-four and may be the oldest man in the platoon except for Staff Sergeant Jones, who is in his late thirties and is as old as my daddy. Ted is a fine squad leader and handles himself like a pro even though he's a draftee like everyone else in the platoon, except Staff Sergeant Jones and myself.

The enemy point man walks almost into Jake's machine gun, and Jake opens fire with a burst that never stops. Everyone in the front positions is pouring fire into the enemy ranks: two M-60 machine guns, three M-79 grenade launchers, and ten M-16s. The rear positions pop off hand flares that give us some light in the heavy rain. As soon as our fire begins, the enemy RPG men fires their rockets. The two RPG rockets explode in our area almost as one. The explosions shake our teeth and stun us, but the only man hit is Rusk. He catches fragments in his right shoulder and arm but does not realize it until the next day. He believed that it was the hard rain hitting his shoulder and arm. Jake is still firing that first burst. It will turn out that his first burst will be five hundred rounds. Daylight will reveal that it made the metal in his gun barrel so soft that the hard rain left metal "bubbles" in the barrel. The enemy had returned some fire at the start, but it has now stopped, and our platoon is still pouring fire into the enemy area. We see no one run away.

Suddenly, a wounded enemy soldier with a hand grenade in each hand stumbles into Lieutenant Price's position. The Lieutenant is talking on the radio; his radioman and the M-79 man are both reloading their weapons. For an instant, it looks bad for the home team; then the medic fires a twenty-round burst into the gook's body, and he falls dead without arming his hand grenades. We check him after daylight and find that his feet had been shredded by Big Jake's M-60 rounds. We don't know how he could walk.

We've got big artillery flares hanging in the air now, and the rain has slacked off. Lieutenant Price and Staff Sergeant Jones get the platoon on line, and we sweep the kill zone. We see enemy bodies lying about and instantly spray bursts of automatic fire into them as we approach them. We'll not take the chance on one of them playing opossum, then opening up on us when we walk past him or throwing a grenade.

We sweep the entire area and locate eight enemy bodies besides the one in the Lieutenant's position. We put rounds into them as we walk by, and one young soldier fires an entire magazine of twenty rounds into each body. Seems like a little bit of a waste of ammo, but we are not worrying about a wounded gook killing any of us. We find four AK-47 assault rifles and three SKS carbines, but there is no sign of either of the RPGs or the other six enemy soldiers. Apparently, they crawled from the area with the rocket launchers and the other rifles. With the amount of fire that was hitting them, they all had to have been wounded. How they managed to get away with as much gear as they had is beyond my understanding. They are good at getting their dead and wounded soldiers and gear from a battlefield.

We saddle up and move from the area when the flares died out. We are carrying the seven enemy rifles, all of which have been hit by our bullets. We relocate to a position about three hundred meters from the ambush location, but we can still observe the area. We set up a circle of security, and Lieutenant Price calls in mortars and artillery fire periodically during the night into our old ambush position. We know that the enemy will attempt to retrieve the bodies of their comrades.

Morning comes, and we move back in and sweep the area again. One of the enemy bodies is missing! He sure didn't leave under his own power, not with thirty or forty bullets in his body. Some enemy soldier really wanted to recover his friend. We sweep into the edge of the swamp and find nothing there as well. We then work our way up to the road, and the trucks pick us up. We head back to the perimeter, and I think about getting a few hours' sleep and maybe some hot chow before we go out again tonight.

We are getting ready to get a little sleep, and Rusk says he cannot get his shirt off. A couple of us move over to help him, and someone says that he is wounded. I have him sit down and send a man for our medic. Our platoon medic returns with the company's senior medic. They help Rusk off with his shirt and see that his right shoulder has been peppered by light grenade fragments. They pick some pieces of steel out of his shoulder. They look a lot like misshaped BB pellets. They then bandage his shoulder. I tell the medics to get Rusk's information and make sure he gets a Purple Heart. Rusk says no, and I tell him, yes, he's going to get his Purple Heart that it will count on his Post Office Test someday. The medics get his info and laugh and say they will see he gets his "Heart."

CHAPTER 32

The Cemetery

November 1968

I'm a twenty-one-year-old Staff Sergeant E-6, and Bravo-2-18 is working out of a small fortified perimeter on a very small black top road in the middle of Second, Eighteenth area of responsibility. I'm well into my second tour with this unit. Second Platoon is working night ambushes.

We leave the perimeter in midafternoon and walk in the opposite direction from where our ambush will be located. We want people to think that we are on a day patrol. We change directions a number of times and hope this will fool the enemy. Our platoon will set up two ambushes tonight. Lieutenant Price leads half the platoon while the Platoon Sergeant leads the other half. I'm the senior NCO with Lieutenant Price's half of the platoon.

We've got one M-79 man on R&R and another in the hospital, so I'm carrying one tonight. The single-shot breechloader with a barrel nearly two inches in diameter weighs only five pounds. The shells for the weapon, however, are four inches long and nearly two inches in diameter. Each of the little shells weighs nearly half a pound. I'm carrying out one hundred shells tonight. Their range is nearly a quarter of a mile, and they hit with about half the explosive power of an American hand grenade. The little shell does not arm itself until it has traveled twenty-nine feet from the barrel of the weapon. This protects the shooter. There is a canister round that's like a giant shotgun shell that the M-79 man uses at close range. I carry ten of these.

I'm humping nearly sixty pounds of weapon and ammo out on this ambush. I'm carrying two canteens in the cargo pockets of my pants, two hand grenades hooked in my belt, and my ten-pound helmet. I've not brought my web gear out tonight. I'm carrying the shells in four claymore bags. Two are hanging from each shoulder with a metal D ring holding the four straps together between my shoulder blades.

There are two kinds of areas in Vietnam. One is a free-fire zone. There are no civilians in these areas, and anyone you see twenty-four hours a day who is not an American or a South Vietnamese soldier is the enemy and is shot at. The second is a non-free-fire zone. There are lots of civilians in these areas, and a curfew is in force between 8:00 p.m. and 5:00 a.m. Between 5:00 a.m. and 8:00 p.m., you can only shoot if you are shot at first, a person has a weapon, or a person runs from you. If you are not an American or South Vietnamese soldier, do not be outside a building between 8:00 p.m. and 5:00 a.m. You will be shot. These are called the rules of engagement. I have no trouble understanding them.

This area we are working now is a non-free-fire zone. There are lots of farmers and lots of villages. The enemy units go into these villages at night for food, rest, and comfort. North Vietnam is stressing about getting ammo down to their units in the South. Food is a secondary concern.

We move into our ambush position after dark. It's a cemetery on a hill overlooking rice paddies to the front, a Napa Palm Line to the left, and a large village to the right. Just inside the Napa Palm Line is an old French plantation house that is mostly fallen down. This looks like a good ambush location. We've got a lot of large tombstones for cover, and if I were the gooks, I'd want to use that old house in the Napa Palm Line as cover in order to stage before moving across the rice paddies to the village.

The last few months our battalion—Alpha, Bravo, Charlie, and Delta Companies—have hurt the enemy badly with ambushes. We've made it very expensive for them to move into villages or factories at night. Therefore, the NVA are getting very crafty about their moves.

I'm in the rear security position with PFC Cliff Bridge, a Specialist 4 named Collins, and a radioman. I have the M-79. The three of them are armed with M-16s. Cliff Bridge has been here about three months and is a fine soldier. He's a small young man from California but always carries two hundred rounds of machine gun ammo without complaining. Often, when we don't have enough men to carry as much ammo as we need, he volunteers to carry four hundred rounds. That's over twenty-four pounds of machine gun ammo, as well as his own gear and rifle. I don't know how he walks with that much weight on him. I'm about twice his body weight and nearly a foot taller than he is, and it kicks my butt to carry four hundred rounds of machine gun ammo.

Lieutenant Price sets up in one of the forward positions, Richard Jacobs with the machine gun in another position, and SSG Jim Morris in another. We each have three men with us. Lieutenant Price has a radio, and so do I. There is another soldier with an M-79 with Morris.

It's a clear night, and Lieutenant Price can see clearly with the starlight scope. He sees an NVA soldier walk by the old French house. He has on a long-sleeved NVA tan uniform shirt and a floppy bush hat. He's wearing shorts, which a lot of the enemies in these swamps do as long pants would stay wet. He's carrying an AK-47 over his shoulder and holding it by the barrel. It's like he's a hunter out hunting and he's at ease, or is he?

Is he alone heading into the village, or is he a decoy to see if we are in the area? Has he got a whole platoon back in that Napa Palm Line covering him, and it's just his turn to be the decoy?

The Lieutenant calls me on the radio and tells me to leave two men watching our rear and for me and my radioman to pull up on line with the three forward positions. I tell SPC4 Collins and Cliff Bridge to watch our rear no matter what happens in the front. I also tell them if they see anyone behind us to shoot them.

I crawl up with my radioman. We stop behind a large tombstone between Lieutenant Price and Staff Sergeant Morris's positions.

The NVA soldier is walking very slowly. He comes to the edge of the rice paddies and starts walking on a rice dyke toward the village. There's still no movement in the Napa Palm Line. We get our hand flares ready to pop to give us light when we open fire.

The NVA soldier is now about halfway across the rice paddies and is about thirty meters to our front walking from our left to our right. Lieutenant Price passes the word to Jake on the machine gun. If we have not seen any more enemy troops by the time the lone NVA gets in front of Jake, then Jake is to kill him. *Sounds like a plan to me*, I think as I open the flaps on two of the bags holding the M-79 shells. I'm lying on my belly behind that large tombstone with just half my head and the M-79 peeking around the side toward the Napa Palm Line.

The lone NVA arrives in front of Jake's position still moving very slowly toward the village. Jake opens up with the M-60, and his red tracer rounds reach out and impale the NVA, who falls into the rice paddy on the other side of the little dyke.

The entire Napa Palm Line lights up with enemy muzzle flashes. Green tracer rounds strike in among us and bounce off tombstones. RPG rockets roar out of the wood line and explode with stunning blasts. One rocket hits a tree behind us. There's at least a platoon, maybe two firing at us. We fire back on them right away, our red tracer rounds crossing their green ones. I fire the M-79, break it open, drop another round in, and fire again. An experienced soldier can fire the M-79 fourteen or fifteen times a minute, and I'm trying to break that record.

The advantage of the M-79 is it's an area weapon, not a point weapon. I'm walking the little shells up and down the line of muzzle flashes in the Napa Palm Line. I only have to look from behind the tombstone every third or fourth shot to make sure that my shells are hitting where I want them to hit. The other guys are putting out twenty-round bursts of fire from their rifles, and Jake is melting the barrel on the machine gun. The Lieutenant is on the radio and has artillery flares hanging in the air and artillery explosive rounds impacting in the tree line. That's when the gooks pull out. They can't stand those big cannon shells landing on their heads.

They are shouting for a medic from Jim Morris's position. Damn, we've got casualties. The medic leaves the Lieutenant's position and crab walks over to Jim Morris's position. Then I hear laughter. What's going on? Then Jim hollers to us that Gillespie has been shot through his canteen. He felt the blow and the wetness going down his side and believed he was shot. Gillespie is a tall Black guy and a good soldier. Even he gets a laugh from the incident.

The artillery flares are still hanging in the air, and some are landing in the village catching thatched roofs of some of the village hooches on fire. The villagers are fighting the fires. The fires are throwing off almost as much light as the flares.

The Lieutenant passes the word. We will leave Jake, his assistant gunner, Bridge, and Collins on the hill to cover us; and the rest of us are going to sweep the Napa Palm Line. Those tombstones have stopped a lot of enemy bullets and saved a lot of us from getting hit, but now we've got to go into that dark Napa Palm Line where just minutes before thirty or forty NVA were firing at us. I gear up and find that I've fired eighty of my one hundred M-79 rounds. I cannot believe that I've fired so much. Did the fight last four or five minutes? It seemed like only one or two minutes to me, but for me to fire that many shells, it would have had to last much longer.

The soldier carrying the other M-79 starts to panic. He is shouting that he can't go on the sweep, because he doesn't have any canister rounds for his M-79 so he'll not be able to engage any NVA at close range in the swamp. I tell him to shut his month, and I hand him two of my canister rounds. He shuts his month but still is not a happy camper and gives me a look that would kill.

We spread out and move across the rice paddies. I feel very vulnerable and afraid. Have the gooks pulled completely out or just moved their position and are waiting for us to expose ourselves like we are doing? We look for the enemy point man who Jake shot down. But he's not behind the dyke. Was he only wounded and crawled into the village, or was he dead and some villagers crawled out and drug him back into the village while we were all firing at the wood line? We will never know.

We move into the Napa Palm Line by the old house. Artillery flares are still in the air, and we see impact sites of numerous M-79 rounds and artillery shells. We find no enemy bodies or equipment. These guys are really good at picking up everything when they pull out. We pull out of the wood line and pick up our guys on the hill, and as the flares go out, we move to another location to wait for morning.

Morning comes, and we move back into our ambush site. We sweep the kill zone. I'm afraid the gooks will be waiting on us. They know our method of operation. We sweep the area and find nothing, not even any expended enemy rifle shells. How could they have picked up their brass? Did they come back just after daylight and just before we got back and police up the area? We'll never know.

We saddle up to head back to our perimeter. None of us are hit, and that's a blessing. Our only casualty is Gillespie's canteen. Then in the distant swamp, we hear a mortar round leave its tube. We all shout, "Incoming!" and hit the ground. The mortar round hits about 150 meters from us in a very marshy area.

We brace ourselves for more mortar rounds, but we get no more "Incoming." Lieutenant Price calls in on the radio and reports the one mortar shell. He is told by higher to hold in place that they are sending an engineer NCO to evaluate the impact point of the mortar round and for us to secure the area.

My jaws are locked. Do they think we made up the mortar round? I gripe to Lieutenant Price about us having to wade out into that dirty standing water and brush attempting to find the impact of the mortar round. The Lieutenant says no, that we do not have to do that. He tells me to hold the guys in place, form a small perimeter, and face out. Lieutenant Price then walks over to a small berm near us, looks over it, pulls a hand grenade off his belt, and throws it over the little berm. The grenade explodes. The Lieutenant then throws a second grenade where he has thrown the first. It also explodes. The lieutenant walks back to us and tells us he's found the impact point of the enemy mortar round. I hope the engineer buys this, and the Lieutenant doesn't get in trouble.

In a few minutes, a helicopter appears over us, and we throw a smoke grenade, and the helicopter lands. A Staff Sergeant E-6 engineer exits the helicopter and comes over to Lieutenant Price and me. The Lieutenant tells him we have found the impact point of the mortar round. The lieutenant and I walk him over to the impact point and point it out to him. He says, "Yes, that is the impact of a sixty-millimeter mortar." I also tell him the direction the round came from. The engineer NCO then turns and walks back to the waiting helicopter and departs.

We then form up and head back toward our perimeter. I think that I was sure right. Lieutenant Price has been made into a fine Platoon leader and really takes care of his men. I make sure that the guys are all aware of how well that the Lieutenant takes care of us. We will not spend half a day wading around in chest-deep water and miss most of our sleep. We'll get back to the perimeter in time to get a decent amount of sleep before we go out on another ambush tonight.

CHAPTER 33

The Curfew

November 1968

I'm a twenty-one-year-old Staff Sergeant E-6 on my second tour with B-2-18. Our platoon is working ambushes out of the Thu Duc Water Plant. As usual, we've divided the platoon in half in order to set up two ambushes in different areas. Lieutenant Price, along with SGT Ted Townsend and SGT Richard Collins, has taken half of the platoon to another area near the factories at Thu Duc. The Platoon Sergeant, along with SSG Jim Morris and I, has the other half of the platoon; and we are moving in the dark and heavy rain to set up an ambush between a village and the Napa Palm Line where the swamp begins.

There are seventeen of us in our group, and our machine gunner is Ken "The Zipper" Bissenden. He's tall, thin, and not as wide as the big M-60 that he carries; but he is a fine and courageous gunner. I also feel very good about working with SSG Jim Morris. He is, by far, the best NCO and soldier in Second Platoon. Morris and I were Sergeant E-5s together, but I had been a Sergeant much longer than Morris, so I was senior. Morris and I made Staff Sergeant E-6 on the same set of orders, but I had much more time in the Army, so I was still senior. But I knew and I think the other guys in the platoon knew that if the Lieutenant ever went down, it would be Jim Morris who got us out of the jam that we were in.

We have talked about how we will set up the ambush before we left our bunker line. We will have three positions facing the Napa Palm Line and one position facing the village. The Platoon Sergeant and SSG Morris will have two of the positions facing the Napa Palm Line, with Ken Bissenden and his gun crew being the third and middle position. I will have the position facing the trail coming out of the village.

It's a long cold, wet walk in the dark until we finally arrive at our ambush site. It's raining so hard that we've not even had any dogs bark at us. We quickly and quietly set up our positions. I'm facing the village with three riflemen and a fourth soldier armed with an M-79 grenade launcher. There's a trail from the village that comes by my position and heads toward the swamp. The nearest hooch to our position is only about fifty feet.

I feel good about being set up and not moving. It's after 2000 hours or 8:00 p.m. There is a curfew for all civilians from 8:00 p.m. until 5:00 a.m. Anyone not an American or South Vietnamese soldier who are outside of a building during the hours of curfew can be shot with no warning. The enemy really likes to move in the dark, and this is an excellent tool to combat his movements. The rain stops suddenly, and part of a moon comes out. This really helps us to see in the dark. Our only starlight scope is with the machine gun, but it does not work very well in the rain. I've got three good riflemen with me and a grenadier.

We are ready in case enemy soldiers come from the village and head toward their base camps in the swamp. We are also ready in case an undercover VC in the village heads out to lead an enemy unit into the village for hot chow and warm companionship.

As we lay in the wet grass and bushes, a male adult Vietnamese steps out of the hooch nearest to my position. He's wearing a long-sleeved white shirt and black pants. He looks like he's in his thirties, and he is looking all around. One of the riflemen with me says, "Sergeant, he's outside the hooch. Let's kill him." I tell him to hold his fire and let's see what the guy does.

The Vietnamese man walks a couple more steps out from the door of his hooch, and the aggressive rifleman beside me says,

"Sergeant, we're legal. Let's kill this guy. He's breaking curfew." I tell the four men with me to hold their fire and if this man walks down the trail toward us, then we will "waste" him.

The Vietnamese man looks around one more time and then urinates on the ground. He then goes back inside his hooch. The rifleman beside me lets out his breath and says, "Damn." I tell him to be cool that the guy may have been checking things out and may be back with his rifle to head into the swamp.

We lay there the rest of the night, and nothing else happens. It starts to get gray in the east, and we pick up our gear and head out before curfew ends. The people in the village probably never knew that we were there. We patrol back toward our bunkers at the water plant as the countryside wakes up. Farmers came out of their hooches and start their daily routines.

As we move back toward our bunkers, the aggressive rifleman from the night before starts to gripe about us not killing the gook who came out of his hooch during the night. I tell him and the other guys that if the man had had a weapon or had gone any farther from his hooch, then we would have shot him. I also tell them that I was a country boy in a house with no indoor plumbing, and I know what it's like to have to go outside during the night to relieve yourself. I tell them that I'm not going to kill a man for going ten feet outside his hooch and taking a leak.

I will never know if the man was an innocent farmer with a full bladder or a VC who saw, heard, or felt something and went back into the hooch. I have never felt bad about my decision. I know it was the right one. The man just did not quite cross the threshold in my opinion to warrant his death. He just did not give me enough reason to kill him.

As we approach the perimeter around the Thu Duc Water Plant, I'm thinking about cleaning my weapon and getting some sleep. Our bunkers at the water plant are prefab bunkers. They are the only ones I've ever seen. There are standing positions in the front of the bunkers with firing slots through which to fight. In the attached rear of the bunker, there are two double bunks built into the walls with a narrow walkway between them leading out the rear of the bunker.

All this is built together and covered in heavy tar paper. This bunker is then placed in a hole in the ground, and *six* layers of sandbags are placed on top of the bunker. It only takes five layers of sandbags to stop an 82 mm mortar round. We just roll up in our poncho liners on the wooden slats in the bunks and sleep like babies.

The perimeter at the water plant is large, so Bravo Company is securing one side of it, and an ARVN unit (South Vietnamese Army) is securing the other side. We've been noticing the last few days that someone is stealing from our bunkers when we are out on patrol. Just the day before I've lost a good knife out of our bunker.

We enter the perimeter, and we all take the round from the chambers of our rifles and head toward our bunkers. I'm sharing a bunker with SGT Ted Townsend, SPC4 Ralph Landweir, and SPC4 George Margus. I enter the bunker first, and there's an ARVN soldier standing in our bunker. I feed a round into the chamber of my rifle and tell the other guys to come in and see what we have. The other three guys come into the bunker and break into grins as they comment on us catching our thief. The ARVN tries to push past me toward the door, and I fire a shot into the ceiling. He stops and just stands there. I tell Townsend to check the ARVN for weapons and search him for any of our gear. Townsend starts to search the ARVN, and he tries to resist. I slap him once with an open hand, and he then submits. Townsend searches him and finds no weapons but does find some small keepsakes that we had stored in our bunker. He recovers these items. The ARVN speaks some English, so I tell him if anything else comes up missing from any of our bunkers we are coming for him. Townsend then grabs the ARVN by collar and drags him to the door of the bunker, kicks him in the butt and tells him "Di Di Mount" (Go away quickly). We then crash in our bunks and get some sleep. Theft from our bunkers ceases.

CHAPTER 34

The Trick

December 1968

I'm a Staff Sergeant E-6 toward the end of my second tour with B-2-18, First Infantry Division. Half of the Second Platoon is on a daytime patrol out of the Thu Duc Water Plant. LT Jim Price has been moved up to Mortar Platoon. We hated to see him go because he was a good Platoon Leader, but he had the seniority to take over mortars.

We've got a new platoon leader, Second Lieutenant Hagan. He's a big guy, maybe bigger than me. So far, he seems like he is going to work out well. He's leading this half of the platoon today, and I'm the senior NCO. The Platoon Sergeant has the other half of the platoon on a sweep in another area.

We've been sweeping for about four hours so far, and it's hot as we come to a small road by a small patch of rice paddies. There are five Vietnamese farmers working in the paddies with garden-hoes. It strikes me as strange that all five of them are on line with the same distance between each of them. On the other side of the paddies behind the farmers is a hedgerow. Something is not right, and I feel jumpy.

Suddenly, we are fired on from the hedgerow. I see a bullet hit the ground a few feet from me. I shout, "Fire between the farmers." We open up on the hedgerow firing between the farmers with long bursts of red tracer rounds. Two of the farmers drop to one knee, but the other three just stand there. I realize that the enemy has set this up with the farmers providing a screen of protection for them.

We are all down pouring fire between the farmers into the hedgerow. As I reload, I see Second Lieutenant Hagan firing a twenty-round burst at the enemy. Richard Jacobs is pouring machine gun fire into the enemy positions as well. The farmers still have not moved.

We hear shouting from the other side of the hedgerow. Some of it is in Vietnamese, and some in English. What the hell is going on? We are no longer receiving fire, so we cease fire but remain ready. The farmers still have not moved. When the firing stops, the ones who went to their knees stand up again, and all are working with their hoes again.

Then one of my soldiers storms up to me screaming about us shooting at farmers. I'm stunned. What is he talking about? The others guys are also looking at him in a strange way. I attempt to shout him down, but he's still screaming. I'm about to hit him with my rifle when Second Lieutenant Hagan rushes up between us shouting for us both to be at ease. He then orders the soldier to move to the rear of the platoon.

Second Lieutenant Hagan then asks me what happened, and I tell him. He then asks me why I didn't deck the guy, and I tell him I was about to when he got between us. I ask him if he heard me give the order to shoot between the farmers, and he says that he did.

Then a platoon of ARVN, South Vietnamese soldiers, comes around from behind the hedgerow walking on the road. I see what has happened now. The enemy has gotten between us and fired on both units, hoping we will get into a firefight with each other. What tricksters these guys are.

The ARVN platoon walks up to us, and the ARVN whom I believe to be the platoon leader speaks some English. He's talking to Second Lieutenant Hagan and me, and I'm telling them what happened. Then another ARVN walks up, and he's enraged. He's screaming and hollering in Vietnamese and pointing to a bullet hole in his pants leg. I tell the ARVN platoon leader to tell him about the trick the enemy has played on us both. The ARVN leader tries talking to his man, but it does no good. The ARVN is still screaming and shaking his finger at me. I've been shot at today, been screamed at by one of my own men, and now this guy. I've run out of patience. I curse the ARVN like a dog. Even if he doesn't understand me, he sees my intent. I'm as angry as he is. I turn and shout to Jake for him to bring up the machine gun that we may have to "grease" these ARVN soldiers. That's the only time I ever see Jake seem uncertain. I then turn on the angry ARVN and flip the safety off my weapon, and I tell the ARVN platoon leader to tell his man to shut up or start shooting. Second Lieutenant Hagan is trying to shoo the ARVN platoon away. I turn and shout for Jake again. The ARVN platoon leader grabs his man, and they begin to leave the way they came. I curse them until they are out of sight with my weapon ready.

We saddle up and continue on patrol. I tell the Lieutenant that either the upset soldier or I am leaving this platoon. Second Lieutenant Hagan agrees with me and says he will handle it when we get back to the perimeter. When we get back to the water plant, the Lieutenant sends the man back to Di An.

That night is New Year's Eve. The Second and Mortar Platoons are securing the perimeter. First and Third Platoons are out on ambush. It's supposed to be a curfew, but the enemy never honors it. I wonder why we do. We have the four ambushes out to keep the enemy from massing near us and hitting us with a ground attack.

It's nearing midnight, and few of us are asleep. We've stayed up talking in our bunkers waiting on New Year's Day 1969 to arrive. Midnight arrives, and some of the men fire hand flares into the air. I see nothing wrong with this. These are nineteen-year-old men under a great deal of pressure enjoying a new year coming in.

The word comes down that all Bravo Company officers and NCOs are to report to the Battalion Commander at his command post. The company commander gets his Lieutenants and Sergeants together and marches us up to the battalion CP. He then reports to the Lieutenant Colonel. The Lieutenant Colonel proceeds to chew the Captain and the rest of us out for a long period of time about the hand flares being fired.

We finally march back to the company area, and the Captain tells us to order our men to not fire anymore hand flares or he will charge us. It all seems "much ado about nothing" to me. I talk to all the men in the platoon and tell them what has happened and to be cool. It's a new year, and we'll have patrols to run.

The next day, I'm with Lieutenant Hagan and half the platoon patrolling an area of pasture and farmlands. This is *not* a free-fire zone. In the daytime, a Vietnamese has to either be armed or run from us for us to fire at him.

We spot a group of about twenty-five men, women, and teenagers about 150 meters in front of us. We head toward them to check their ID cards. As we walk toward them, they walk away. We pick up our step, and so do they. We begin shouting to them, "Dung lai" (Halt) and "Lai dai" (Come here). They ignore us and keep going. We begin trotting after them, and they do the same. I tell an M-79 man to put a shell well in front of the group. He fires the shell, and it lands about fifty meters in front of the group. They stop dead still. We approach them with our weapons ready and start checking ID cards. We find four military age males with short haircuts and no ID cards. They are not armed, so we call for "white mice" (ARVN military policemen).

We wait, and in about thirty minutes, two white mice arrive in a jeep. They dismount and began questioning the four suspects. One of the white mice begins shouting and pointing his finger in the face of one of the suspects. The ARVN then slaps the suspect. The ARVN then turns to us and tells us that the four suspects are all NVA soldiers. Someone asks how he knows, and he says "by the way they speak." Another one of the guys asks how he can tell that by their speech. I reply that I guess that "the North Vietnamese and South Vietnamese speech is as different as two Americans from New York and Alabama." The American says he sees what I mean.

The ARVN tie the four suspects' hands behind them and load them into the jeep and leave. We search the area where we have followed the group. We are looking for any discarded weapons but find none. They may have seen us first and ditched their weapons before we saw them. They were using the group of villagers as cover to try and escape us. Well, that's four more NVA soldiers in a POW camp.

CHAPTER 35

The Swimmers

January 1969

Second Platoon is working day patrols. We are sweeping the swamp attempting to locate enemy base camps. Lieutenant Hagan has half the platoon in this sweep while the Platoon Sergeant has the other half of the platoon on a sweep in another area.

I'm a twenty-one-year-old Staff Sergeant E-6 on my second tour. I'm the senior NCO working with the Lieutenant's half of the platoon. I'm getting toward the end of this tour and my time in the army. I've been torn about whether to re-up or not. The re-up bonus for a six-year hitch for an E-6 is $6,000. That's when you could buy a brand-new Corvette for $5,000. I have almost decided to get out. I've always wanted a career in law enforcement; and during my time at Fort Benning, Georgia, in between my Vietnam tours, I've found out just how boring the peacetime Army is. Also, you have ninety days after getting out that you can re-up and still get the bonus and keep your rank.

The swamp is nasty. The mud stinks, and it's at least ankle deep at all times, sometimes deeper. The trees and brush are thick, and it's hard to see more than a few feet. There are numerous streams and creeks to cross, and there are lots of mosquitoes and leeches. We are working in two files, Lieutenant Hagan has one, and I have the other. Specialist 4 Spaulding and Sergeant Richard Collins are in the first and second positions in the Lieutenant's file.

Suddenly, Spaulding and Collins open fire on automatic. Lieutenant Hagan and I lurch forward, and Sergeant Collins shouts to us that they have fired on several men armed with rifles and wearing brightly colored swim trunks. The Lieutenant shouts for us to get the men on line, and we press forward.

The unit is on line, and we are pushing through the mud when we get glimpses of the enemy soldiers. They are wearing brightly colored swim trunks! What is this, the Olympics?

We all fire on them, and they fire back with carbines. There's no AK-47 fire; that's a blessing. We keep pushing, slipping, falling, and firing. They fire back as they run. I can't believe that we've not hit any of them, but I've seen no blood trails.

A loach helicopter arrives above us. It's a small two-man helicopter, but it does have one M-60 machine gun mounted on the outside on the passenger's side. I think that we've got the little SOBs now. The chopper will kill them from above with the machine gun. The chopper makes a pass. The machine gunner fires a couple of short bursts, and then it jams. Damn, if it wasn't for bad luck, we would have no luck at all. The chopper keeps making passes at the enemy, and the passenger is firing a .45-caliber pistol! They don't even have an M-16 in the chopper to back up the M-60.

We are still after the enemy, breathing with our mouths open. We are firing twenty-round bursts from our rifles; and Burns, the machine gunner, is burning belts through the gun. The M-79 men are popping off little shells when they can get an opening in the underbrush. The Lieutenant is doing little firing now and is just shouting into the radio attempting to get us some support.

We break out onto the banks of a creek about thirty feet wide. A VC in burgundy swim trunks and carrying a carbine is just crawling onto the opposite bank. He's not thirty-five feet from Spaulding and Sergeant Collins. They each fire a twenty-round burst, and the VC flops to the ground riddled with bullets; blood is everywhere.

Just then a South Vietnamese navy patrol boat pulls up beside us on the river to our left. The Lieutenant shouts for me to take half of the men, get on the boat, and cut the enemy off down the river.

He shouts that he will keep the other men and the machine gun and lay down a base of fire on the wood line across the stream.

I grab my radioman and half a dozen other men, and we climb onto the riverboat. I tell the South Vietnamese boat captain to take us down the river, and we head out. We go around a bend in the river, and there are two VCs standing in the river with their hands up. One is wearing electric-blue swim trunks, and the other is wearing emerald-green swim trunks. I throw my rifle up and cover them, and the South Vietnamese boat captain is shouting in English for us not to shoot them. I shout at him that we are not going to shoot them. We are just covering them.

We pull the boat up beside the two VCs, and they are shaking like leaves. We pull them onto the boat and see all they have are their swim trunks. I tell the boat captain to ask them where their rifles are. He does, and they seem to not know what he's saying to them. I tell him to tell them that either we get the rifles back or we shoot them. He panics and is shouting that we can't do that. I shout at him that I don't intend to shoot these prisoners. I just want them to think we are if we don't get the rifles. This angry shouting between the boat captain and me seems to convince the two VCs. They are now very willing to show us where they dropped their rifles. I tell four of the men to take one of the VCs onto the bank of the river and recover the rifles. The other three men and I will cover them, and if they run into more VCs, we'll come ashore and back them up. I tell the boat captain to tell the VCs on the boat, if he runs, he will be shot. I also tell the GIs if the VC runs to kill him. They drop into the water with the one VC and climb onto the bank and enter the brush. In minutes, they are back with two rifles. They wade back to the boat and climb aboard.

We tie the two enemy soldiers' hands behind them, and I direct the boat captain to take us back to the rest of the unit. I've already called the Lieutenant on the radio and told him we have two POWs and their weapons. He has stopped the rest of the unit from firing.

We come back around the bend and climb back onto shore with the Lieutenant and the others. Everyone seems happy about our success. We've killed an enemy soldier and captured two others. We've also recovered three carbines. I walk over to Sergeant Collins and tell him that he and Spaulding did some good shooting when they killed that

VC in the burgundy swim trunks. Collins shakes his head and says that Spaulding killed the gook that he, Collins, was spraying the bushes where the other enemy had disappeared into. I walk over to Spaulding and tell him that he did a good job. He tells me, "Thanks."

The Lieutenant says we need to recover the dead enemy and his weapon from across the creek. I tell him that I will do it. I drop my helmet, web gear, and shirt. I keep my rifle and tie our rope around my waist. I then swim the thirty-foot creek. I come out on the other side of the creek and ready my rifle as I walk up on the enemy soldier. He's lying on his back covered in blood. He's been shot six or seven times. I secure his rifle and tie the rope around one of his ankles. I then grab the rope and tell the guys on the other side to pull us across.

They pull the dead VC and me through the water and out onto the bank on the other side. The water washes all the blood off the enemy's body, and somehow he now looks obscene with all the bullet holes and no blood. We ask our Kit Carson Scout to ask the two VC prisoners how many of them were involved today. They insist it was just the three of them. We ask them what they were doing, and they say that they were a messenger team carrying verbal messages. We ask them what messages, and they say the dead VC was the leader and only he knew the message. We ask them where they were going, and they say only the dead leader knew where they were going. We don't believe a word they say, but what the hell?

The Lieutenant calls in a Huey helicopter, and we send the two POWs and the three rifles to the rear. We then saddle up and prepare to continue our patrol. Before we do, I tear the First Infantry Division Patch off my left shoulder and drop it onto the body of the dead VC. We've been doing that for some time, so the enemy soldiers will know who killed their fellow soldier. It's a personal thing. The patch slides off the VC's body and lands on the ground. One of the guys picks it up and quickly puts it on the VC's body.

We use the rope, cross the creek, and continue our patrol. This will be my last firefight in Vietnam. In a couple of weeks or so, I'll be home and out of the Army. In a few months, I'll be in the Memphis Police Academy.

CHAPTER 36

Going Home

January 1969, Di An, Vietnam

My hitch in the Army is up. I'm a twenty-one-year-old Staff Sergeant E-6 finishing up my second tour with this fine unit. I haven't fully completed my second tour, but now it's either time to reenlist or go home and get out of the Army. I'm torn. I've made E-6 on my first hitch, but that's because of the war and the rapid growth of the Army. Still if I re-up, I will get a $6,000 bonus. Doing it while stationed in Vietnam will mean it will be tax-free. This was when a brand-new Chevrolet Corvette can be bought for $5,000. I'm not a Corvette fan, but you can buy a decent small house for $12,000.

I do recall how boring my time at Fort Benning was between my Vietnam tours. I fear being this bored for the next seventeen years until I can retire. I'm afraid that would be a long hard seventeen years. I have another option. I can go home and leave the Army and still have ninety days in which I can go back in, retain my rank, and still get my bonus. The only drawback is that the bonus would be taxed if I was in the States.

I have always been interested in a career in law enforcement. I'm thinking that career would not be boring, because you would never know what would happen from one minute to the next. It's a tough decision.

I make the decision to get out and make a final decision before the ninety days are up. I say goodbye to the guys in the platoon and head to the repo depot at Long Bien after processing out at division. I then process out at Long Bien, and after a couple of days, I board a jet with nearly two hundred other soldiers headed home.

The plane takes off, and I notice a big "bump" as we take off. I wonder what it could be. I have no idea. I'm busy with my thoughts.

We continue eastbound in the air as many thoughts go through my head. I'm uncertain about my decisions. I'm glad to be alive and not crippled, but I will miss the excitement and, most of all, the guys. I wonder if guys in law enforcement are anywhere near as tight as guys in an infantry platoon in combat.

We approach the island of Guam, where we have been told that we will land and gas the plane. I hope that we will be able to get off the plane and stretch our legs. I start noticing that the half-dozen beautiful flight attendants have fear in their faces. I get a very bad feeling. If these older ladies (some must be twenty-five years of age) are afraid, there must be a good reason.

We approach the air strip, and I see seventeen firetrucks lined up beside the runway. My hard face comes on. There is apparently something wrong with the plane. Damn! Two tours in combat in Vietnam and four Purple Hearts, and I'm going to be killed in a plane crash. I set my jaw, tighten my seat belt, and look straight ahead.

The plane lands, and there seems to be no problem. After we get stopped, I can breathe again. The flight attendants seemed very relieved. I am too. They let us exit the plane to go into the terminal. When we get to the ground, we see that one of the tires on the plane is torn in pieces. They tell us that when we took off in Vietnam, the tire blew. I'm glad that they didn't tell us about it when it happened.

We learn that we will be on Guam for a couple of hours while they change the tire on the plane. That will give us time to goof off and relax. I need that. This may be the only time that I'm going to be here.

We load up on the plane and fly east into the dark. I sleep in my seat and awake when we land in Hawaii to gas the plane. We do not get to deplane, and a lot of the guys do not wake up. I watch the crew gas the plane through the window. We then take off, and I go back to sleep.

I wake as we approach the coast of California. A few of the guys cheer. I just smile. This is "old hat" for me. We land at Travis Air Force Base, and they bus us over to Fort Ord to process us out. Most of the guys on the plane are being reassigned to other Army posts. About thirty of us are getting out of the Army. They tell the thirty of us if we are going to put in for any disability, we will be here four or five days. If we are not, then the process will take about twenty-four hours with chow and latrine breaks. The guys being reassigned will be out of here in a few hours.

None of us want to be here for four or five days. There is one other E-6 besides me and seven or eight E-5s. The rest of the guys are all Specialist 4s. We line up standing at a long table with a mountain of paperwork. There is an E-7 on the podium walking us through all the forms. It goes on for hours with breaks. It's apparent that the Army lives on paper. We finally finish and then are issued dress green uniforms with long sleeves and coats. They will replace our short-sleeved uniforms. I'm glad. It's wintertime and cold.

We are then transported to the San Francisco Airport, and I walk in carrying my bag. Then I see them! Two hippies are standing in my way and looking at me with sheer hate. They seem to step over to block my path. They are both as tall as I am but lankier built. I would guess both would be about 185 or 190 pounds. One has black long hair and a beard and sharp features. The second has long blond hair and a beard. His features seem softer than the dark-haired hippies. The blond guy seems to be looking for directions from the dark hippie.

I've been hearing how these hippies have been harassing and even attacking soldiers returning from Vietnam. These guys are sizing me up. I walk right up and get in the face of the dark hippie. I smell two things, body odor and marijuana. I've never seen such hate in anyone's face. My nose is an inch from his nose. I see a men's bathroom to my right. I look at the bathroom and then back at the hippie. I point toward the men's room with my chin. He looks at it and nods his head yes. I turn and walk into the men's room and see that it has two stalls, two urinals, and two sinks with just enough open area for three men to "work." I throw my bag, coat, tie, and cap on the counter by the sinks; turn; and wait on the two hippies. They have picked the wrong soldier to bully. I just hope that neither of them has any kind of weapon. I sure don't, not even a pocketknife. My left leg begins to shake uncontrollably. Where are these two guys? I've got a plane to catch. I only have a few minutes to handle this problem.

I walk to the door of the men's room and look around. I do not see the hippies. They have thought better of the situation and left. I think that they are looking for a nineteen-year-old, 140-pound Specialist 4 to bully. I quickly put my coat, tie, and cap back on and pick up my bag. I search for the hippies, but they are gone.

I barely make it to my gate in time to board my plane. We fly to Dallas, and I change planes. I then fly into Memphis. My stepfather is waiting for me at the airport. He tells me that my mother is in the hospital but that she is going to be all right.

We drive to the hospital, and I visit with my mother, and her doctor comes in. He sees my coat hanging on the coatrack with all my ribbons and my Combat Infantry Badge. He smiles and tells me that he was in the Korean War. I ask him if he was a doctor then. He tells me no, that he was an Infantry Platoon Leader. I call him homeboy, and we bump shoulders. You never know where you will run into a "grunt."

During the next few weeks, I work a small job and work on my big decision. I decide on a career in law enforcement, and in a while, I enter the Memphis Police Academy.

EPILOGUE

March 1997

I'm a fifty-year-old grandfather with a slight limp. I'm working as a railroad policeman in Shreveport, Louisiana. I worked as a Memphis, Tennessee, policeman from 1969 until 1982 and loved the job, but the pay was low, and I had to work part-time jobs. In 1982, I had the opportunity to go to work as a railroad policeman. After that, I didn't need to work part-time jobs. In 1995, the railroad police transferred me to Shreveport.

It's a cool March morning, and my wife, Louise, drops me off at the Shreveport Airport. I'm flying to Los Angeles International Airport, where I will join other former members of the First Infantry Division. We will then fly to Vietnam to visit old battlefields that we fought on thirty years before. My wife hopes that this will put to rest some of the demons that I live with every day. Only recently has the USA established relations with our old enemy.

I arrive at LAX and find that it will be nearly twelve hours before the plane takes off for Hong Kong. In Hong Kong, we will change planes and then fly into Vietnam. I'm going to have to nap sitting up as I wait.

More guys start showing up. None of them was in Bravo-Second, Eighteenth during the war. They were from all over the division. Sergeant Major Frost was in WWII and missed the Korean War due to being stationed in Germany. Then for a year in the sixties, he was the Command Sergeant Major of the Quarter Cavalry in the division. We have a second retired Sergeant Major that was a Korean War veteran and also served in the Quarter Cavalry in Vietnam. Both of these retired Sergeant Majors have brought their wives along. I'm surprised that someone has their wife with them. I guess I'm still thinking that Vietnam is a combat zone even though I know it's not.

Retired Sergeant First Class Malone is a Korean War veteran. He also served two tours in Vietnam. One of those was with First, Eighteenth, our sister battalion. He then retired and had a second career as a park ranger in California. Doc Halladay was a combat medic in another battalion. Dwight Perry was a grunt in the Twenty-Eighth Infantry Regiment. Desila was a company clerk, "in the rear with the gear," but he was there. Jack Cave was a mortician. (I did not know that the division had morticians in Vietnam.) Another guy was a commo man in the rear. There are several other guys, some combat troops and some support troops.

Our plane arrives, and we load up. I find that Dwight Perry, Jack Cave, and I are sitting together. All three of us are a little "wide in beam," so it's crowded. I doze in my seat as we fly across the Pacific in and out of darkness and daylight.

It's morning time as we see Hong Kong in the distance. There are mountains around the city and the harbor. Our plane will have to go in on a very steep landing path. That makes me very nervous. I don't want to die in a plane crash. I want to see my grandchildren grow up. We land and deplane. It's a huge terminal. I also see many police officers on patrol in pairs. They are all carrying submachine guns. That also makes me nervous. I hope there is no trouble. I do not want to be in the middle of a firefight unarmed.

We have a couple of hours, and most of us grab a Coke, burger, and fries at the food courts. We then pick up another couple who have been waiting on us in Hong Kong, Paul Nelson and his wife, Ginny. They are both tall with blond hair and seem like supernice people. I find that Paul was in the division band in Vietnam. (I did not know we had a band in Vietnam.) Paul asks me where I thought the buglers came from at ceremonies for troops killed in action. I tell Paul that I just thought that they found a soldier who could play the instrument and purchased the bugle from a pawnshop. He laughs.

Our plane to Vietnam arrives, and we load up. It's a smaller plane than the one we came in over the Pacific. It's still large, however. All the passengers on this plane are Asian, except our group.

They feed us a really nice meal of seafood as we fly across the Gulf of Tonkin.

We land in Vietnam and prepare to go through customs. The country still smells like rotten cantaloupes. I'm feeling really beat and note that the custom officials do not look like happy campers. I tell the guy who set up the trip that the customs officials are going to mess with us. This is his business, and he has done this a number of times. He tells me that they are not going to mess with us. He says they are going to mess with Vietnamese people who are coming back to visit family. As I watch, I see that he is right.

We clear customs, and there are two buses waiting on us. One for our luggage and an air-conditioned bus for us. This is great getting in the cool air. We start moving in traffic. Most of the traffic is motorbikes. I see no Lambrettas. That was the tiny three-wheeled buses that were everywhere when I was here in the sixties. I'm tired and beaten down with jet lag.

As we slowly move through traffic, I see on the sidewalk on my left a uniformed NVA soldier with an AK-47. My reflexes take over, and I shout, "NVA on the left," and start to duck to the floor. The guys laugh, and someone says, "Ed, I think they are just VA now." I'm embarrassed and blush. I shake my head and laugh with the guys. I'm glad I wasn't armed. Learned responses can stay with you a lifetime.

We arrive at the Rex Hotel and check in. It's an older hotel but beautiful and elegant. A lot of news people stayed here during the war. I find that they have a nice restaurant on the flat roof. This is the dry season, so no rain.

The guy in charge of the tour has a nice dinner set up for us with entertainers. I would rather just go to bed and sleep; but I tough it out, eat the gourmet meal, and try to listen to the singers. I keep nodding off. Finally, it is over, and we head to our rooms. I'm sharing a room with Jack Cave. We enter the room, and I crash on one of the beds without even taking my clothes off. Ten hours later, Jack wakes me and tells me he's going to breakfast on the roof with some of the other guys. I tell him I'll soon join them.

I shower and shave and head up to the roof. I find Jack and some of the others guys at a table and join them. I order breakfast and coffee. The guys tell me that the coffee is much too strong. I also order a pot of hot water and cut the coffee by half. It's pretty good coffee then. The breakfast is good as well.

We load on the bus at 0900 hours and drive toward the Di An area. We've got a twenty-four-year-old Vietnamese man on the bus as a translator. He was born the year the US Army left Vietnam. His English is excellent. We also have a retired NVA colonel on the bus whom the government has put with us. He's a small guy with eyeglasses and a frozen smile. We are told that he speaks no English. I tell the other guys that he may speak better English than any of us.

We drive to our old base camp at Di An. We are not allowed on the base because the Ninth Vietnamese Division is stationed there now. Our old opponents now live on our old base camp. I'm sure that none of the guys we fought in that unit are still in it. For one thing most of them are either dead or crippled or old. We drive around the area and I see many things I recall. We drive by the water plant at Thu Duc. The tower is still there.

We stop at a nice little roadside cafe and eat lunch. We then drive back into Saigon and visit the War Museum. The museum is all slanted against the Americans. I expected no less. We return to the Rex Hotel and get cleaned up.

We then all go to a nice dinner. We are told that the next day we will go the Vietnamese Veterans Association and meet with our former enemies. We are also told that to belong to this group, you have to have been an officer in either the Viet Cong or the North Vietnamese Army. So no enlisted men, no grunts. Just hard-core commies who toe the party line. I don't want to do this, but I have no choice. I must admit I'm a little curious about these people who I fought so long and in many ways still do.

The next morning, we bus to our meeting and walk in. There's a long table with water bottles all around. One side of the table is full of middle-aged and older Vietnamese men and one woman. We sit down at the table, and I notice that the guy running the tour has had two of my bigger friends sit on each side of me. He knows that I don't like this idea and I don't like these people. They killed my friends. Some would say that was thirty years ago. I would say it was just last night.

They then introduce the "enemy" to us. The woman is an enemy doctor. The little dried-up gook with the green baseball cap is the retired commander of the Fifth NVA Division. I'm looking at the "big" guy across from me. He is huge for a Vietnamese, about five feet eight and 160 pounds with a European face. I decide that his father had to have been a Frenchman when the French owned this country. They introduce him as the retired commander of the Ninth Enemy Division. He speaks some English. He's staring at me. Does he recognize me from some long-forgotten battlefield?

They then introduce all of us, our units, and when we were there. When they announce that I was there twice, the old retired Ninth Division general's eyes light up. He's staring intently at my hard face.

They then have us each say a few words that are then translated to the gook officers. When it's my turn, I list all the locations and all the battles where I fought his unit. He looks me dead in my eyes, and he never blinks.

In a few minutes, we take a break, and everyone mills around. The old French-looking retired general walks up to me. I don't like the man, but he is a general. I come to attention like a good soldier would do in front of a general. He then asks me why I was in Vietnam longer than most Americans. I answer, "Because I liked the work, sir." He then tells me that many more of his comrades were killed than mine. I smile and say, "I'm well aware of that, sir." The old general turns and walks away.

Before leaving to return to the Rex Hotel, we have a picture taken with our former enemies on the front steps of the Vietnamese Veterans Association. The retired NVA general looks around at the group and says, "Surrounded by the First Infantry Division again!"

The next day, we drive up to the Loc Khe area where our Third Brigade was stationed. We find that we are not allowed on this base either because the Fifth NVA Division is stationed there. We do drive around the area and visit many battlefields, some of which I was involved in.

We get all our film developed across the street from the Rex Hotel. There is a nice, clean-cut, middle-aged Vietnamese man who handles our business at the photo shop. He speaks English. He tells us he was a lieutenant in the South Vietnamese Army when the war ended. The NVA sentenced him to prison for the crime of fighting against them. He served nine years in prison before being released.

The next day, we drive up to Quan Loi, and I find my collapsed bunker up from the bar where Ben Garza and I went and collected the dumb AWOL soldiers one dark night. The bar is now an abandoned building. We walk among the rubber trees. These are new growth rubber trees, not the ones that were there in the sixties.

The next day, we go to the tunnels at Chu Chi. They have made it into a theme park. One is even big enough for a big American. The other guys go through it, and I do, too, feeling like a fool. Well, hell, this is my vacation. I'm seeing the countryside from an air-conditioned bus with a cooler full of cokes and beer. Most of all with no fear. It's so pleasant not being afraid. I don't ever recall a minute when I was here in the sixties that I was not at least afraid, many times terrified.

The next day, we travel to the Black Virgin Mountain. I fought around that mountain a number of times on my first tour. They have made this a theme park as well. It costs fifty cents for a Vietnamese to enter the park and two dollars for non-Vietnamese. They've got kids rides and a Ferris wheel. They also have a footpath where you can walk to near the top of the mountain. Some of the guys are going to walk the trail. I'm not. I break out a lawn chair and sit in the shade of the bus. I watch kids play and think about being here in the sixties and think about the other guys whom I served in combat with.

Over the next days, we visit a number of battlefields and walk the ground. Many of these fights I was in, and some of the areas send a chill up my back as I remember enemy bullets snapping by my ears. We enter one area that Malone recalls right away. His company was in a big fight here, and he gets very excited.

We have gotten a few dirty looks while we have been here, but the vast majority of the people have been very nice to us. They've told us that nearly half the people in Vietnam have been born since we left. It just doesn't seem like it's been that long. For me, it hasn't been. I live it every day.

Before we know it, our two weeks are up. We check out of the Rex Hotel and head to the airport and climb on a plane to Hong Kong. We get on an even bigger plane there and cross the Pacific. We land in Los Angeles. We all shake hands and head to terminals to catch planes to different cities. I fly to St. Louis and change planes there for the final leg of my trip to Shreveport. I'm burned down with jet lag. I get up graded to first class but go to sleep before we take off. I don't awaken until we land at Shreveport.

What have I learned from this trip? I know that the war is really over. Intellectually, I knew it was over before I went. Emotionally, I did not believe it. The war was going on both times I was there and both times I left. I now know that it's been done nearly a quarter of a century. It's real for me every day and night, but I know that the real war is over except in my dreams. I know I did all I could, twice. The politicians gave it all away after we won it on the ground. I hope that all fifty-eight thousand dead Americans haunt those same politicians. Two hundred and fifty thousand ARVN (South Vietnamese Army) also died. But recently released files from North Vietnam says that a million and a half NVA and Viet Cong soldiers died. What does that tell you about who "won" the war?

Would I do it all again? *In a heartbeat!*

1966
1st Sgt. Bill Perry and his Radio
Men waiting on helicopters

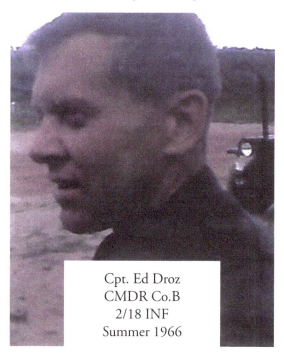

Cpt. Ed Droz
CMDR Co.B
2/18 INF
Summer 1966

1968 Richard Jacobs
with M-60 Machine Gun

Jan 1967
"Country" Mike Wallace and Ed Fedrick

1969
A soldier cooks in the field.
Note his drying out his feet.

Summer 1966
Ed Fedrick. Taken at Di An Base Camp.

2012 reunion in Memphis TN. L to R. Ben Garza,
Ed Fedrick, Doug McVey, Liborato Gonzales in front.

1967
Photo of "Big Red One"
that Engineer cut in Jungle.

Summer 1966, Loc Rhe Platoon Leaders
1 LT. Charles Fletcher
1 LT. Robert Leary

Left is Ed Fedrick with Ben Garza at Di An.
Note the little square canvas box behind these guys.
This is an outside piss tube, you pee in this only

Platoon Ldrs Co. B, 21/18 INF
LT Lockery, 1LT Leary, 1LT Milner. 1LT Fletcher

SG Ben Garza
Platoon CO. B
18 INF
1966

2nd Platoon Co. B
2/18 INF
Fall 1966

1968

Some of 2nd platoon in from an operation and cleaned up. Standing Left to Right, Morrison, Vanderburg, Burna, Nine, Ed Fedrick, Sanchez, Spridling, Snell, Jacobs, LT. Price. Knelling Left to Right, Quintano, "Ski", Litrum, Townsend, Marcus, Cardenas, Bridge and Jewell

Feb 1967

McVey on left facing camera. George Arnold with helmet, left profile. Lambrett in background without helmet. Jim "The Swede" Norberg Facing camera on the right.

Enemy Paymaster killed on Jan 13, 1967 by
Ed Fedrick on "Operation Cedar Falls"

Sept. 1966
Base Camp "Bearcat" Willie Johnson on Bunker.
Standing Left to Right, Sanders, McVey, Gonzales, and
Jim "The Swede" Norberg, George Arnold kneeling.

B company 2nd 18th
1966–1967 in Di An. Nov 1966—Standing Left to
Right, Ed Fedrick, Douglas McVey, Scott, kneeling
L–R, De Jesus and Bickett, Gonzalas in background.

2nd platoon B CO
Late 1966 with XO Leary L to R Standing, SSG Bass, LT. Leary,
SSG Garza, SSG Evans, Sgt. Arnold—Kneeling, SSG. Caluiro.
Sgt. Mul Chency and PLT. Sgt. John Hall the Runs Sac.

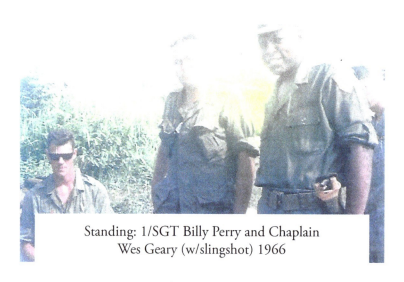

Standing: 1/SGT Billy Perry and Chaplain
Wes Geary (w/slingshot) 1966

Fall of 1966, Wellie Johnson on the Bunker. Standing L to R. Louis Sanders, Doug McVey, Leborato Gonzales, Jim Norborg. Kneeling is George Arnold. The Hot LZ.

Douglas McVey

Fall 1968
Sgt. Richard Collins at Di An.

Memphis Tennessee, May 18, 1976
Policeman Ed Fedrick has been shot
Four times in a gunfight. He is being
Assisted to a waiting ambulance by
Officers Jim Johnston and John Molnar

Fall 1968
Ted Townsend at the Thu Due Water Plant

Chaplain Wes Geary and others
with a captured VC, 1967

Nov 1968
Ed Fedrick at Di An with wounded left elbow with purple heart

1968
SSG Ed Fedrick in Front on B-2-18 orderly room, Di An

Ed Fedrick and Jerry Sweat
1966
@ Loc Khe

Ed Fedrick and Mulchaney
1966
@ Di An

Ed Fedrick and Ben Garza
1966
Di An

Nov 1968
Ed Fedrick at Di An.
Note bandage left elbow, 4th purple heart

Wes Geary, Jr., Ed Fedrick, Colonel Wes Geary (Retired), Bill Perry
(Captain, USA), Command Sergeant Major Bill Perry (Retired)
Frisco, TX

Walt Ehlers, Congressional Medal of Honor, and Ed Fedrick

1968
L–R Company, Ski, Morris, Bisenden, Kney

Fall 1968,
2nd PLT. B-2-18 Squad leaders and PLT. Sgt. Standing L–R, Sgt.
Townsend, SSG. Morris, SSG. Fedrick,
Kneeling L–R Sgt. Collins, SSG Jones.

Fall 1968
Left–Right
Atkins, Turner, Porter, at the Thu Duc Water Plant

Fall 1968,
Snell and Ed Fedrick with cutdown AK-47

Ed Fedrick and Ben Garza
Reunite in 2005

Seated—Tony Tardugno (Medic), John Nykiel.
Standing—Rick Dimas, Ed Fedrick, Richard Jacobs,
Johnny Anderson, Namen Carter, Mike Binkley

Seated—Ken Bissenden, Cliff Bridge, Ed Fedrick
Standing—Richard Jacobs, Jim Morris

Ed Fedrick, Liberato Gonzales, Ben Garza
2006 Reunion

Ed and Louise Fedrick
1992

1999
Ed Fedrick at Liberato Gonzales' Home in New Mexico

Ed and Louise Fedrick
At a 1st Div. Reunion Dinner

Ed and Louise Fedrick
2003 First Infantry Division Reunion

ABOUT THE AUTHOR

Edward Fedrick was born in Carthage, Mississippi, and grew up in Memphis, Tennessee, where he attended Treadwell Grade School and Middle School and graduated from Tech High School in 1965. After an attempt at college, he and his best friend, David Wing, joined the army on the buddy system. David went on to become part of the military police in Vietnam and Ed went to the infantry.

During Ed's two tours of duty in Vietnam, he sustained wounds four separate times and was awarded four Purple Hearts.

After the war, Ed served his community for more than forty years in law enforcement. During which time, he was wounded on two separate occasions and awarded two Police Purple Hearts.

Ed and his wife, Louise, live in rural Middle Tennessee with one of their four adult children and loving pit bull mix puppy. They are blessed with six grandsons and three great-granddaughters. Ed's life now involves tending to his herd of miniature goats, flock of chickens, miniature horse, and miniature donkey. When asked when he was last in Vietnam, Ed will tell you, "Last night," as the thoughts of war are ever present in his mind.

CPSIA information can be obtained
at www.ICGtesting.com
Printed in the USA
LVHW071232010521
686193LV00019B/1179

9 781636 304700